Praise for *The Real Estate Entrepreneur and Cliff Perotti*

"Perotti's first-hand knowledge provides practical guidelines, critical information, and comprehensive strategies for running a successful and profitable business. The comprehensive range of *The Real Estate Entrepreneur,* its time-tested techniques and authoritative guidance from the author, make it an indispensable resource."

Ginny Shipe, CAE
Chief Executive Officer
Council of Real Estate Brokerage Managers

"The journey to success—for each of us, our industry and consumers—is dependent upon the very concepts that Perotti so clearly identifies and defines in this text. Whether you are about to start your own real estate company or you are reviewing the strategic direction of your existing company, *The Real Estate Entrepreneur* is a definitive roadmap to success."

Jim Kinney, CRB, CRS, GRI
President, Rubloff Residential Properties
Chicago, Illinois
2004 Illinois Realtor of the Year

"*The Real Estate Entrepreneur* . . . knowledge critical for anyone who owns a real estate company or who is thinking about owning a real estate company. In particular, it is a roadmap for real estate professionals who are deciding whether or not to 'cross the line' into ownership."

John Yen Wong, CRB
2004 President
Council of Real Estate Brokerage Managers

"Cliff Perotti is the kind of leader who has helped individuals and companies to realize their untapped potential. His passion for the real estate industry is evident and his contributions, both in this text and through his work . . . are great."

Andrew Zsolt
President
Coldwell Banker Terrequity
Toronto, Ontario, Canada

"As the 'next generation' owners of an independent, family-owned real estate brokerage, we have faced both challenges and opportunities during the ownership and management transition of our real estate company. Perotti's experience, guidance and positive energy have helped us to not only avoid the pitfalls, but also enabled us to capitalize on the opportunities. Most importantly, he helped us focus on the important things in order to develop clarity of vision about where we're going and how we're going to get there."

Steve Holman
President
Droubi Real Estate
San Francisco, California

The Real Estate ENTREPRENEUR

Everything You Need to Know to Grow Your Own Brokerage

Cliff Perotti
CBR, GRI, E-PRO, SRES
President, TheBrokerCoach.com

McGraw-Hill

New York   Chicago   San Francisco   Lisbon   London
Madrid   Mexico City   Milan   New Delhi   San Juan
Seoul   Singapore   Sydney   Toronto

1 2 3 4 5 6 7 8 9 0 DOC/DOC 0 9 8 7

ISBN 13: 978-0-07-148434-3

ISBN 10:   0-07-148434-5

This publication is designed to provide accurate and authoritative information in regard to the subject matter covered. It is sold with the understanding that neither the author nor the publisher is engaged in rendering legal, accounting, futures/securities trading, or other professional service. If legal advice or other expert assistance is required, the services of a competent professional person should be sought.

—*From a Declaration of Principles jointly adopted by a Committee of the American Bar Association and a Committee of Publishers*

REALTOR® is a federally registered collective membership mark which identifies a real estate professional who is a member of the NATIONAL ASSOCIATION OF REALTORS® and subscribes to its strict code of ethics.

McGraw-Hill books are available at special quantity discounts to use as premiums and sales promotions, or for use in corporate training programs. For more information, please write to the Director of Special Sales, Professional Publishing, McGraw-Hill, Two Penn Plaza, New York, NY 10121-2298. Or contact your local bookstore.

This book is printed on acid-free paper.

Library of Congress Cataloging-in-Publication Data

Perotti, Cliff.
  Real estate entrepreneur : everything you need to grow from sales associate to
real estate broker / Cliff Perotti.
     p. cm.
  Includes bibliographical references and index.
  ISBN 0-07-148434-5 (pbk. : alk. paper) 1. Real estate business.
2. Real estate agents. I. Title.

HD1375.P387 2007
333.33068—dc22
                                                                    2006103340

This book is dedicated to my wife, Lisa;
my daughters, Corinne and Callie;
my mother, Patti;
and my departed son, Ryan;
all of whom bring the gifts of laughter, support,
love, inspiration, and purpose to my life.

CONTENTS

ABOUT THE REAL ESTATE INDUSTRY

"It is often said that 'the real estate industry is unlike any other.' It's a statement that is both true and false. In truth, it is an observation that few industries welcome and foster the entrepreneurial spirit as real estate does. On the other hand, it is a statement lacking accountability, as it is dangerously false to think the real estate industry is immune to the pressures of change and the power of the consumer.

"A real estate company is known not only by the marketing image it formally crafts, but perhaps even more by the reputation of its associates, the delivery of its services, and the degree of commitment to serving the consumer—an increasingly knowledgeable consumer who expects assurance and accountability. Without a definitive roadmap and guidance, many would-be broker/owners struggle—at great expense to the individual, the consumer, and frankly, to the reputation of the industry."

Jim Kinney, CRB, CRS, GRI
President, Rubloff Residential Properties, Chicago IL
National Association of Realtors Presidential Liaison to Ireland
2004 Illinois Realtor of the Year
2001 Realtor of the Year, Chicago Association of Realtors

"Today's world is filled with countless managers who react or respond to the ever-changing landscape. What the real estate industry really needs are leaders who will help forge a new direction in the landscape and blaze a new trail as technology and e-commerce continue to change how we do business.

"As our industry landscape changes, true leadership will become more critical than ever. Creating companies and holding them together to achieve their goals will continue to become more challenging in the world of a 'work at home' office environment, rent-a-desk commission structures, and Internet-focused communications, all of which serve to limit personal contact. Successful organizations are the ones where the leaders are clear on and committed to their vision, and can positively guide their organizations in spite of these challenges. Leadership includes relentlessly communicating core values, setting the tone and example, and establishing the minimum standards for the company to achieve."

Andrew Zsolt
President
Coldwell Banker Terrequity
Toronto, Ontario, Canada

ACKNOWLEDGMENTS

It would not have been possible for me to write this book on my own. Every day that passes, I realize more and more how much life is a collaboration of efforts, with each individual adding his or her own brand of magic to the mix in order for positive movement to occur. This book is no different. I would like to acknowledge the ongoing editorial support of Corinne Revel, my daughter, who read each and every word of this publication, correcting my language and telling me when something sounded, well, stupid. Also part of my editorial team was Jan Aksztulewicz, whose experienced eye for organization kept the structure of this book together.

It is important to also acknowledge that this work is a product of my life experience. I must acknowledge the important contribution of Patti Collins, my mother, who helped me start my first business at age 16 and who taught me how to read a set of company books. She instilled in me the passion for life that I carry with me today. Also, without her continually pushing me into acting lessons at a young age, I would not be the seminar speaker I am today, or the teacher, and thus, not the author. In other words, I wouldn't be me.

A special thank you goes to Dianne Wheeler, my editor at McGraw-Hill. She is one great lady! As one of her many authors, she has guided me from innocent writer to published author (a challenging task for sure). Dianne has championed my cause all along the way, believing in this book and its importance to our industry. There is no classroom that teaches you how to work with an editor; it is a learning experience. I am grateful that I had someone as talented and patient as Dianne.

And finally, I acknowledge the sacrifice and commitment demonstrated by my loving wife, Lisa, while I was writing this book. It has been said that behind every great man is an even greater woman. For 16-plus years, Lisa has been my rock. She tolerates my craziness and inspires my laughter.

Cliff Perotti

INTRODUCTION

Welcome to the world of the real estate entrepreneur! I commend you on the decision to enter the dynamic, exciting, and rewarding career of real estate brokerage ownership. This book is designed to help you in the earliest stages of the brokerage journey, with the desired outcome being to save thousands of dollars in wasted hours or to avoid countless minor mistakes that can act as setbacks to your achieving a successful real estate company. Regardless of whether you're a real estate veteran or neophyte broker, the information in this book will prove to be a valuable resource in helping to launch a new real estate company.

The world of the real estate broker is not just a job; it is a lifestyle. While traditional jobs are generally Monday to Friday, working 40 hours per week with weekends off, real estate frequently has weeks of 60-plus hours with weekend work being part of the routine. Yet the real estate lifestyle allows the broker to have flexible hours, offering the opportunity to participate in family events or have a nice midweek golf date. A well-run, successful real estate brokerage will allow brokers to make a positive contribution to their families' financial security, the lives of their agents, and to their community.

WHY I WROTE THIS BOOK

I am an entrepreneur. I have an entrepreneurial spirit. I love to start, acquire, develop, own, and sell business opportunities. One of my attorneys once called me a "serial entrepreneur," and while I laughed at that phrase initially, I realized how the truth resonated. I started my first business at age 16, and I have had some sort of business enterprise on my plate ever since. In my first year of business, I was described in local papers as some sort of business prodigy, with the goal of making my first million by the time I was 21 years old. While it took 20 years longer than I expected to make that million, the same flame still burns within me, as it does for countless freedom-seeking entrepreneurs.

At age 17, my adventurous spirit led me to attend my first real estate seminar. Like countless attendees to such seminars before and after me, I was looking for the great secrets to real estate that would make me gazillions of dollars with little effort. The speaker was a flashy real estate guru with some serious gold bling-bling around his neck. He was confident, funny, entertaining, and obviously successful. Right? He had to be. He had a microphone, and people were giving him money to hear more words from him on dozens of cassette products. I was 17. What did I know?

I do remember noticing that he wasn't particularly brilliant or clever and that he spoke only of boring "secrets" like appreciation, leverage, tax benefits, increasing demand, and limited supply. I walked out of that seminar saying, "So what? Real estate's boring."

In looking back, I realize that I was not ready for what Mr. Bling-Bling was telling me. Little did I understand how the candle of my passion for real estate was lit in that brief, cheesy experience. Most real estate brokers or agents can talk of the moment, like my seminar experience, when the real estate seed was planted into their minds and hearts. Unlike the flashy fields of professional sports or acting, I certainly have yet to meet anyone who in high school said, "I want to be a real estate broker!"

So a few years later, with entrepreneurial spirit in tow, I took my California real estate salesperson exam at age 24 and I never looked back. I found a home in real estate sales. I really loved, and still do love, the rewarding sense of accomplishment I get when I help people find the ideal home to live in, or even raise a family in. I love the challenges that real estate presents.

A bit of luck and persistence led me to a certain level of success in real estate sales. About a year later, I had a conflict with my broker/company, and I became convinced that I could run a better company and treat my salespeople more equitably. I then obtained my broker's license and started my own small brokerage in San Francisco. Some version of this story has been repeated countless times over the years throughout the United States. I often wonder how many start-up brokerages occur because an agent's prior company failed to provide adequate value to the agent or because the firm had an unreasonable or unfair policy.

With ink-wet broker's license in hand, I started out on the path of leadership and unlimited earnings potential, or so I thought. I soon discovered that before I could hire my legions and conquer the marketplace, I had to do a lot of work setting up my office, getting business cards and letterhead, creating marketing pieces, and performing a ton of other administrative activities. While these tasks were essential and would take a lot of my time, they didn't directly pay the bills. I found myself working longer days to get everything accomplished, and my income initially suffered. But a strong sense of purpose and faith kept me moving forward.

Over the 22 years that followed, I opened or acquired six real estate companies, ran a successful top-producing team, and trained hundreds of agents to build their own individual businesses. Furthermore, I came to recognize that there was no publication designed to reduce the number of mistakes and help the broker launch a new company or office. (Until now, that is.)

HOW TO USE THIS BOOK

Consider this book a resource or a how-to manual. It's designed to walk you through all the stages of setting up a brokerage. In addition to vital information designed to help you achieve a successful start-up company, there are several key elements designed to bring the material to life and increase the impact. These chapter elements are:

- **Tales from the Real World.**   These are examples or stories of important learning experiences that come from mistakes or successes of actual real estate brokers or managers. The names used in these examples have been changed to protect the not-so-innocent.
- **Coaching Corner.**   This element contains key messages from me to you, the reader, offered as if I were your business coach. You can take them or leave them, at your own peril. I do understand that sometimes we simply have to reinvent the wheel in order to truly comprehend its importance.
- **Personal Exercises.**   These should be completed before you move on to the next chapter. You'll need to keep a pen and paper handy, or preferably a word processor, to write your responses to these exercises. Some of these exercises are introspective thinking kinds of exercises, while others are actual tasks to complete. These assignments are a critical element of this book because they help take the information "off the page." They help create *action*.

You will get the most out of this book by treating it as an interactive experience; that is, write in it, highlight items of importance, do the exercises, talk about it, and think about it. By experiencing this book fully, you will absorb the concepts faster and to a greater depth. As a resource book, certain chapters may hold greater interest to each individual; for example, if readers have a background in financial accounting, they may view the financial management chapter as more interesting than the chapter on recruiting.

WHAT SHOULD YOU EXPECT FROM THIS BOOK?

It's important to start by taking a moment to explore your expectations of this book (see Personal Exercise I.1). The concept of clarity is one that is repeatedly presented throughout, and brokers should be clear about where they want to go, where they've been, and the specific details of how something is to be done.

Brokers often start their business in an irrational moment of anger or frustration with their current broker, believing that they can do things better. They run out and have some signs made, open a bank account, and work out of their home until they figure out how it is all going to work. Let's *not* go down that path. If you are reading this book after doing exactly that, then take a deep breath and look at your expectations of this book by completing Personal Exercise I.1.

PERSONAL EXERCISE I.1

EXPECTATIONS

Please answer the following questions before proceeding.

1. Why do you want to start a real estate company?
2. If you have a spouse or partner, how does he or she feel about your starting a real estate company?
3. Why are you reading this book?
4. What are the 10 most important questions you are hoping to get answered by reading this book?
5. How will you determine whether this book has helped you?
6. How much time will you commit to read this book? Do you have a deadline for completing this book? If so, what is that deadline?

Now that you know what you want from this book, let's get started.

SO YOU WANT TO OWN YOUR OWN REAL ESTATE COMPANY

The thing always happens that you really believe in; and the belief in a thing makes it happen.

—FRANK LLOYD WRIGHT

One of the most commonly discussed statistics in the real estate business is that over 75 percent of the people who pass their real estate exam end up leaving the real estate industry, walking away from all their hopes and aspirations for success in this industry. Couple that with the reality that over 50 percent of start-up businesses fail within two years, and you begin to see that you will be facing some enormous challenges as you start a real estate business.

THE BROKERAGE STATISTICS

In a 2002 survey of its more than 4,500 members, the Council of Real Estate Brokerage Managers (CRB) learned some interesting facts about its members, who consist of real estate company broker/owners and managers. Here are some of the key points revealed by that survey:

- The average age of a broker/owner/manager is 55.
- The average number of agents in a company is 40.
- The average broker/owner has two offices.
- The average number of agents per office is 20.
- 57 percent of the companies are losing money.
- 75 percent of the broker/owners have to sell real estate, in addition to owning and managing their companies, in order to pay all their company and personal bills.
- 80 percent of the broker/owners are previously licensed real estate salespeople.

CRB members are some of the most well-trained, experienced real estate brokers in the industry. How can a majority of these very "successful" real estate brokers be losing money? That's a good question and one that is answered for you in this chapter. Also, don't let the "odds of winning" discourage you in any way from pursuing your dream of brokerage ownership; these are just survey results that should give you cause for pause and reflection. Before leaping into the world of company ownership, you should understand the realities of the world to which you are about to commit your personal focus, time, energy, and finances.

Be aware that one of the most common reasons that new brokerages fail is that there was not a careful enough evaluation of both the benefits and pitfalls of such business ownership prior to the broker leaving his or her current company and launching the new vision. Thus, before getting into the particular details of starting and running a company, it's appropriate to first review and analyze the pluses and minuses of owning and running a real estate firm, from the perspective of one who has "been there and done that," so to speak. If, after considering this information, you still feel that absolute passion and burning desire to move forward with your own firm, then by all means move onward. The path and decision are yours; just make your move with an accurate view of your future world.

LIFESTYLE CHANGES

What are the differences in lifestyle and daily activities that you can expect when going from the life of a salesperson to that of a broker/owner? Think about the typical life of a real estate salesperson. There is a significant difference between the lifestyle of a new licensee and a veteran salesperson. The same can be said of a new broker/owner and a veteran broker/owner.

A new licensee's life starts with taking classes and an enormous amount of training and then progresses to focusing on prospecting for new clients. The new licensee then transitions into listing and escrow work. A typical week might include an open house; some door-knocking; putting together a direct mail campaign; touring homes; attending sales meetings; sitting on "floor time" or at the "up desk"; negotiating a sales contract; handling loan applications; overseeing inspections; and getting documents signed for closing. A typical workday for the new licensee might start at 9 a.m. and end at around 5 or 6 p.m. Let's see how that differs from the day of an experienced agent.

An experienced sales associate's workday might start at around 9:30 or 10 a.m. The agent isn't being lazy, for typically she has been at the gym, had a cup of coffee or tea, and may have even accessed the multiple listing service (MLS) online from home to check on the newest listings. The agent has also most likely already checked her e-mail from her laptop at home. This agent arrives at the office ready for work. She checks her voice mail and calendar and begins getting on the phone, talking with her clients or touching base with her "sphere of influence" contacts. Her world is filled with past customers, many of whom are her personal friends, who provide her with several new leads per month. Her prospecting activities are more personal in focus at this stage of her career, so she schedules visits to her past customers, lunches, coffee meetings, and dinners in small groups. She typically still maintains a consistent direct mail campaign, a lead-generating Web site and two to three open houses per month, depending on the number of listings she might have at the time. Personal time is integrated into weekly activities, whether it's a pedicure or a golf game, or time with the kids at a soccer game. Ah, the good life!

The most notable changes to expect between being a salesperson and being a broker/owner will be the initial demand for longer work hours and a reduction of personal time. This is because in addition to regular sales duties, the broker/owner must accomplish the tasks and activities of a new business owner. Starting any business is demanding, requiring an enormous amount of energy and focus. Starting a real estate company is no less challenging, except that most new brokers also have to initially maintain their personal sales production in order to support their family *and* their new business. Time management and energy management become critical issues for the new broker/owner. The new broker/owner should expect to arrive at the office at around 8 a.m. and depart somewhere around 5:30 or 6 p.m. Some broker/owners are in the office between 6:30 and 7 a.m. because they've discovered that it's a great time to review files, do business planning, and so on without interruptions because no one else shows up at the office until 8:30 a.m.

Additional responsibilities that may have to be addressed in a typical week will include recruiting; brand development; employee development and training; creating policies and procedures; planning for sales meetings; developing and implementing a training program; *more* recruiting; reviewing contracts and solving transaction problems; interviewing prospective employees or agents; dealing with insurance issues; meeting with your agents' customers for counseling; attending training classes to upgrade knowledge about running a business; bookkeeping problems; and even *more* recruiting. A new broker should concentrate no less than 10 to 15 hours per week on recruiting activities, in addition to all the other things that need to get accomplished. So when does this hectic life let up? Good question.

For an experienced broker/owner, the typical workday still starts around 8 or 9 a.m. at the latest. As a successful businessperson, the veteran broker/owner most likely has an administrative assistant that helps with the bookkeeping, administrative tasks, and time management. Hopefully, the experienced broker/owner has a sales manager to help with training, reviewing contracts, and recruiting. An experienced broker/owner will tell you that he spends more time "putting out fires" than anything else on a day-to-day basis. The sense of being constantly absorbed in problem solving for your agents is widely recognized as one of the key time management challenges for most broker/owners. An established, well-organized broker/owner generally has a different, less stressful lifestyle and spends more time on leadership development, training, business planning, business development, recruiting, and other things that go toward improving the firm.

Figure 1.1 shows a comparison of the lifestyles of a new licensee, a veteran agent, a new broker/owner, and an experienced broker/owner.

FIGURE 1.1 Lifestyle Comparisons

Category	New Licensee	Experienced Agent	New Broker/Owner	Experienced Broker/Owner
Primary focus	Making enough money to stay in business.	Maintaining revenue stream while enjoying lifestyle.	Getting business going. Surviving! Selling to pay bills.	Being the company leader by working on improving the business in the areas of strategic planning, recruiting and training, financial management, and marketing.
Weekly activities	Prospecting for leads, holding open houses, sitting on floor time, sending out direct mailings, contacting friends and family, attending training classes.	Maintaining referral base of past clients, holding open houses, sending out direct mailings, creating listings, and making listing presentations.	Same as experienced agent, *plus* running weekly sales meeting, recruiting new and experienced agents, developing systems for office, conducting training sessions, supervising ads and company marketing, putting out fires. Being a manager for the agents.	Same as new broker/owner, but with no selling *and* holding weekly staff meetings (with assistant manager, administrative assistant, marketing director, etc.), attending conferences and training programs, holding the company together. Being a leader for the agents.
Challenges	Learning fast enough, finding business, financially surviving.	Working smart, managing transaction volume while maintaining a personal life.	Juggling personal time with the time needed to build a company. Having an outside life.	Helping agents to become more productive, building market share, maintaining and increasing profitability.
Typical compensation level	Lowest	Highest	Next lowest	Next highest

5

THE FINANCIAL TRUTH

Most real estate brokerages, as a business, lose money. The lack of profitability is not really talked about very often among brokers, but when it is, you quickly learn that most brokers have had to, at one time or another, tap into their savings or home equity in order to keep their real estate companies afloat. Furthermore, for broker/owners who are actively selling, it's not uncommon that they can't take home a particular commission check because the company needs it in a slow month. Typically, there is a cycle to the cash flow of a real estate office, with January–February being rough cash flow months (because the broker has a fixed overhead to pay monthly and closings are lower in these months) and April–June being good cash flow months because of a higher number of closings. The fall (September–November) can also be very strong secondary cash flow months. So why mention this cycle? If you are the broker/owner, you'll be faced with some simple lifestyle questions, such as, "Financially, should I take my three-week family vacation during the winter, spring, summer, or fall?" or "Economically, should I plan to be away from the office during the slow times or the busy times?" Or better yet, "Should I take multiple, shorter, weekend-type vacations or one longer, annual vacation?" But the real question most often asked is, "When can I afford to go on a vacation?"

But fear not! All is not financial ruin! A properly run real estate brokerage can be very lucrative. The financials of some 50-agent companies in major metropolitan areas reveal over $1 million per year in profit for the owner. So yes, you can make good money owning a real estate company. There is also the financial benefit that is derived from brokerage ownership in having opportunities to make good real estate investments. While such investment activity doesn't show up on the financials of the company, it certainly is an economic benefit to you the owner.

THE TRUTH ABOUT AGENTS

Once you open an office and start recruiting agents, you will no longer be one of the agents. It's a cruel fact of life that once you are the person responsible for paying the bills, training the staff, reviewing agent contracts, and hiring or firing agents, you will be fondly (hopefully) referred to as the broker. In other words, you will no longer be "one of the guys." There is no way to avoid this reality, and you must get used to the fact that, while you like your agents and enjoy an occasional social event, you will no

---

Tales from the Real World

FRIEND OR AGENT?

John opened a boutique firm with $60,000 borrowed from his home's equity. He recruited 10 agents, including his best buddy, Phil. Phil had two years' experience and was formerly a licensed contractor. Everything at John's office was going along smoothly, and Phil was becoming a rising star.

One day, John got a phone call from an upset client of Phil's. The client explained that Phil, during the purchase of the home, saved the client $500 by personally performing the property inspection. The client had never purchased a house before, but Phil was a licensed contractor, so she felt confident in his abilities. During his inspection, Phil discovered some minor items that needed repair, but was generally satisfied with the condition of the property. The client was happy and purchased the property.

Thirty days later, the sewer line backed up into the house. The client called a local plumber to clean out the line. The plumber recommended using a videoscope to look into the sewer pipe to determine if there was a significant problem. The video showed a severe break in the sewer line that required $5,000 to fix. The client was now demanding that John pay her a total of $10,000 to cover the cost of the repair and for the negligent inspection performed by Phil. John told the client that neither he nor the company was going to pay for Phil's activities as a contractor. The client hired an expensive lawyer and filed a lawsuit against the real estate company, John, and Phil.

When John talked with Phil about the claim, Phil acknowledged doing the inspection to save the client money, at the client's request. He further told John that he didn't carry any insurance as a contractor. John's errors and omissions insurance carrier advised him that it would not cover Phil for his contractor-licensed activity, but that it would at least defend John and the company. The insurance company reminded John that his policy had a $5,000 deductible.

An arbitration ensued, with a demand that grew to $60,000. Phil had to hire his own attorney, who asserted that John was responsible because he never told Phil not to do contractor inspections. John insisted that Phil's contractor activities were beyond the scope of a real estate agent's duties. The claim settled for $25,000, with Phil paying $15,000 and John paying $10,000.

What would you do, if you were John?

---

longer be their close companion or friend. There are some exceptions, of course, but these are rare. This is because you are both financially and legally responsible for the agents who will occasionally do things that you feel are inappropriate or possibly even illegal.

THE RESPONSIBILITY OF LEADERSHIP

Step into the role of the broker/owner and you will be taking on the responsibility of leadership. Your employees will be trusting in your ability to continually pay their wages. The agents who join your company will be relying on you to be fiscally responsible for the viability of the company so that they can continue to earn a living and support their personal goals. And members of your own family will be relying on you to make good business decisions so that you can support them. That's a whole lot of responsibility! Strength of character and commitment to your vision will be tested many times by those around you. (See Personal Exercise 1 below.) For your family's sake, as well as your own, you must stay true to your course. As the leader of a company, your employees think of you as a lighthouse on a foggy night; lighthouses can't go out.

Your staff will look to you to move with certainty about your vision and a passionate heart. During the tough times that will inevitably occur, this responsibility of leadership will be a gigantic source of stress for you. You will have to learn to deal with that stress, without being in a funk that can negatively affect your agents, staff, or family. You should revel in your abilities to make it through these tough times. Just keep your eye on the ball and stay focused. Later in this book, we talk more about keeping up your positive leadership attitude and ways to overcome stress. For now, just be aware of what's waiting for you down this road.

The good news is that there are also good times ahead. The excitement of creating and realizing your own business vision is unparalleled! Your decisions and actions will influence the lives of dozens of people, if not hundreds. With a true heart, honorable intentions, and actions congruent with your stated intentions, this influence will be a positive one on the world; it can be your legacy. Here are some good things that real estate brokerage ownership can offer you:

- The satisfaction from helping hundreds of people realize their dream of home ownership
- Being respected by family members, employees, agents, peers, and customers
- Becoming a presence in the community; donating time and resources to local organizations and worthy causes
- The flexibility of being your own boss

- The enjoyment of fresh learning opportunities and new experiences
- The opportunity to build a consistent revenue stream

When all is said and done, recognizing these positive aspects of the business and enjoying the little moments of gratitude have kept me going for 22-plus years in this business.

PERSONAL EXERCISE 1

WHAT WOULD YOU DO?

As a leader of a real estate office, you will be faced with many interesting challenges and situations that require you to make difficult decisions. Here's an exercise to help you evaluate your decision-making skills. Answer each question.

1. What would you do if you have a new licensee, whom you nurtured and trained for six months, come and tell you that she is leaving the company and joining a competitor who has offered to pay her 15 percent more on her commission split?

   _____
   _____
   _____

2. What would you do if the police arrive at your office and serve your best, most prominent agent with papers for violating fair housing laws?

   _____
   _____
   _____

3. What would you do if you find out that one of your agents has forged the signature of a client?

   _____
   _____
   _____

4. What would you do if you get a phone call from one of your agents who has been arrested for drunk driving with one of your clients in the car?

   _____
   _____
   _____

5. What would you do if one of your agents asks you to give a referral to a personal friend who helped to secure a recent closing?

   _____
   _____

TRUST YOUR INSTINCTS

As in life, you should learn to trust your instincts and ignore the pressures of your pocketbook. Remember that time when you interviewed a potential home buyer and agreed to work with the buyer in spite of your body giving you a warning message in the form of an upset stomach? A couple of weeks later, that same buyer tells you that he just bought a house from another broker who was really nice to him at an open house. Sound familiar?

Too often, we don't listen to that little nagging voice, that upset stomach, or that pain in the neck when we should. The result is, of course, a disaster in the form of lost time, lost reputation, or lost energy. We've all made compromises at one time or another because we have families to feed, bills to pay, or egos to soothe. In your new role as a broker/owner, temptation will typically show up as potential recruiting opportunity of an agent who has strong production but a toxic personality.

Coach's advice: Stay true to yourself and stay focused on the kind of company you want to build. When your gut says, "Something's not right here," believe it! Stall for some time so that you can think things over and make the right decision.

KEY POINTS

Here are the key points to take with you from this chapter:

- The real estate brokerage business is not a slam-dunk business. You will have to work hard.
- There is always room at the top for a successful brokerage.
- Real estate brokerage ownership is a lifestyle, not just a business.
- The job of real estate broker/owner is different from that of being a good salesperson. Don't assume your success in real estate sales will instantly translate into your being great at brokerage ownership.
- Make sure you have financial reserves and staying power before launching into your new brokerage. Lack of capital, which later translates into lack of staying power, is a common reason for brokerage failures.
- With few exceptions, agents will be your *agents*, not your *friends*.

- Take leadership responsibility seriously. Be the beacon of light for your people.
- Through the growth and development of the real estate brokerage, you will influence many people and your community.
- You're going to *love* this business!

C H A P T E R

2

CLARITY OF
VISION

*Good business leaders create a vision, articulate the vision,
passionately own the vision, and relentlessly drive
it to completion.*

—JACK WELCH

Before you start any business or other enterprise, you should define your current situation. Taking inventory of current personal assets, both real and perceived, will help give you a clear picture of your starting point. Personal Exercise 2: Your Starting Point provides a fairly personal set of questions for you to answer. Some of these questions will be easy, while others will require some contemplation. The key is to complete the entire assessment.

13

PERSONAL EXERCISE 2

YOUR STARTING POINT

Personal Information
1. Full birth name and date of birth.
2. Your current age.
3. At what age would you like to be "finished" working?
4. What are your height and weight?
5. How do you feel about your overall physical condition?
6. How is your health?
7. What could you do to improve your health and physical condition?
8. What are the top five personal goals that you would like to accomplish in your life?
9. Write down five words that describe you.
10. Write down those things that are going on in your personal life that you think may affect, either positively or negatively, your efforts to open a real estate company.

Personality, Values, and Energy
11. What are the values you hold as most important? (List three to five.)
12. If you had/have children, what are the values that you would want those children to cherish?
13. What are the notable differences, if any, between the answers to questions 11 and 12?
14. How closely does your everyday behavior match your values? If there are disconnects, what are they?
15. Describe your level of energy.
16. What could be done to increase your energy level?
17. What's really important to you in life?
18. How fully engaged do you feel in life?
19. Looking back at your life, what are the top three lessons you feel you've learned?
20. Describe the general persona you have in public.
21. Now describe how that persona differs from the person you really are.
22. What differences do you see between the two?
23. On a scale of 1(depressed) to 10 (ecstatic), how happy are you?
24. What could make you feel happier?
25. Describe the personality traits of people you like to be around.
26. Describe the personality traits of people you do not like to be around.

Your Real Estate Career
27. How and/or why have you selected real estate as a career?
28. Write a brief résumé of your real estate career.
29. What attracts you to owning a company instead of just selling real estate?
30. What are some of your strengths as a new broker/leader of a company?

31. What are some of your weaknesses as a new broker/leader of a company?
32. How will you overcome these weaknesses?
33. What kind of real estate activity do you like to do (e.g., residential sales, investments, property management, mortgage brokerage)?
34. What is the target market area where you would like your company to work?
35. What is your average number of sales or transactions in a year?
36. What is your average annual income in real estate?
37. What thoughts have you given to the area of recruiting agents to your company?
38. What thoughts have you given to training new agents in your company?
39. What do you think makes a successful real estate company?
40. What if your company doesn't succeed? What will you do?

Financial
41. What is your current financial situation? (Write down the thoughts that come to mind about your finances.)
42. How much will it cost to start your company and keep it running during the first year? How did you arrive at that estimate?
43. How will you pay for the start-up costs and operation of your company during the first year?
44. How long will you be able to last, if your company doesn't generate any revenue?
45. What is the most money you have ever made in a single year of your working in real estate?
46. How much money do you need to make annually to (a) simply cover your expenses and (b) achieve your personal goals?

Other
47. Write down any other information you have thought about as part of this starting point assessment.

YOUR VISION—WHERE ARE YOU GOING?

Having defined a starting point, or you current situation, it's time to create a statement of where the business is going. This is known as a vision statement. A company's *vision statement* is a written descriptive statement that includes several key elements that, collectively, define and answer such questions as, "Who are we?" "Why are we doing this?" and "What do we hope to accomplish?" It should set in place the ideal for your company. Think of a company's vision like a baseball field; it establishes the playing field and boundaries of your company's activities (i.e., what type of business your firm will and won't do).

Brokers often make the mistake of simply starting a business without creating a company vision. A common story for start-up brokers is that they got into a disagreement with their prior brokerage and then walked out and opened their own company, working out of a room in their house or from a small office. Such brokers are typically on a shoestring budget and must immediately focus on simply working their current transactions. These brokers don't spend any time creating a company vision statement because they are too busy or perceive a vision statement as a complete waste of time. After all, they *know* what they want to do. Why should they have to write it down? Fast-forward a few years, and this broker is losing money without understanding why. Avoid this experience by having a clear vision for your company. Personal Exercise 3 will help you define your vision.

PERSONAL EXERCISE 3

DEFINING YOUR VISION

1. What are the three to five core values or principles that you want in your company? (Core values are the foundation, such as the company's integrity, ethics, idealistic standards, etc.)
2. What greater purpose is the company to serve? Why does it exist? (Don't get trapped into thinking that your company exists for the purpose of just selling houses; you can do that without the company.)
3. What does your company stand for?
4. Write down three to five "outrageous" objectives or goals for your company. (e.g., to be the number one company in my marketplace, to have 60 percent of the market in Sherman Oaks subdivision, to have 1,000 agents, etc.).
5. Write a very detailed, textured description of what your office will look and feel like in four to five years. (When I say "textured," I mean hitting all of the senses, so be sure to include comments about the location and exterior look of the office, colors of paint on the walls, the type of furniture in the office, the appearance of your agents and staff, the smells in the office, the sounds in the office, etc.)

The answers from this exercise should be in alignment with the personal values you expressed in Exercise 2, representing a congruence between who you are as a person and where you want to go with your business. Any misalignment will result in an unexpected result for the company because your personal core values will generally remain unchanged, while the company you develop will gradually adapt to match and reflect those personal core values.

| **Tales from the Real World** |

A COMMON VISION

A manager took over a 52-desk branch office of a large company that only had nine agents, including the former manager who was being replaced. The office had been decimated by the recruiting activities of a competitor and lost 35 agents and over $150,000 within six months. The situation seemed so abysmal that the new manager recommended that the company simply close the branch, which it was unwilling to do.

The new manager called a meeting of the nine agents left in the office. He had a flipchart on which he had written "#1." The agents arrived at the meeting expecting to be told that the office was going to be closed, but what they heard was something completely unexpected.

The manager told the agents that his vision was to create the "#1" office in the marketplace. He was not interested in the office history, past performance, or agent losses; these were not important now. What *was* important was that each agent must agree to the following three commitments, or he or she should resign at the end of the meeting:

1. Stay with the office, denying all recruiting invitations or luncheons.

2. Excel in the performance of their jobs; whining was not welcome.

3. Actively help the manager recruit when called upon to do so.

The manager gave the agents 10 minutes to decide, and in about 3 minutes they agreed to the conditions and asked where they could begin. They were fired up!

Eighteen months later, the office was fully staffed with 52 agents and was in fact the number one office in the marketplace thus demonstrating the power of a common vision.

Personal Exercise 4 puts it all together in one simple cohesive paragraph—the vision statement. This statement should be inspiring and will act like a beacon in the night, showing you clearly what needs to be done in times of doubt. Once completed, this vision statement should make you feel energized, like you want to immediately go out and jump into doing it. Any less of a result means that the vision statement is not compelling enough. Be patient; it may take a few attempts to get a vision statement to the point where it feels right.

YOUR VISION STATEMENT

Using some of the information from Exercise 3: Defining Your Vision, create a paragraph that will be your company's vision statement. At the very least, this vision statement should answer the following questions:

- Who are we?
- Why are we in business?
- What is our product, service, or purpose (i.e., What do we do?)?
- How do we do what we do?
- Where do we conduct our business (marketplaces)?
- What are our philosophical values?

Your Vision Statement:

_____
_____
_____
_____
_____
_____
_____
_____
_____
_____
_____

CLARITY IS THE KEY

The likelihood of your personal company dream becoming reality is directly related to the clarity of your vision for the company. This principle is easy to understand in a different context.

A person sees an old friend and wants to get together for a luncheon in the near future. Which approach is most likely to result in a lunch meeting?

Approach 1. "Hey, it's good to see you. Let's do lunch sometime."

Approach 2. "Hey, it's good to see you. How about I call you next week, and we set a time to get together for lunch?"

Approach 3. "Hey, it's good to see you. How about lunch Tuesday at noon at Fred's Café?"

Approach 3 is most likely to be the approach that succeeds because it's the *clearest* and most specific of the three options.

To ensure any desired outcome—whether it is an appointment, a family commitment, a company vision, or sending someone to the moon—clarity is the key. Writing down a company vision helps you clarify what it is you want, thus adding to the likelihood of the vision actually being realized. This mere act of writing down a vision statement also gets it out of your head and into the world, allowing others to read it and join in the mission to fulfill the vision. Write your vision statement down and begin to give it some real power!

KEEP YOUR VISION

There will inevitably be times when you become overwhelmed by business pressures, family obligations, or just plain old life. During these times, it's really hard to stay in touch with your vision, and it's very easy to have a company's movement and progress stall until you personally get back on track. The best advice I can give for such situations is to embed your vision into your psyche before you are faced with the tough times. By doing so, you will continually feel the presence and motivation of your vision, even if at only a subconscious level, and you will regain your personal focus quicker.

Imbed your vision statement into your psyche by reading it once per day for a 30-day period. This daily, two-minute ritual will help you maintain clarity of vision and will ensure faster movement toward the vision.

COGNITIVE DISSONANCE

With a vision in place, you look around and see that you have a distance to go to realize that vision. You may experience some anxiety about the enormity of the task ahead or feel overwhelmed by all the work to be done. This emotional experience is very common and to be expected. It is a result of something called *cognitive dissonance*—an internal response that occurs when the world around us does not match the world that our brain sees.

Once a vision becomes very clear in the mind, becoming empowered by passionate thoughts, the brain triggers all the positive emotional responses as if that vision actually existed in reality. But the brain has a problem when what is seen today doesn't match what it's been focusing on and empowering. There is disconnect in the brain, and discomfort (dissonance) is experienced. This is cognitive dissonance.

If, for example, a person loses a high-paying job that is needed to maintain a certain lifestyle, the person's brain starts to become uncomfortable because it knows it should be an employed person (vision), but now finds it's not (reality). Given the difference between the vision and the reality in this case, the person feels great discomfort and anxiety. The person then gets busy to make the reality (unemployed) match the vision (employed), scouring employment ads, going to interviews, and so on until employment is once again found. After taking a new job, the person's dissonance quiets down because now the reality (employed) matches the vision (employed). The discomfort experienced is upsetting in a very physical and real sense. (While in this "in-between" emotional state, some people become so upset that they may find themselves at the doctor's office seeking medication.)

Successful businesspeople who are creative and motivated learn to live with cognitive dissonance. Worthwhile goals require change and stretching beyond comfort zones. In order for you to achieve even greater successes in anything, you must become familiar with the "uncomfortable" world of cognitive dissonance. Welcome the uncomfortable, for it will be the clue that growth and movement are close at hand. Think of this feeling as the "pain" or stiffness felt the day after a great workout at the gym; even though the muscles ache, it somehow feels good.

While we all feel some discomfort when we experience cognitive dissonance, it is the required catalyst for the process of success. Given the internal disparity between what we see and what we say we want to achieve, our brain then goes to work, looking for solutions to the problem. Once your brain goes to work to solve the problem, it's likely that actions won't be far behind.

Don't try to hurry through a dissonant period. Be patient. Allow the answer to a problem time enough to materialize and evolve. This is the hardest thing for "Type A" people because they want the answer now. They don't like being "in between" any decision. Some people are so impatient that they constantly try to shortcut the process, which leads to forced and inappropriate decisions, resulting in their ultimately getting off track. While a forced decision may get an immediate result, it is often the setup for a different problem later on.

SITUATIONAL GRAVITY

Another challenge that will show up is the principle of *situational gravity*, which is the force that pulls on a person, attempting to keep the person at rest, that is, in his or her current situation. In order to overcome gravity of any kind and to create movement in a person or company, energy is going to have to be exerted. Take the example of a man sitting on a couch, watching television. If he continues to sit there, he exerts very little energy. However, if he wants to get up to do something, he has to exert a lot of energy to overcome his own gravity (typically accompanied by complaining of some sort). But what is the source of this "gravity" that seems to want the man to remain on the couch? It is the force of his current "situation." It's easy and comfortable to stay on the couch; it's hard work to get up and get moving.

Teenagers offer another easy example of situational gravity. Most teenagers try to establish their vision of "adult" status as quickly as possible. They can see and feel a great pull toward this new vision of themselves, but the world around them (friends, parents, siblings, other relatives, neighbors, etc.) tends to treat them as if they are still children—bigger ones, maybe, but still children. This is because these people around the teenager subconsciously want the world around them to stay as they currently know it. Otherwise, they themselves will have to change and treat the teenager in a different way, with different interactions, different rules, and so on so that everything that these people knew as the "way it is" would be gone and a new "way it is" would be thrust upon them.

Remember a time when you were personally excited about a new opportunity (a new job, a new love, a new apartment, etc.) and you told a few friends, only to be met with a lackluster, "Great," or unenthusiastic, "That's nice"? This false enthusiasm is nothing more than those around you being internally bothered by the change it will mean to their relationship with you.

Situational gravity acts to keep us in our current situation. It is caused by the force and energy of the very situation itself, including the environment. Our relationships with other people will also be affected by our change and growth created by our moving toward a new vision. Figure 2.1 illustrates this concept. As a situation changes because of movement toward a vision, the past situation starts to exert an emotional force, not unlike the pulling of a rubber band. As the vision gets closer, the past situation will pull harder and harder, until it breaks. This occurs once the vision is achieved and thus becomes our new current situation.

FIGURE 2.1   Situational Gravity

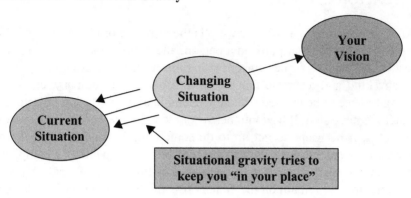

KEY POINTS

- Examine all the elements of your current situation before you launch your new business.
- Define your vision for your company *before* launch. Make sure is it extremely clear and textured (look, feel, smell).
- Your vision statement should be in writing; make sure it includes the core values that you want to see reflected in the business.
- Clarity is the key. A clear vision has a greater likelihood of becoming reality than an unclear vision.
- Cognitive dissonance occurs. Expect it. Look forward to it. It's a sign of growing and learning.
- Situational gravity will be working against all change—business or personal. It will try to keep things as they are. Understand it. Recognize it. And keep moving.

3

USING A
NICHE

*You specialize in something until one day you find it is
specializing in you.*

—ARTHUR MILLER

Home buyers and sellers tend to think of brokerage companies as "niche" or specialty companies. Consumers identify easily with a well-defined company image, that is, estate sellers prefer to work with an estate company, while condo buyers want to work with a condo specialist. While the consumer's perceived benefit of working with a specialty company may, in fact, not be accurate, the perception alone is enough reason for a company to establish itself in a niche during its start-up phase. Often, a company's niche is determined by the style of the broker.

THE BROKER'S STYLE

An experienced real estate agent spends years establishing a personalized business model and customer base. In that process, the agent develops a certain style and method of business. This personal style attracts certain types of clients and causes the agent to gravitate toward certain types of homes or properties to list and sell. When this same experienced agent launches a new real estate company, that firm will be a reflection of the agent's already-established style. If a broker were to attempt to form a company outside his personal range of style, it would be a potential disaster because the broker would be working in unfamiliar, uncomfortable territory. This would create additional personal challenges, since the focus of the new company would feel "unnatural," decreasing the brokerage's likelihood of efficacy and success.

Personal Exercise 5 will help define your style as a broker. If you have no prior real estate production, then answer the questions by looking forward and thinking about your future company.

PERSONAL EXERCISE 5

STYLE CONSIDERATIONS

1. Describe the type of clothes you wear at work (e.g., designer suits, jeans, necktie, T-shirt).
2. Describe the type of car you drive and its condition.
3. What are your favorite restaurants (e.g., McDonald's, Outback, Ruth's Chris Steak House, some little bistro)? And why?
4. Describe the neighborhood you live in. Is it affluent, middle class, or something else?
5. What is the average sales price of the properties you sold in the last 12 months?
6. In what geographic areas have you sold properties in the last 12 months? And what percentage of your closings have been in each of these areas?
7. Is there one or two geographic areas that you specialize in within your marketplace? If so, where are those areas?
8. Describe your typical customers. What is their typical income level? What kind of hobbies do they have; how do they spend their personal time?
9. How and/or where do your customers generally find you?
10. What are some of the attributes or character traits you look for in clients before you agree to work with them? Why?
11. Is there a type of client you simply won't work with? If so, describe that person.

12. Describe the type of agents you like to work with in the marketplace. Give a couple of specific names of agents you really like.
13. Describe the type of agent you don't like to work with in the marketplace. Give a couple of specific names of agents you really don't like to work with.
14. Is there a main type of product you list and sell (e.g., single-family dwellings, condominiums, office buildings, etc.)? If so, describe the type of product you sell more than others.
15. What companies and/or agents are competitors in your marketplace?

ELEMENTS OF STYLE

There are some basic elements to consider when creating the style of a company. These elements are:

- Price range
- Geographic area
- Customer base
- Agent pool
- Product type
- Competition
- Personal preference

Individually, these elements are just reflections of different aspects of a broker's personality. Together, they define a very clear style that will attract prospects and agents who resonate with that style. Determining a company's style is not an exact science; it is more of an intuitive process.

Price Range

Most agents state that they would love to sell upper-end, expensive estate properties. For example, in a marketplace and with an average sales price of $300,000, the high-end marketplace might be in the range of $700,000 or more—maybe even $1 million. An agent's desire to list and sell million-dollar homes may be diminished when the agent realizes that as much as $3,000 to $4,000 may have to be spent on marketing each listing. While this does not mean that a company should exclude high-end properties from its marketing strategy, it does mean that it should consider all the implications when it pursues a certain price range as a niche. So what price range is optimal for a start-up company? (See Personal Exercise 6.)

Determining optimal target price range for a company begins with an examination of the marketplace, which involves a breakdown by price

---

| Tales from the Real World |

WORKING THE UNFAMILIAR

Broker Mary had a small firm in a suburban commuter community about 30 miles from a major city. A "big city" agent, Phyllis, relocated to Mary's community and joined her firm. Mary had never done any business in the city because she was a country person; she didn't like big cities—not part of her style. Although Mary felt uncomfortable about it, Phyllis brought several city listings to Mary's firm.

Mary felt unsure about the unusual marketing procedures and specific disclosures and forms that were required during the marketing and selling of Phyllis's city listings. She was hopeful that Phyllis would instruct her about the unique aspects of these city transactions, which Phyllis did—except for a minor energy disclosure that Phyllis forgot about.

After the close of escrow on one of these city properties, it was discovered that Phyllis had forgotten to provide the required energy disclosure. This resulted in Mary's firm being sued for $6,500, the amount needed to retrofit several energy-saving items that had been required to be cleared by the seller but which Phyllis had forgotten to discuss.

Mary settled the claim by paying for the retrofit repairs. She also learned a valuable lesson about working in markets that were unfamiliar to her: don't!

---

range of homes that have sold. Most multiple listing services (MLSs) can generate a marketplace report for the previous 12-month period that shows closed sales transactions, separated by price ranges (see Figure 3.1).

Once a broker has obtained the overall market activity by price range, the personal track record of the broker should be compared to the overall market activity. This will reveal whether or not the broker is selling in the average price range of the market, or whether the broker is selling properties that are at the higher or lower end of the market.

PERSONAL EXERCISE 6

YOUR TARGET PRICE POINT

1. What will be your new company's target average price range?
2. How did you determine this?
3. List your other thoughts pertaining to your company's target price range.

FIGURE 3.1   Anytown, USA: Sample Report of Closed Sales by Price Range

Price Range	Number of Closed Sales	Percent of Closings
$0–$200,000	550	25%
$200,001–$400,000	725	34%
$400,001–$600,000	410	34%
$600,001–$800,000	105	15%
$800,001–$1,000,000	14	6%
$1,000,001–$1,500,000	6	5%
$1,500,001+	1	4%

If it is discovered that a broker is selling properties in the lower end of the market, then the flavor and style of the broker's own personal transactions is revealed; for example, perhaps the broker enjoys working with first-time buyers or starter condominiums. On the other hand, if it is discovered that a broker has a large number of transactions at the higher end of the price ranges, then perhaps the broker has a more financially affluent sphere of influence and the broker gets a large number of leads from members of a yacht club to which the broker belongs.

Either way, an experienced real estate broker has an established price-range style and needs to understand that this style will be a part of any real estate company started by that broker.

Geographic Area

An interesting phenomenon of the real estate business is that it is still a local business. No matter how large a company grows or how "virtual" it becomes, it still benefits from having offices close to the location of the homes that it intends to sell. While this is changing to some degree as our industry becomes more computer-oriented and mobile, the reality is that home buyers and sellers often gravitate toward a company that has a high presence in the local marketplace. Therefore selecting an ideal geographic area to focus on is important and begins by analyzing data from the local MLS that is broken down by geographic markets. Figure 3.2 shows an example of marketplace activity in Marin County, California, broken down by geographic area.

An examination of Figure 3.2 reveals two geographic areas that should be considered as potential target areas for a company. These are Mill Valley and San Rafael because they have the greatest number of closed units. This

FIGURE 3.2   12-Month MLS Market Activity Sample

Town	Units	Total Volume	Average Sales Price
Belvedere	19	$65,126,000	$3,427,684
Corte Madera	31	$25,121,500	$810,371
Fairfax	38	$29,978,050	$788,896
Greenbrae	32	$29,457,275	$920,540
Kentfield	26	$44,674,000	$1,718,231
Larkspur	34	$41,376,700	$1,216,962
Mill Valley	209	$279,585,087	$1,337,728
Nicasio	2	$3,530,000	$1,765,000
Ross	19	$60,788,500	$3,199,395
San Anselmo	90	$98,375,153	$1,093,057
San Rafael	305	$276,399,368	$906,227
Sausalito	52	$62,556,500	$1,203,010
Tiburon	71	$146,977,184	$2,070,101
Total market closings	**928**	**$1,163,945,317**	**$1,254,251**

means that there is more business to go around and a greater likelihood that a company would be able to survive in these areas in its early stages. A broker may prefer the higher-end homes of Mill Valley over the "bread and butter" starter homes of San Rafael. While the example given is in a very high-end marketplace overall (average sales price of $1.2+ million), the point being made is applicable to any marketplace. In addition, a price-range focus will often determine a geographic area focus.

As a broker considers the geographic area within which to focus, it is also important to examine his or her historical production (comparing the broker's personal production history to MLS activity). This includes reviewing such personal factors as where the broker lives, does the broker already participate in any particular community activities, is the broker already highly visible in a geographic area, and so on. (See Personal Exercise 7.)

PERSONAL EXERCISE 7

YOUR GEOGRAPHIC AREA

1. What will your new company's target geographic marketing area be?
2. Why have you selected these areas?
3. What other thoughts do you have pertaining to the company's target geographic market area?

Customer Base

A broker may not engage in discriminatory practices. However, any marketing executive would encourage a company to understand the behaviors and characteristics of its target customer base. Some of these characteristics may have already been determined when the broker selected a target price point or geographic area.

For example, if a broker's target geographic area consists of vacation properties on a lake with an average home price of $1 million, then the broker will want to target customers who can afford such properties and have an interest in lakefront homes. Furthermore, the average customer in such a marketplace might have an annual income in excess of $200,000 per year, enjoy certain hobbies such as fishing or water skiing, drive certain cars, use certain products, read certain publications, and so forth. This type of information can help a broker focus the marketing efforts of the company in order to obtain prospects who fit the profile.

There are two primary ways to gain information about customer trends: (1) from the customer directly or (2) from third-party sources. When gathering customer database information, it's important to remember that information gathered from a source closest to the customer is more accurate than information found in general statistical data.

In gathering customer data, a broker should start with the closest source possible—past customers. A survey of these past customers should be conducted through telephone calls, by mail, or by e-mail. Because of their ease of use and the ease with which they can be customized, and the rapid response they generate, e-mail surveys are the most effective survey method. There are several cost-effective e-mail survey services available on the Internet that allow a broker to create surveys online in about one hour. Once a survey has been developed, e-mail addresses are manually entered or uploaded and, with a simple click of a mouse button, the survey is sent. As people respond, results can be viewed online within minutes. See the sample survey in Figure 3.3.

For third-party sources of customer information, start with the U.S. Census Bureau. Every 10 years, a census is conducted throughout the United States, and the results obtained are readily available at your library or online. The census will reveal such information as average income, average household size, and job sectors. An additional source of information is the local chamber of commerce, which typically has consumer and business information about a specific marketplace. Begin your data gathering of customer information with a sample survey.

FIGURE 3.3   Sample Initial Customer Survey Questions

- Where were you living before you bought your current home?
- Before you purchased your current home, did you rent or own your residence?
- What is your household income? Are there one or two wage earners in your household?
- How long were you looking for a home before you made your purchase?
- How did you find your current home?
- How did you find the agent that sold you your current home?
- How did you select the company that sold you your current home?
- What hobbies do you have?
- What publications do you read?
- Did school districts play a part in your decision of where to live?
- What Internet sites did you use when looking for a home?
- What was your original target price range before you purchased a home?
- What price did you pay for your home?
- What were a couple of the key factors in the selection of your current home?

Once brokers have done some questioning and analyzing of the behavior patterns of their past customers, they can then apply the company's target price range and geographic focus to determining the customer base (see Personal Exercise 8).

PERSONAL EXERCISE 8

YOUR CUSTOMER BASE

1. What is your target customer's profile?
2. Why do you believe this profile to be accurate?
3. What other thoughts do you have pertaining to your target customer?

Agent Pool

Another key element in a company's style is the local agent pool from which the company will be recruiting agents. When considering the total pool of agents available, a broker should consider the agents' experience, socioeconomic makeup, and the geographic marketplaces they have served. For example, if a broker is in a community of only 20 real estate companies with four to six agents each, that broker will have a more difficult time recruiting agents than if the broker was in a marketplace of 2,000 real estate agents spread out across 300 companies. The potential agent pool for a company is important because these potential agents, as they are recruited, will complement or detract from the image of the company. (See Personal Exercise 9.)

PERSONAL EXERCISE 9

YOUR AGENT POOL

1. How many licensed agents are in your marketplace?
2. What is the average number of units sold by an agent in your market (total number of sales in the market divided by the number of licensed agents)?
3. How many companies or brands are in your marketplace?
4. What percentage of the agents in your marketplace has less than three years of experience? This represents approximately how many agents?
5. Given your company's target price range, how many agents in your marketplace sell houses in this price range?
6. Given your company's target geographic area, how many agents sell houses in this geographic area?
7. Describe the type of agent that you want to work in your company.
8. Write down names of any agents that come to mind that fit this description.
9. Write down any other thoughts pertaining to your agent pool.

Product Type

The simplest element to consider in determining a company's style is the type of product that will be sold or represented. Typically, a broker who is starting a company has real estate sales experience with a focus on a certain type of product such as single-family homes, condos, or commercial investment properties. It stands to reason that if a broker has a great depth of experience in selling one type property, this focus should be maintained in the broker's start-up company. It would be risky and make little sense for a broker to start a company selling commercial condominiums if the broker has no experience, desire, or interest in that particular product. (See Personal Exercise 10.)

Competition

The nature of competition from other firms is an essential element to consider in determining a real estate company's style. By understanding the strengths and weaknesses of competing companies, a broker can assess the opportunities that may exist in the market and how to differentiate his or her firm's services. Differentiation in the minds of agents (who may be potential recruits) and customers is essential to a brokerage's success. (See Personal Exercise 11.)

YOUR PRODUCT TYPE

The breakdown of the historical product type of your sales is as follows:

Type of Product	Percentage of Your Sales
Single-family homes	_____
_____	_____
_____	_____
_____	_____

You expect your company to have the following breakdown of product sales:

Type of Product	Percentage of Sales
Single-family homes	_____
_____	_____
_____	_____
_____	_____

YOUR COMPETITORS

Identify the names of the top five to ten competitors in your marketplace. Rate each company on a scale of 1 (low quality/competitiveness) to 10 (high quality/competitiveness) for each of the categories shown.

Company	Market Share	Location(s)	Facilities	Leadership	Training	Marketing Tools	Agents	Image
1.								
2.								
3.								
4.								
5.								
6.								
7.								
8.								
9.								
10.								

Personal Preference

While it is necessary that we are all careful not to engage in discriminatory practices, it is only human nature that brokers will have personal preferences about the personality types with whom they choose to work. This is an important consideration because the brokers' personal preferences will influence the nature of the company owned or managed by them. For example, a broker may not like working with high-end customers and may prefer first-time buyers, or a broker may enjoy selling condominiums and avoid listing mobile homes. (See Personal Exercise 12.)

PERSONAL EXERCISE 12

YOUR PERSONAL PREFERENCES

1. What personality types of clients do you like working with?
2. What personality types of clients do you not like working with?
3. What types of properties do you like selling?
4. What are the types of properties you don't like to sell?
5. What price range do you prefer to sell properties within?

BRINGING IT ALL TOGETHER

Having examined the individual elements that influence a company's style, it's time to bring it all together in a clear and comprehensive description of the niche the company will serve. Personal Exercise 13 will help you write a thorough description of the niche or style that your company will fill.

PERSONAL EXERCISE 13

BRINGING IT ALL TOGETHER FOR YOURSELF

1. What type of real estate product will the company focus on selling?
2. Who is the company's target customer?
3. What will the company's target price range be?
4. What geographic area(s) will be served by the new company?
5. Who are the primary competitors for the company?
6. What is the niche to be filled by the company?

BE TRUE TO YOURSELF

You are who you are. If you have no interest in selling a certain type of property, don't sell it. If you don't want an office in a certain location, don't locate there. Thoreau once said, "Be true to thine own self and it follows, as the night the day, thou canst not be false to any man."

The clue lies in your passion. If you are passionate about a particular niche market, then you will do well working that niche. If you are simply doing what the other guy is doing, you are doomed to failure or, worse, mediocrity.

By determining your company's style, personality, and what sort of specialization it has, you won't be as tempted to take listings that are not in your product or geographic specialization. And if you do, at least you'll know the potential risk of venturing outside the company's niche.

This doesn't mean that your company can't expand its culture and reach. But such expansion should result from careful planning and an understanding that makes it clear what changes will be required of your agents and staff, as well as the financial commitment needed from you.

So, if you are considering adding mortgage placement to your services, don't do it simply because an agent in your office has a great idea to make more money, but do it because it fits your company's vision, business plan, and niche.

Work from a place of vision!

KEY POINTS

- By targeting a specific niche, a start-up company will increase its likelihood of success.

- A niche is determined by the style of the broker/owner, and there should be congruence between the niche pursued by a company and the personal style of its broker.

- A company's style should be thought out before the firm is established.

- Factors that influence a company's style and niche selection are (1) price range, (2) geographic area, (3) customer base, (4) agent pool, (5) product type, (6) competition, and (7) personal preferences.

CREATING A BRAND

*Once you have got a brand image, it is the most valuable
thing you can have. It gives instant value, credibility,
reliability and reassurance.*

—SIMON ANHOLT

B efore a new company announces itself to the public, it needs to
create an image or brand. A company's brand is important for
several reasons:

1. It is a reflection of what a company represents.
2. It communicates a message about the company.
3. It establishes continuity in the company's marketing message.

4. It increases retention in the minds of customers.

5. It can be a source of pride and esprit de corps for the broker and agents.

CREATE A TEXTURED EXPERIENCE

The most common misconception among brokers is that a brand is merely a logo or something that appears on a sign or a business card. While these items are part of a company's identity package, a brand is a more comprehensive textured experience of the company's presence in the marketplace. A *textured experience* suggests that consumers do not make a decision to work with a company based simply on what they see. Their decision is based on what they hear, feel, smell, think, and experience as they come into contact with a company. This is especially true in real estate because of a consumer's highly charged emotional state around the home buying/selling experience. For example, imagine a real estate company that designs an elegant logo, beautiful signage, high-quality business cards and letterhead, four-color custom brochures, and an advertising campaign all of which speak to the elegance of its prestigious service. A potential customer visits the company's office and sees a letter missing from the company's building signage, an empty receptionist station with a half-eaten sandwich on it, and a waiting room with worn-out furniture. The customer is greeted by a company agent who is dressed in stained blue jeans, scuffed tennis shoes, and an old sweatshirt. When this potential customer explains to the agent that he has an appointment with the broker, the agent takes a couple of steps away from the customer and yells into the office, "Hey Mary. There's some guy here to see you!" The potential customer has now had a *textured* experience of this company's brand, and it says, "We are all promises, but no substance."

Every consumer has been a frustrated customer at one time or another. This type of negative textured experience might have occurred in some restaurant, where the horrid service overshadowed the excellent quality of food or in a department store where its high-quality clothing is soon forgotten because of an unhappy and rude salesperson. The key here is congruence. In other words, all of a company's branding elements must be congruent (in alignment) with each other, or potential customers will sense the disorganization and subconsciously equate this chaos with the level of service they will receive.

In real estate, the most commonly experienced elements of a company's brand are:

- Company name
- Logo
- Motto/positioning statement
- Business cards
- Stationery
- Signage
- Listing presentation
- Postcards
- Web sites
- Procedures

COMPANY NAME

The selection of a company name is one of the most important decisions a new broker faces. A long-standing debate in real estate is whether or not a company should contain the broker's name.

The advantages of using a broker's own personal name include:

- If the broker has established a professional history in the marketplace, the company name will be easily recognized by past customers and other agents.
- Past customers will generally be impressed by the transition from a prior company into a new one that carries the broker's name.
- If the broker continues to personally sell real estate while running the company, the broker will experience some spin-off recognition benefit because as the company agents market the company name, they are unintentionally marketing the broker as an individual producer. (See Personal Exercise 14.)

The disadvantages of using a broker's own personal name include:

- As a practical recruiting consideration, some agents will not want to join a firm if its name is the same as someone against whom they have repeatedly competed for listings.
- If the broker actively sells real estate, then the company's agents may become suspicious of how prospect leads are distributed because they are insecure and threatened by the fact that the broker's name is more visible than their own. (This perception, regardless of accuracy, is something to watch out for and avoid.)

- If the broker is a controversial character in the marketplace, it may not be wise to have a company carrying the broker's name.
- If a broker's name is difficult to spell or remember, then the consumer will have a hard time spelling or remembering the company name.

PERSONAL EXERCISE 14

USING YOUR NAME IN THE COMPANY NAME

Write your full or last name in each of the spaces provided below. When you are done, read each potential company name aloud. Do any of these names feel right to you? If so, circle it or them.

- _____ Real Estate
- The _____ Company
- _____ & Associates
- _____ Associates
- _____ & Company
- The _____ Group
- Team _____ Real Estate
- _____ Realty
- _____ Properties
- _____ Estates

If a broker's personal name is not going to be used, then a company name will have to be created from scratch. There are two ways for brokers to create a company name: (1) hire an advertising agency or (2 create the name themselves. Hiring an advertising agency will be costly, typically running from around $25,000 to $35,000 for a name. This cost, as well as the personal nature of a company name, causes most brokers to create their own.

Most brokerage names are tied to the marketplace they serve in some way; for example, Tech Valley Homes, Lakes Edge Realty, Bodega Bay Homes. Another type of company name is found by using Greek or Latin root words in the name, giving a deeper meaning to the company's presence, for example, Palmaris Properties (*palmaris* means "worthy of receiving the palms," which refers to an ancient Greek ceremony for recognition of excellence). Creating a name is an intuitive process and may take a few days. It is a process of writing down names, weeding through them, trying them out on friends and family members, and then listening to their feedback, which typically reveals perceptions missed by the broker. It's better to hear objections or concerns about a company name in the early stage of development, prior to printing expensive letterhead or using a name that may be a problem. (See Personal Exercise 15.)

PERSONAL EXERCISE 15

THE COMPANY NAME

Step 1. List as many potential names as you can think of for a real estate company.

Step 2. Keep this list around for a few days and add, change, or remove names from it as you become inspired to. Don't rush this process; it may even take a couple of weeks.

Step 3. Select your favorite three to five names from this list.

Step 4. Run these favorite names past a few of your family members, trustworthy agent-friends, and past customers for feedback as to what they think and why.

Step 5. Select the name about which you feel passionate and for which you received positive feedback.

LOGO

Think of a logo as the visual equivalent of the company. In a split second, it represents the essence of the company. When designing a logo, it is important to remember that not everyone is good at everything. If graphics is not a broker's strength, then the help of a professional should be sought. Here are some guidelines to consider for logo design.

Use a Graphic Artist

Find a local graphic artist to help develop a logo and identity package. A good graphic artist can usually be found by asking friends and fellow business associates for a recommendation. If you can't get a referral, then consider searching the Internet for graphic artists in the local marketplace. The Internet allows you to view a graphic artist's work. A broker should conduct an introductory meeting with a graphic artist, during which the graphic artist should ask a lot of questions about the broker's company, image, vision, and core values. A good graphic artist must learn this information in order to properly create a logo design. If the graphic artist is not asking probing questions, the broker should select a different artist.

Within one to two weeks, the graphic artist should come up with four to six samples of logos. While it is possible that one of these first few logos will be ideal, it is more likely that they will serve to clarify an image in the broker's mind, thus providing the seeds of the ultimate logo. Often, the final logo will contain various elements from these first few sample logos.

Depending on the market, a broker can expect to pay as little as $1,000 to as much as $20,000 for a good logo design. This cost should include a broker's complete identity package, that is, letterhead, business cards, envelopes, and signs.

Consider Reproduction Aspects

A common mistake made in logo design is that the logo is too complicated for easy reproduction in a variety of media. A logo may look great at the top of a letterhead, but it may not reproduce well in newspaper advertising. If a logo looks great on signs but fails to be well represented in a magazine, the continuity of the company image is lost. Also, a broker needs to remember that the agents in the company will be using the logo in their own marketing materials. If the logo is difficult to work with, does not reproduce easily, or is too costly to reproduce, these agents will take shortcuts and end up creating a poor-quality version of it. This diminishes the branding effectiveness of the logo. In working with a graphic artist, a broker needs to discuss all the potential uses of a logo and look at samples of how the logo will appear in different applications.

Use Color—Maybe

Studies have shown that the use of color in the logo increases its retention in the customer's mind. However, the use of multiple colors merely for the sake of using color is not always a wise tack to take. A full-color logo will dramatically increase the cost of reproduction in business cards, letterhead, and other stationery. An overuse of color can make a logo look tacky and may deliver the wrong message to prospective customers. A two-color logo may effectively create the desired impact, while keeping reproduction costs manageable.

Explore Available Resources

There are numerous Web sites that create draft logos online. Web sites such as www.logomaker.com can help a broker create logo concepts, if not the final logo version. (See Personal Exercise 16.)

LOGO IDEAS

Using a blank pad or an online logo design Web site, create three to four draft ideas of a potential company logo. If you like anything you create, show it to your graphic designer for his or her input and enhancement.

MOTTO/POSITIONING STATEMENT

If a logo is a visual representation of the company, then the motto or positioning statement communicates the company's core values in a few brief words or a simple sentence. Here are a few examples that are not real estate–related mottos:

Visa: It's everywhere it you want to be.

Nike: Just do it

Avis: We try harder

Burger King: Have it your way

Maxwell House Coffee: Good to the last drop

Hallmark Greeting Card Company: When you care enough to send the very best

Here are some examples of real estate–related mottos:

Hobbs/Herder Advertising: The real estate marketing specialists

Team Perotti Real Estate: Experience the difference

Tech Valley Homes Real Estate: The forward-thinking company

BJ Droubi & Company: Best agents, best listings, best service

While a company doesn't have to have a motto, a motto may help to differentiate it from its competitors and can provide a strong message to the company's agents and customers. The key to a good motto lies in its simplicity. It should be one sentence or a phrase that summarizes the essence of the company or its value proposition.

To create a motto, a broker should start by looking at the core values set forth in the company's vision statement where it is not uncommon to find a phrase or an inspiring short sentence that represents the essence of the company. (See Personal Exercise 17.)

PERSONAL EXERCISE 17

A COMPANY MOTTO

1. Write down two to three sentences that summarize your company's services or value proposition, that is, the benefit of working with your company.
2. Reread the sentences you just wrote and summarize them into one strong sentence or phrase.
3. Have you just created your motto? If not, adjust the sentence and rewrite it into a motto that is straightforward, simple, and clear.
4. Get feedback on the motto by showing it to friends and family members. Revise as appropriate.

BUSINESS CARDS

Even in this electronic or digital age, a business card is still one of the most predominate branding devices a company has. There is a real sense of confidence that is present when an agent hands a prospect a highly professional business card. Here are some thoughts to help save you time and avoid mistakes in creating a business card.

Too Busy

Too many graphics or too much information on a business card can visually confuse a customer and undermine the purpose of the business card, which is to provide *essential* contact information. Occasionally, brokers make the mistake of using the business card as a billboard opportunity for one of their listings, or they include a catch phrase to solicit referrals. This is inappropriate, especially when it is most likely that the business card is being given to someone who doesn't know the broker. A business card is an efficient, professional communication tool, not a chance to be graphically cute—unless "cute" is the target market segment a broker is pursuing.

Photos or Not?

Many years ago, it became the fashion in real estate to put personal agent photographs on business cards. The rational thinking behind this movement was inspired by a study that revealed that the use of a photograph increases retention in the mind of the consumer by as much as 25 percent. Given the number of real estate agents contacted by typical consumers, how will they remember whom they talked to if they don't have a picture to refer to?

Agent photographs on business cards have evolved into a more personal statement for some, who decided to include family members or pets in the photo. This sort of photograph on a business card can present a less than professional appearance. Wouldn't it be a bit strange if your attorney or doctor gave you a business card with his or her photo on it, or a personal photo with family members? What kind of statement does such a business card make? It's just food for thought.

If a company is going to use agent photos on business cards, the broker should insist on the use of a professional photographer. Avoid pictures that include pets or family members. Brokers and agents alike need to think for a moment about congruence, company image, and the message communicated by the business card.

Vertical or Horizontal Layout?

The orientation of the business card really doesn't matter. However, consideration should be given to the presentation folders a broker is going to use; do they have horizontally oriented card cuts in them? (Most do.) Vertically oriented cards will require that they be stapled to the inside of such folders.

STATIONERY

The same issues identified for business cards also apply to business stationery or letterhead. Again, a broker should consider obtaining the services of a graphic artist for design assistance. If a broker is working on a shoestring budget or is otherwise unable to use the services of a graphic artist, then a broker may want to think about using the services of an Internet-based printing company.

Given the quality of good four-color laser printers today, a broker may consider designing letterhead using a word processor template. A graphic artist can usually set up a version of letterhead in a word processor. When a broker thinks of company agents using letterhead carelessly or sending out mailings on letterhead, it may be cost-effective to keep letterhead in an electronic format. A self-printing solution is not advised for the envelopes used by a company because of the need to maintain a reasonable level of quality.

A graphic artist will be able to recommend a printing company. Costs will vary depending upon the type of business card, quality of stationery paper, number of colors, and so forth. As an alternative solution, here is a list of several Internet-based printing companies that specialize in business cards and letterhead.

www.PrintDepartment.com
www.BusinessCardsOnline.com
www.VistaPrint.com
www.PrintsMadeEasy.com
www.OvernightPrints.com
www.iprint.com
www.PrintingForLess.com

SIGNAGE (YARD SIGNS AND OPEN HOUSE A-FRAME SIGNS)

The next element of the branding package to consider is the property sign. Statistically, over 17 percent of home buyers find their potential home via the property sign in the yard. For this reason, signage is extremely important to a real estate company. There are a few key factors to consider when designing a company sign.

Readability

One of the most common mistakes made by brokers is that they design signs using logos that are easy to read on business cards or stationery but that do not translate well to signage. It is important to remember that logos always look smaller on a yard sign than they do on paper or other mediums. Furthermore, script-type lettering in a company name may look so small on a sign that it becomes unreadable from only a few feet away. Ideally, a sign should be readable from at least 100 feet away, representing a distance of four houses away from the sign.

Material

Signs are made of a few different types of materials. The best material to use for yard signage is a polyurethane or polypropylene, which is weather resistant, scratch resistant, and lightweight and allows for easy installation.

GET OUT OF THE WAY

Developing the company name, logo, and marketing materials is often an area where you might have a tendency to get a little crazy with your creative design ideas. Don't get too cute or clever because your new image could create an impression that you don't take your business seriously. No one will appreciate you representing yourself as the "Duke of Real Estate" or the "Queen of Development."

Also, avoid getting your ego overly involved in this process. While you will be leading this company, you should avoid creating a brand that is so much "you" that it becomes a deterrent for outside agents whom you may want to recruit and who have spent a lot of money developing a personal marketing image that is focused on them.

Some companies use metal signs, which are not recommended because of how easily they are scratched and because of their sharp edges that could cause damage if blown free from the sign post.

Phone Numbers

What phone numbers should be on a company's sign? The main office phone number? The agent's personal phone number or direct line? Or a generic 800 number that goes to a call center? The answer will depend on a company's philosophy and how the broker prefers to have incoming sign calls handled.

If a broker wants all calls generated by a sign answered by a floor desk agent, then the main office phone number must be on the sign. The problems with floor time are: (1) Not all agents are skilled at handling incoming calls, and (2) brokers often assign newly licensed agents to floor time, meaning that the brokerage's costly leads (typically costing $50 to $75 a call) are being handled by the least experienced agents who are going to have a lower closing ratio for appointments than will more experienced agents. From the customer's perspective, the listing agent is the most knowledgeable person to answer questions about that listing. Experienced listing agents are most likely to be better closers when handling property inquiries, and they tend to screen prospects better, avoiding wasted time. Given the high costs of marketing, companies need to think about conversion ratios.

Personalized property signs that use a listing agent's direct telephone number exclusively on the sign will thus take advantage of the listing agent's closing abilities, while providing the added benefit of reducing telephone traffic for the company receptionist. In the event of the agent's unavailability, today's customers are accustomed to leaving voice-mail messages with their contact information. Knowledgeable buyers and sellers are more interested in getting accurate information from the right agent than they are concerned about giving out their contact information. The use of personalized signs will help a brokerage increase its agent productivity, which translates into greater revenues.

As a final option, a brokerage can use an automated call center phone number on its signs. Each listing or advertisement would be assigned a three- to four-digit extension number, and customers calling in would enter the appropriate extension number for the desired listing, thus allowing them to hear recorded information about the particular listing. Customers who are interested in obtaining further information or a viewing of the property can leave a message, or they can press "0" and be connected to a live person.

Web Site Address

All signs should have the company's Web site address on them. This allows prospective customers to obtain further information about the company or its listings from the comfort of their own home or office.

Sign Makers

Signs can be made by any local sign company, and if a broker needs a sign made quickly, a local company is the ideal solution. However, there are several national sign makers that specialize in real estate signs, who will provide the most economic solution for a broker. The following list, though not all-inclusive, will give a broker a good place to start:

Lowen Sign Company: www.lowensign.com
Oakley Signs & Graphics: www.oakleysign.com
Dee Sign Company: www.deesigncompany.com
Build A Sign: www.BuildASign.com
Real Estate Signs: www.RealEstateSigns.com

LISTING PRESENTATION

A listing presentation is a package or booklet that contains information about market conditions, the company, the agents, and the marketing efforts that will be made on the seller's behalf. Depending on the company brand and its target price range for listings, the presentation package could be an elaborate four-color presentation or a more modest two-color presentation. A brokerage should consider developing a listing presentation for its agents using Microsoft PowerPoint, which enables agents to use an interactive laptop presentation. Also, the individual slides within this presentation can be printed out, thereby creating a handout that matches the laptop presentation. As a side benefit, once sellers know that they are about to receive a copy of the presentation, they tend to pay more attention to the agent's discussion during the actual presentation.

Franchise organizations will provide their brokers with choices and options for listing presentation materials. A nonfranchise start-up company has to create its own initial listing presentation package. A listing presentation should address the following key areas:

- Introduction and overview of the presentation
- Current market conditions
- Information about the company
- Information about the agent
- Information about marketing strategies
- Information about pricing strategies
- An area to insert the CMA (comparative market analysis)

While a broker could take the time to develop a highly personalized PowerPoint presentation from scratch, templates are readily available that can be easily adapted and personalized. Figure 4.1 is a table of template PowerPoint listing presentations and sources for accessing them.

POSTCARDS

A key element to include in any branding effort is the development of marketing postcards and other direct mail pieces. These are typically postcards for "just listed" announcements, "just sold" announcements, or open house invitations. Given the ease, availability, and quality of online printing

---

HOW TO WASTE TIME AND MONEY

A successful broker needed a listing presentation package to help his agents obtain listings. He developed a massive 47-page print presentation that impressed and pleased his agents. This legendary presentation was designed to be used in its entirety by his new licensees, or piecemeal by his experienced agents, who just needed some additional handouts to add to their current presentations. It took six months to complete this epic, four-color listing presentation and cost over $20,000 to produce. The agents were happy and the world was good.

Then one day the broker discovered that agents were hoarding packets of certain pages from the presentation and creating a shortage of the most preferred pages. To make matters worse, less than 10 percent of the agents were actually using the presentation. The agents told the broker that while they liked the presentation, it was now in need of updating, and they also preferred their own materials because they could put their own individual photos on their own materials, something they could not do with the company's presentation. The broker went to work creating a more flexible presentation that could be updated easily and offered personalization potential. In six months (and for an additional $10,000), the broker proudly distributed a word processor version of the presentation on a CD-ROM that allowed each agent to personalize the materials using their own computer. The agents were happy, and the world was good.

Then one day the agents complained that the broker needed a PowerPoint presentation so they could use laptops in presentations, especially since a competitor was giving away such a presentation to its agents. The broker went to work creating a PowerPoint presentation. Two months later, the broker handed the agents a new CD-ROM with a customizable PowerPoint presentation that could be personalized by each agent and printed out in color as a "leave-behind" for their sellers. The agents were happy, and the world was good.

But then the broker overheard some older agents talking in the lunchroom. They were complaining about the new PowerPoint presentation because they didn't know how to use it. They further said that they wouldn't use it anyway because it contained too much information. Besides, they said, they worked only by referral anyway.

The moral of the story? A broker can't please everyone in the company.

---

services for postcards, a broker no longer needs to spend a lot of time trying to develop a company postcard program. Figure 4.2 is a list of online postcard providers. Additional providers can be found by searching the Internet.

FIGURE 4.1   Listing Presentation Sources

Product	Producer	Cost	Where to Buy
Homeselling and Marketing Presentation	TheBrokerCoach.com	$89 for CRB members $139 for nonmembers	www.CRB.com
Company Presentation	Achieve Ace Ltd	$130–$400	www.agentpresentations.com
Top Presenter 2	Top Producer Systems	$299	Google the term "Top Presenter 2" for a list
Top Producer 7i	Top Producer Systems	Monthly fee	www.Topproducer.com

FIGURE 4.2   Postcard Providers

Company	Where to Find It
PrintDepartment.com	www.PrintDepartment.com
VistaPrint	www.VistaPrint.com
ReaMark	www.reamark.com
Image Media	www.imagemedia.com
Real Estate Postcards Online	www.realestatepostcardsonline.com

WEB SITES

A company Web site is a critical element of a broker's branding efforts. In a 1999 survey by the California Association of Realtors, it was revealed that 93 percent of buyers stated that they are "very likely" to use the Internet in the purchase of their next home. A majority of prospective sellers, buyers, or agents will look at a company's Web site to learn about the firm and compare it to other companies. In other words, without an adequate Web site, a brokerage may lose potential customers.

A challenge for most brokers in designing a Web site is that most brokers have limited or no technical knowledge of what makes a Web site successful. A broker may not understand the subtleties of keywords, titles, first paragraphs on a Web page, and so on. The good news is that a broker doesn't have to become an expert in Web pages in order to create an effective Web site for the company because an entire industry has sprung up to handle such matters. There are numerous Web site template companies that will provide a broker with an instant Internet presence. In selecting a Web site template provider, the broker has to make sure that the selected template Web site provides the right benefits for the brokerage. The key factors to look for when selecting a Web site provider or package for a company are:

- **Customer support.** Does the company provide *real* 24/7 support? Or at the very least, does it provide support during some portion of the weekend? Invariably a Web site will have problems on the weekend during heaviest traffic times.

- **Search engine assistance.** Does the provider help with search engine optimization? If not, the broker will have to hire an online marketing company to help with this issue. Because there are thousands of real estate companies and agents with Web sites, getting the broker's company to the top of the search engine page is critical to increasing brokerage exposure and Web site results.

- **Lead generation system.** Does the Web site provide a lead generation system? Lead generation systems, once considered exceptional services, have become the standard and should be incorporated into the company's Internet presence.

- **IDX compatibility.** Is the Web site IDX-compatible? IDX is an interface platform that allows a broker's Web site to pull listing information from a multiple listing service. This allows a brokerage to show active listings, including those of other companies, on its Web site. In some parts of the country, IDX interface with the MLS data is not allowed by the MLS provider. But, more and more, IDX integration is becoming the norm.

- **Informational reports.** Does the Web site provide a series of informational reports on the listing or buying of properties for consumers? A large amount of content on a Web site creates "stickiness," meaning that potential customers must return to the site repeatedly to obtain useful information.

- **Easy updating and adaptability.** If a Web site is so difficult to update that the broker or the broker's staff put off doing updates, then the broker should consider a different template company. It is not unreasonable for a broker, prior to committing to a specific provider, to have the Web site provider walk through a sample of updating a Web page or uploading photographs for listings.

FIGURE 4.3   Template Web Site Providers

Provider	How to Contact
iHouse Marketing	www.iHouseweb.com
Myers	www.myers.com
RealtyDrive	www.realtydrive.com
Total Real Estate Solutions	www.totalrealestatesolutions.com
Z57 Internet Solutions	www.z57.com
Agent Image	www.agentimage.com
Blitz Development	www.blitzdevelopment.com
Rapid Listings	www.rapidlistings.com
Consulnet	www.consulnet.ca
Link U Realty	www.linkurealty.com

Figure 4.3 is a list of providers that can at least be the starting point for a broker's investigations. Monthly costs and setup fees have been intentionally omitted because they don't remain constant.

PROCEDURES

While policies and procedures for an office are discussed later in the book, it is appropriate to consider some specific procedures that can add to or detract from a company's brand. These are procedures that affect a customer's experience in working with a company and are important to consider because they can either create a sense of congruence and continuity in the minds of your clients, or a sense of fragmentation and chaos. Specifically, the procedures that should be addressed in writing are:

- **Maintaining the appearance of the front office.** A procedure should be implemented regarding the appearance of the front office and who is responsible for maintaining it in an uncluttered and professional state. While a cleaning service will take care of the waiting room front office at the end of the day, a staff person should keep this area uncluttered during the workday because it creates a lasting impression in the minds of clients.
- **Greeting customers when they come to the office.** A procedure should establish the exact greeting a broker wants staff to use with all people that enter the office. For example, a broker may want staff members to greet new arrivals as follows: "Good morning, welcome to

ABC Realty. How may I help you?" It is also important that this procedure sets forth the manner in which customers are to be greeted; for
example, the customer should be greeted with a smile and looked
squarely in the eyes. A staff person who greets a customer with a positive, polite, and professional demeanor can add to a company's brand
image in that customer's mind.

- **Initial answering of phone calls.**   The exact wording, manner, and
  vocal tone to be used by staff members when answering incoming
  phone calls should be expressed in writing. A broker may decide to
  have staff members answer the phone with a particular phrase, especially if that phrase is part of a marketing strategy; for example, "It's a
  great day at ABC Realty! This is Mary. How may I help you?" An
  important procedure to include here is exactly how to handle calls from
  someone who is irate or upset.
- **Showing customers to a conference room.**   A company may want to
  have a procedure for how its staff members should direct customers
  to a conference room. Should the staff member walk the customer
  to the conference room? Should the customer be offered water, coffee,
  or tea? Should the conference room door be closed once the client
  is seated?
- **Handling customers in the waiting room.**   Consideration should be
  given when a customer or co-op agent is in the waiting room. In such
  cases, inappropriate or confidential topics should not be discussed, and
  staff members should use caution in their conversations.

While some of these procedures may seem trivial, a brokerage only
gets one chance to make a first impression.

KEY POINTS

- A broker should take some time in selecting a company brand. It's better to spend too much time on this issue than to regret a brand selection
  that ultimately does not fit the firm.
- Use of an independent graphic artist to create an identity package will
  provide access to fresh ideas and an outside perspective.
- Online resources for printing of marketing materials should be used
  as often as possible to provide the greatest amount of diversity in
  marketing materials at the lowest cost possible.

- Procedures that set forth the ideal experience that a customer should have in the initial office visit or first telephone contact are a part of a company's branding package; it does no good to tell a customer how great a brokerage is if the phones are improperly answered or the company waiting room looks like a messy bedroom.

5

TO FRANCHISE OR NOT TO FRANCHISE

It's about creating strength in numbers, finding common ground and supporting each other . . .

—JANE KIM

A broker has the choice of whether or not to affiliate with a national franchise. Since image, style, and competitive forces vary dramatically from one marketplace to another, there is no hard and fast rule to follow; a broker must evaluate the benefits, cost, and style associated with the various franchises. This chapter discusses the benefits and drawbacks of becoming a franchise office. Since franchisors adapt their systems to meet market forces, a broker who is serious about joining a franchise should investigate all the options available for his or her marketplace.

THE BENEFITS OF A FRANCHISE

The benefits discussed here are not necessarily the same benefits that a
franchisor might expound upon in the process of actively selling a franchise
to a broker, but rather those benefits specifically mentioned by numerous
franchise brokerage owners.

- **Perceived stability.** As a franchise real estate office, a new brokerage carries a greater perception of stability in the local community than
  that of a new independent firm. This could help a broker in recruiting
  and in initial business development.
- **Existing systems.** A franchise offers its franchisees a significant number of proven systems, policies, commission models, and other tools that
  can save a broker countless hours of having to create everything from
  scratch. Often, these systems are like modules that simply have to be
  plugged into the broker's office.
- **Training.** A large franchise will have regional live, Internet-based, or
  satellite-broadcast training programs for brokers and their agents.
- **Marketing tools.** Access to marketing support is one of the most
  common reasons brokers join franchise systems. A franchise typically
  provides a wide variety of marketing tools, suppliers, and vendors that
  a broker can easily tap into, thereby saving the broker countless hours
  of unnecessary research and allowing the broker to stay focused on the
  day-to-day running of the business.
- **Recruiting materials.** While franchisors will not do the recruiting
  for a broker, they typically have a variety of recruiting materials that
  are of high quality and can be customized for a broker's company and
  marketplace.
- **Management support.** A broker may receive management support
  from a franchise system in two ways: (1) franchisor business consultants and regional leadership or (2) networking with other franchisees.
  The amount and type of support varies widely across franchise systems
  and often depends largely upon the regional leadership of the particular
  franchise in your particular marketplace.

While franchise benefits such as national networking, national television ads, or relocation divisions offer lots of "sizzle" for potential franchisees, a broker may not experience any direct benefit (e.g., increased
market share or increased recruiting ability) from such programs and
should not select a franchisor based solely on these items.

THE CHALLENGES OF A FRANCHISE

The following challenges will not prevent a broker from being successful. However, it is a reality that there are challenges in working with a franchise system because by affiliating with a franchise, a broker is essentially bringing a silent partner into the business and sharing the revenues generated by the franchise office. The key challenges of being a franchise office include:

- **Value proposition.** A typical complaint from franchisees is the cost of the franchise fee. These complaints are merely a symptom of a shaky value proposition being delivered to the broker by the franchisor. Brokers don't object to paying franchise fees when they are receiving benefits in excess of the franchise costs. On the other hand, franchisors do not always "deliver the goods." Brokers considering a particular franchise system should talk with existing franchisees to determine if the franchisor is delivering its promised value proposition.
- **Perception versus reality.** Not all franchises are the same. Some franchises will provide a high level of support and all the programs a broker could possibly want or use, while other franchises may only sell the broker a brand name and provide very little assistance. A broker should remember that what is *perceived* about a particular franchise may not, in fact, be the *reality* of that franchise.
- **Growth restrictions.** When a brokerage joins a franchise, it acquires the rights to use the franchise brand in a specific zip code or for a specific office location. In order to protect the quality of a franchise brand, the franchisor may retain control over neighboring zip codes. This affects the rights of the franchisee to expand into additional offices, which is especially important if a broker has growth ambitions or potential acquisition opportunities.

In addition to the above issues, there is another important issue that must be dealt with concerning franchises—the franchise fee. There are essentially four types of fees that a broker could pay to a franchisor. The first type of fee is the initial franchise purchase, which typically ranges from $0 to as much as $50,000. This initial charge is paid for the right to join the franchise system and also covers initial setup costs for the franchisor.

The second type of fee is the *off-the-top fee,* which is the fee that a broker will pay on every transaction or every revenue dollar generated by the

FIGURE 5.1 Nonfranchise Office versus Franchise Office Comparison

	Nonfranchise Office	Franchise Office
Gross commission income	$1,250,000	$1,250,000
Costs of sale		
Franchise royalties	—	$62,500
Sales associate commissions*	$875,000	$831,250
Total costs of sale	$875,000	$893,750
Gross profit (company dollar)	$375,000	$356,250
Operating expenses	$312,500	$312,500
Net operating income	$62,500	$43,750
Difference between nonfranchise		
and franchise net operating income		$18,750
Percent of profit paid to franchise		30%

*Sales associate commissions are less with a franchise because they are calculated *after* the payment is made to the franchisor.

broker's company. For a start-up office, this type of fee will typically range between 4 and 8 percent of gross revenues. A problem pertaining to the off-the-top fee for most new business owners is that they don't understand its relationship to their profitability. When a broker agrees to pay 5 to 6 percent off the top, the broker is paying potentially 20 to 50 percent or more of the company's bottom-line profit. A sample comparison of a franchise office to a nonfranchise office and how the franchise fee affects the bottom line is shown in Figure 5.1.

There are hundreds, if not thousands, of real estate offices in the United States today that pay franchise fees and are doing quite well. However, a broker needs to be fully aware of the impact that an off-the-top franchise fee represents to the company's bottom line.

The third type of franchise fee a broker can expect to pay is referred to as a *marketing fee,* or a *national marketing fee.* This type of fee can be on a per transaction basis, for example, $50 per transaction closed, or on a percentage basis of revenue, similar to an off-the-top fee, though a marketing fee of this type might be in the area of only an additional 1/8 to 1/4 percent.

The fourth type of franchise fee that a broker could pay is a *per licensee fee,* that is, a monthly fee for each agent on the broker's roster. This type of fee applies to desk fee types of franchises and is usually in the range of $25 to $50 per agent.

WHAT TO LOOK FOR IN A FRANCHISE

The key in selecting a franchise is to perform adequate due diligence. A broker should start by calling various franchises and asking for an appointment with someone in their franchise sales department. In this initial meeting, the broker should allow the franchise sales representative to

PERSONAL EXERCISE 18

QUESTIONS TO ASK A FRANCHISOR

1. What are the top five reasons to select your franchise over another?
2. What are your franchise's goals for growth in my market area, and what specific efforts are being undertaken, or are going to be undertaken, in order to achieve these goals?
3. How will you, as my franchisor, help me recruit agents or search out potential acquisition/merger opportunities?
4. What are the total fees that I can expect to pay as a member of your franchise system?
5. As my operation grows, do I receive a discount in my franchise fees?
6. Is there a master franchisor that I will be working with in my market area?
7. What are my restrictions regarding opening or acquiring additional offices?
8. Who owns or controls the franchise zip codes, or market areas, around my office or in the marketplaces that I might want to expand into?
9. What are the specific training programs that will be available for me or my agents?
10. How often are training programs conducted in my market?
11. What marketing support will I receive?
12. Will you give me the names of three franchisees so that I may discuss their experience within your franchise system?
13. Who is the business consultant that will be supporting my office?
14. What procedures would I have to follow for approval if I buy another company?
15. If I sell my company, what are the buyer's options relative to the franchise?
16. How long is my franchise agreement and how is it renewed?
17. What are the three most common complaints expressed by your franchisees?
18. How will you support me in making the announcement about my affiliation with your franchise?
19. What are my options if I am unhappy with the franchise in the first few months?
20. What sort of financial support might be available to me if my business gets in financial trouble?

give his or her best show about the franchise system. After hearing from all of the franchises that interest a broker, a second appointment should be set up with the top two to three franchises, during which the more difficult questions should be asked, as shown in Personal Exercise 18.

FRANCHISE MODELS

There are several types of franchise models available today, with new models arriving on the scene every year. Some of the newer franchise models are bringing with them new ways of looking at our industry, but they remain unproven and are deemed a higher risk for a start-up company. While there is no way to provide a complete list of all of the franchise models available, the primary models can be examined. Each of these models has its own strengths and weaknesses. It is up to each broker to investigate thoroughly which of these models might be most appropriate for his or her business.

Traditional Commission Model

The *traditional commission model* is the most common franchise model and is seen in such franchises as Century 21 Real Estate, Prudential Real Estate Affiliates, Coldwell Banker Residential Real Estate, or a dozen other well-known national brands. These franchises have grown up over the last 50 to 80 years at a time when the traditional commission model was highly profitable and agent commission splits within the company averaged close to 50 to 60 percent.

   Under the traditional commission model, the brokerage revenues come from the gross commissions generated by its salespeople. This gross commission income (or GCI) is shared first with the franchisor through payment of the off-the-top fee, then secondarily with the sales associate responsible for the transaction. This leaves an amount referred to as *gross profit* or *company dollar* and represents the amount of money the broker-age has left to pay its operating expenses and generate profit for its owner.

   For a start-up company, the key to a traditional commission model office is to keep the gross profit (or company dollar) at a minimum of 21 to 35 percent of the gross commissions received by the company. This task is easier said than done in today's climate, where agents are demanding bigger commission splits than ever before.

The primary benefit of the traditional commission model franchise is that it is commonly accepted, understood, and supported, thus creating no barriers to recruiting agents from companies with similar commission structures. Furthermore, the cash flow for this sort of office is good if it is in a high-end marketplace or in a marketplace with a high volume of sales units. As the company's agents make more money and produce more sales, so should the broker's profits grow.

Desk Fee Model

The *desk fee model* has been the primary model used by such major franchise players as Realty Executives and RE/MAX. The desk fee model is designed to accommodate top-producing agents who prefer to control their own expenses and commissions with the idea that they will ultimately end up retaining a greater portion of the commission than they would at a traditional commission model company.

In the desk fee model, the brokerage derives its primary revenues from rental fees or "desk fees" paid by the agents for the use of the brokerage's name, phones, desks, and brand. These desk fees vary widely across the United States, from as little as $100 per month to as high as $2,500 per month and are typically a reflection of the services provided to the agent by the brokerage. The franchisor will help a broker determine what desk fee prices should be charged in order to achieve some target profitability.

The benefit of the desk fee model franchise is that the brokerage receives consistent monthly revenue from its agent base, assuming agents pay their monthly fees in a timely manner. A broker needs to have some skill in enforcing collection of monthly fees, or company revenues won't be consistent. This can be a challenge during softening or slow markets, when agents might not have the cash available to pay monthly fees.

In an effort to increase recruiting competitiveness, some desk fee franchises have modified their policies to support local franchisees in offering other commission models as well as desk fee options for their agents.

Recruiting Model

Realizing how important recruiting was to the growth and profitability of a brokerage, some entrepreneurial brokers developed the *recruiting model,* which compensates agents and brokers for recruiting additional agents into

---

Tales from the Real World

OBTAIN AND READ ALL PAPERWORK!

John was a manager for a major franchise. As a reward for John's recruiting efforts, the master franchisee gave John an opportunity to acquire a troubled franchise office in an upper-end marketplace. The broker did not charge John an initial franchise fee, since the franchise fee had already been previously paid by the master franchisee.

John was given disclosure documents, which he reviewed carefully for any potential references that might affect his ability to grow his new company into a multioffice organization. John discovered no such limitations and further noted that there were no other franchise offices in the immediate surrounding towns. John was excited by the opportunity to carry the franchise brand into untapped neighboring marketplaces.

John set out to recruit agents into his new office. Within 90 days, John had reenergized the office, recruited additional agents, and found a high-end boutique firm to acquire. John worked out the details of this potential acquisition with the owner and brought his plan to the master franchisee, seeking franchise approval of this new office addition to the system.

John's excitement was soon diminished when the master franchisee would not approve of the acquisition because the boutique office was in a town that the master franchisee wanted to retain for itself. This information had never been disclosed to John. John hired an attorney and began a battle with both the master franchisee and the franchisor, claiming failure to adequately disclose and explain the franchise growth restrictions, especially given the fact that John had expressed interest in growing into a multioffice organization.

It was discovered that the master franchisee had neglected to provide John with the list of zip codes and towns that were reserved for the master franchisee's expansion exclusively. Disillusioned with the entire experience, John no longer wished to be a part of the franchise and agreed to settle his claim by simply unwinding the franchise purchase agreement. John soon went to work for a competing company.

---

the franchise. Two major franchises that work with this model are Avalar Real Estate and Keller Williams Realty.

The basic concept is that a reward is offered for recruiting agents into the company. Once an agent or broker has been recruited into a franchise office, a certain percentage of the franchise fee paid from that new recruit's gross production is ultimately returned to the agent or broker responsible for recruiting that agent. The financial incentive for recruiting another agent typically ranges from 0.5 to 1.2 percent of the gross commission income generated by that new agent. In the case of Keller Williams Realty, an additional small recruiting bonus is paid on the proportionate percentage of the profits generated by any agent recruited. Furthermore, in the recruiting model franchise, a broker can also collect bonuses for additional agents that are recruited by the new recruits, similar to a multilevel marketing concept, potentially creating a passive "down line" revenue stream from agents recruited, then from other agents recruited by those agents.

The benefit of a recruiting model franchise is that it creates financial incentive for recruiting and encourages agents to proactively recruit on the broker's behalf. This sort of motivation can help a small office experience explosive growth.

The downside of a recruiting model franchise is that it often attracts agents that may be more interested in recruiting and creating a "down line" revenue stream than they are in listing and selling real estate. A broker may want to think carefully about hiring an agent who wants to join the company simply because of the recruiting incentive; this may be a clue that the agent may not be a very solid sales producer. If an office becomes filled with agents who are mediocre producers, trying to recruit better agents will be difficult. Depending upon the franchisor, the recruiting model franchise may in fact become a retirement model for an agent or broker.

Retirement Model

A common question for experienced agents and brokers is, "How can I retire?" The *retirement model* has been created to answer that question. Over the years, an agent builds a book of business in the form of hundreds of past clients. In the retirement model, a system is provided so an agent or broker can pass on this book of business to a successor and collect fees on all future business generated from the client base that has been passed on. As in the recruitment model, it is not uncommon that a retirement model franchise may also include some reward for recruiting agents. One of the more popular retirement model franchises available today is Exit Realty.

High-Density Model

Imagine a real estate office with over 1,000 real estate agents, but occupying only about 2,000 square feet of office space. Agents in this type of office would not actually have permanent desk space, but might have "hotel" workstations that would allow them to plug their laptops into the office network or Internet. This type of office may have numerous conference rooms, a large work room, a reception station, and an office for the broker, and possibly an administrative assistant. Thus, all agents working for this company would be considered satellite agents. This sort of office is a *high-density model*.

Given the rising costs of office space, increasing agent splits, and the need to recruit even larger numbers of agents in order to achieve profitability, it is easy to understand how this high-density model came into existence. In a high-density model, agents typically pay only a monthly fee and a minimum off-the-top percentage of their gross commission income to the broker, allowing them to retain 95+ percent of their commissions earned. Agents do have to pay all their own expenses, but the broker will receive the monthly stipend from each agent, plus additional profits from the close transactions.

The high-density model franchise is being met with skepticism by the traditional brokerage community because the brokerage community cannot understand how a high-density broker can adequately manage hundreds, if not thousands, of agents with any sort of accountability and quality. There is a fear that this widened span of control will result in more lawsuits or claims because of less supervision, though this in no way has been proven.

The benefit of the high-density model franchise is that the broker can expect a consistent level of monthly income from the agents while maintaining a relatively low fixed-cost overhead for the office.

ALIGNMENT IS ESSENTIAL

It is critical that you select a franchise system that is in alignment with your core values and that shares your business philosophy. If you select a franchise simply based upon its flashy presentation or the personality of its regional leadership, you could make a critical mistake that would affect the staff's enthusiasm in your own office. If you are "on fire" about your franchise selection and a real believer in the value of the brand, it will be easier to explain a solid value proposition to potential agent recruits. This positive attitude will be felt by agents in the interview process and will be contagious.

Selecting a franchise that is *not* in alignment with your core values means constant resentment of franchise fees and infrequent use of franchise programs, translating into no enthusiasm about your brand during recruiting interviews. So be true to yourself.

KEY POINTS

- A quality franchise should provide support in the areas of brand recognition, office operational systems, marketing, recruiting, training, and consulting.

- While franchisors receive only 5 to 7 percent of company gross commission income (GCI), this amount translates into 20+ percent of a broker's total company profit.

- A broker should evaluate the value proposition that a franchise is bringing to the table.

- A broker should investigate the franchise limitations that may affect future growth of the broker's company into a multioffice organization.

- A broker should have an attorney read franchise documents before signing them.

- A broker should select a franchise that is in alignment with the broker's method of doing business and core values.

CHAPTER 6

YOUR OFFICE
LOCATION

*The three most important factors in buying a home are
location, location, location!*

—UNKNOWN WISE PERSON

There are several key issues for brokers to consider when selecting the ideal location for their first office. These are best discussed from the most general issue to the most specific issue.

SELECTION OF MARKETPLACE

If a broker has determined a specific company niche, it is likely that he or she has also decided on the specific town or marketplace for the new office;

for example, a broker with the niche of homes with boat docks might want to be located near a marina, or a broker who loves snow skiing and selling the outdoor lifestyle might locate the office in a winter vacation area. For most start-up brokers, the location decision is often made by reviewing where the broker has done most of his or her sales; for example, if a broker sold more homes in the Pacific Heights area of San Francisco, then his or her first office might be based in that area.

However, a broker's past production, while a perfectly valid reason for selecting an office location, is not the most objective. A broker may also consider market activity in various neighborhoods or towns. By using statistical data available from the local multiple listing service, a broker can get a clear understanding of market activity. (See Personal Exercise 19.) Market statistics for the previous 12 to 24 months should be examined for each neighborhood or town in the broker's marketplace. By comparing this statistical activity with the broker's niche, it is possible to discover a natural town or marketplace "fit" for the brokerage.

In Figure 6.1, let's assume that a broker had a personal track record of sales in the $200,000 price range. If this broker intends his or her new firm to stay in this price range niche, in which town should the broker open an office and why?

Given the target price range niche, Hollow Point may be the best choice. Prices in Port Caper are lower than the target price range. Hollow Point offers 50 percent more in sales volume than does Port Caper, with only 10 percent difference in closed units. This translates to a nominal risk from increasing the target average sales price to the $250,000 in Hollow Point to produce an overall 50 percent increase in potential sales volume. Opening an office in Stoneridge would require a different culture from what the broker has historically worked in.

A broker should also consider competition from other real estate companies in a particular neighborhood or town. A strong competitor in the

FIGURE 6.1   Using Data to Select a Marketplace

Town	Average Sales Price	Number of Closed Units in Last 12 Months	Amount of Closed Volume in Last 12 Months
Stoneridge	$600,000	100	$60,000,000
Hollow Point	$250,000	195	$48,750,000
Port Caper	$150,000	210	$31,500,000

area could mean that it will take longer to get a start-up company noticed; on the other hand, a strong competitor could mean that consumers are in need of a brokerage option to represent them. Overall, it is definitely easier to capture market share if there is no dominating brokerage presence in the immediate area.

PERSONAL EXERCISE 19

EXAMINING YOUR MARKET DATA

Using your multiple listing service (MLS) data, determine the top three towns or neighborhoods for locating a brokerage office based upon:

1. Your target niche
2. Price
3. Number of units sold
4. Competition

STREET LOCATION

Serious thought needs to be given to the street location of an office. (See Personal Exercise 20.) In the past, consumers generally walked into real estate offices to seek assistance with finding a home. This customer behavior pattern may not exist in all marketplaces, however. In addition, lower rental rates are causing a trend in residential real estate companies to move into actual office buildings. Here are some factors a broker should consider when selecting a street location for an office:

- **Visibility.** Twenty years ago, it was considered foolish if a real estate office did not have ground-floor visibility on a major traffic artery. However, with the increasing mobility of buyers and sellers and the impact of the Internet on customer behavior, some brokers feel that visibility is not as important as it used to be. Several companies in urban marketplaces are located in high-rise office buildings or in office parks, with little or no visibility.

    The style of a broker's company or franchise brand may influence the need for a high-visibility location. As a final thought, most real estate agents prefer a location that has high visibility, easy access to freeways, and easy access to and from their cars. Thus, an office with higher visibility may be a recruiting enticement for potential agents, which is a consideration that any start-up broker may want to keep in mind.

- **Foot traffic.** In the marketplace being considered, will buyers and sellers walk into a real estate office for assistance if it is located in a high-foot-traffic area? For three years, a brokerage in a high-foot-traffic small town carefully tracked how much business it received from walk-ins, and it discovered that 5 percent of the company's volume came from walk-in traffic. Given this fact, a high-foot-traffic area may be desirable for a real estate company.
- **Signage.** The type and size of sign exposure that a broker will have at the office location are important. Signage is how buyers and sellers will initially find the office location. It creates a sense of frustration for clients if they have a hard time finding an office because of poor signage.
- **Parking.** The parking issue is a strange one. In some marketplaces, brokers have lost agents because of the lack of available parking at their company. In other marketplaces, it's highly unusual to have any parking, other than on-street parking, for a company. A broker will have to assess the importance of parking for the company.
- **Accessibility.** The issue of accessibility (i.e., how easy is it to get to the office from a freeway, major artery, or local landmark) is important. If an office is located on a one-way street or on a street with a median barrier, how easy is it for potential clients to turn their vehicles around if they have inadvertently missed the office? In other words, how easy is the in and out access to the office? When you're considering accessibility, it is also important to remember that some of the company's

DETERMINE STREET LOCATION

Considering the issues of visibility, foot traffic, signage, parking, accessibility, and personal preference, list your top three street locations in the target market areas as shown:

Market Area 1
a. (Best street location 1)
b. (Best street location 2)
c. (Best street location 3)

Do the same for your top three market towns and neighborhoods.

customers may have limited mobility or be handicapped and that these customers will have special accessibility needs.

- **Personal preference.** Ultimately, the broker has the final say about the office location. If a broker has any personal preferences as to street or building choices, these should be taken into consideration when selecting the home of the company. Don't ignore your personal preferences, or you may not be excited about going into the office every day.

DETERMINING OFFICE SPACE REQUIREMENTS

Having selected the physical location for the new office, the broker is now ready to plan the physical facility. A broker must first understand how the facility will be used and how those uses will dictate the office requirements. For example, is a waiting room necessary? How large should the conference room be? Figure 6.2 provides some minimum guidelines to use in determining the amount of space needed for a new office. (See Personal Exercise 21.) Again, these are only guidelines and are designed to give only ballpark space requirements.

Assume that a broker wants to build an office for 25 real estate agents, a manager/broker, 3 staff members, and a conference room that holds 6 to 8 people. Using the guidelines in Figure 6.2, the broker would need to accommodate 20 percent of the agents in private or semiprivate offices. The new licensees can share a desk facility during their first year. This target ratio of 20 percent new licensees means that five agents will share desks.

PERSONAL EXERCISE 21

DETERMINE SPACE REQUIREMENTS

Using the information provided in Figure 6.2, determine the ideal square footage range for your office. Remember to consider the following:

- How large do you want your company to be in the first two to three years?
- What are the space expectations of potential recruits?
- What space is provided for agents at your competitor?
- Where will you conduct agent training sessions?
- Where in the office will your agents be able to have a private conversation with a client?
- Top producers typically make up 10 to 15 percent of an office's agent mix.
- New licensees typically make up 20 to 30 percent of an office's agent mix.

FIGURE 6.2   Minimum Space Requirements

	Square Footage Needed
Workspace	
• 48-inch desk (small)	35 square feet
• 60-inch desk (normal)	40 square feet
• 72-inch workstation	54 square feet
Conference Rooms	
• Small (4 people)	100–130 square feet
• Medium (6–8 people)	140–180 square feet
• Large (10–20 people)	220–350 square feet
Offices	
• Individual (1 person)	100–130 square feet
• Shared (2 people)	225–300 square feet
Reception Area	
• Small	70–80 square feet
• Medium	100–150 square feet
• Large	200–? square feet
Workroom Area	
• Small	100–150 square feet
• Medium	150–250 square feet
• Large	250–350 square feet
Restroom Area	
• Small	20–25 square feet
• Medium	30–50 square feet
• Large	75–100 square feet
Hallway Load	
• Minimum	10 percent additional
• Average	15 percent additional
• Spacious	20 percent additional

Given the example in Figure 6.3, the broker should look for a physical space of about 2,931 square feet. While this is only a rough guideline, if the broker looks for 2,900 to 3,200 square feet of space, the range will allow for unusually shaped buildings or eccentricities of a particular space. Armed with the space requirement, the broker is ready to begin the search.

FIGURE 6.3   Space Estimating Example

Description	Square Footage	Comment
Manager/broker office	225	2-person size
Staff members	162	3 staff members: 54 square feet
Reception area	100	Medium size
Workroom area	150	Medium size
Conference room	160	Medium size
Top agent offices	730	3 total offices
Other agent desks	972	5 shared + 15 other
Restrooms	50	2 small
Total space	**2,549**	
Hallway load	382	Using 15 percent
Total office minimum need	**2,931**	

SEARCHING FOR OFFICE SPACE

The search for commercial office space is accomplished by either (1) enlisting the services of a knowledgeable commercial broker or (2) doing it yourself. Typically, a start-up broker looks to save money by representing himself or herself and getting the leasing commission. There is nothing wrong with this if the broker has at least a minimal level of experience in negotiating leases. If not, then using a commercial broker is recommended.

Assuming a broker is going to represent his or her own company, the broker needs to realize that most available office spaces are not listed in the residential multiple listing services. This means that the broker must put in more legwork to find potential locations. A broker should start by driving through the towns, neighborhoods, or streets that have been predetermined as ideal for the new office location. The broker should note any "for lease" signs and the names of brokerages representing particular properties. Typically, a broker might spend three to seven days driving and/or walking the target areas to gather information and get a real sense of the available space.

The broker should also check his or her own MLS as well as a couple of Web sites, including loopnet.com and CCIM.net, for potential listings. By spending a day or so visiting all the available spaces and talking with all the various brokers, space that is not yet available, but is coming up soon, may be discovered. Remember, some commercial brokers leave "for lease" signs up on buildings, even though they don't have any current vacancies because they often have tenants who will be departing within the next three to six months.

FIGURE 6.4   Questions to Ask a Landlord or Leasing Agent

1. When will the space be vacated by the current tenant?
2. What is the rental rate for the space?
3. Is there a "load factor," on top of this rental rate (i.e., net rentable space versus net usable space)?
4. Are there any other pass-through charges in addition to the rent?
5. What is the landlord's target length of lease wanted?
6. What is the minimum length of lease the landlord will consider?
7. What sort of options would the landlord consider?
8. Will the landlord consider an option to purchase the property?
9. What build-out or improvements is the owner or landlord willing to make?
10. How long will it take the landlord to prepare the space for occupancy?
11. Is the property capable of handling high-speed or broadband Internet access?
12. Where do the phone lines enter the building? (Could affect cost of putting phones at every desk, if the landlord is unwilling to make any improvements.)
13. What is the condition of the electrical system in the building? (If the property has old electrical service, such as fuses instead of circuit breakers, this could indicate electrical risks for computers and machinery.)
14. Has the property had any plumbing or drainage issues? (Plumbing or drainage issues could cause a serious problem.)
15. What are the businesses that are adjacent to this office space?
16. How long have the adjacent businesses been there, and when do their leases expire? (Gives an idea when an additional space may be available, if needed.)
17. Will the landlord divide the space? (If a smaller space is desired.)
18. What sort of up-front monies will the landlord expect in any lease proposal?
19. Are there any hazardous materials issues on this space or in the building?
20. What else do you need to know about this space or the property?

Finally, the broker should schedule appointments with owners and/or leasing agents to view the interior space of each office that the broker has identified as a serious possibility. During the showing of the space, there are some key questions that a broker should ask, as shown in Figure 6.4.

THE LETTER OF INTENT

Once a desirable office space is found, the landlord or leasing agent will expect the broker to prepare a document called a *letter of intent,* which is simply a letter that sets forth the general terms and conditions under which the broker will lease the space. Before writing a letter of intent, it is a good idea to ask the landlord or leasing agent for a floor plan of the space. This helps reduce confusion as to what space is being leased and where the landlord is to install walls, electrical outlets, computer wiring, phone jacks, and doors. Figure 6.5 is a sample letter of intent to lease an office space.

A broker may wish to employ the services of a space planner before submitting any proposed improvements to the space, especially if the broker has never designed an office before or is unclear about real space needs. A space planner will typically cost between $2,000 and $4,000 for a small office.

FIGURE 6.5   Sample Letter of Intent

Please find the following offer on behalf of ABC Realty to lease the office space located at 200 Anystreet, Suite 250, Anytown, CA 94925 under the following terms and conditions:

1. **Landlord:** John Doe, et al.
2. **Tenant:** ABC Realty
3. **Premises:** 200 Anystreet, Suite 250, Anytown, CA 94925, an office suite of approximately 2,653 square feet.
4. **Use:** ABC Realty, a residential real estate brokerage
5. **Term:** Three (3) years with one three (3) year option.
6. **Rent:** Monthly gross rent shall be $7,826.00 for the first year ($2.95/sq ft).
7. **Tenant costs:** All utilities (gas, electricity, and water); janitorial costs within the premises; delivery of all wet and dry trash from the premises to the common area trash receptacles; maintenance of fixtures and facilities within the premises.
8. **Landlord costs:** Landlord's common area maintenance (CAM) items include the following: common area utilities, maintenance of common areas, building operations, and trash removal from common area receptacles.
9. **Increases in rent:**
   a. *Initial term.* The Monthly Gross Rent of $7,826.00 shall remain fixed for the first year, and then be subject to increase upon each anniversary year, based upon the Consumer Price Index (CPI) for the area.
   b. *Option periods.* On the anniversary of the Rent Commencement Date of year four, the Monthly Gross Rent shall be adjusted to reflect the Market Rent in accordance with a procedure to be specified in the Lease. The Monthly Gross Rent beginning on the anniversary of the Rent Commencement Date from years 4 to 6 shall be increased based on the CPI (SF/Bay Area Office/Clerical Wage Earners) with an annual minimum of 3% and an annual maximum of 5%.

(Continued)

FIGURE 6.5   Sample Letter of Intent (Continued)

10. **Improvements and actions to be completed and paid for by Landlord:**
    a. Replace existing carpeting in all office areas where there is currently carpeting. Tenant to select carpet color. Carpet to include commercial padding.
    b. Repaint certain walls/ceilings, as selected by Tenant, with colors selected by Tenant.
    c. Three parking spaces to be designated for Tenant's exclusive use.
    d. Landlord to provide refrigerator, microwave, and dishwasher in kitchen area.
11. **Improvements to be completed and paid for by Tenant:** Maintenance of all fixtures and interior facilities.
12. **Signage:** Tenant shall be allowed nonelectric window signage at the exterior entrance of the premises.
13. **Landlord's contingencies:** Tenant to submit, within seven (7) days of acceptance hereof, financial statements, and other documents needed to demonstrate that Tenant has the financial capacity to undertake the subject transaction, which Landlord shall have five (5) days from receipt thereof to approve/disapprove.
14. **Lease commencement:** The lease term is to commence approximately October 15, 2008.
15. **Rent commencement:** Rent shall commence on November 1, 2008.
16. **Deposit:** The Tenant will pay a security deposit of $15,652.00 when the lease is signed.
17. **Commissions:** A leasing commission of $7,043.40 (2.5% of lease value) shall be paid by Landlord to ABC Realty upon the execution of lease. An additional commission of 1% of the total lease amount for each extended option period shall also be paid to ABC Realty by Landlord upon exercise of any such options/extension(s).
18. **Confidentiality:** Both parties acknowledge and agree that all of the information contained herein and exchanged through the course of negotiations shall remain confidential.
19. **Indemnification:** Tenant and Landlord agree to indemnify, defend, and hold harmless each other against and with respect to all claims, costs, expenses, obligations, liabilities, damages, recoveries, including interest, penalties, engineering consultant fees, and attorneys' fees that each party shall incur or suffer which arise, result from, or relate to any toxic pollutant or contaminant existing in, on, or beneath the property (or groundwater) or any improvement or equipment on the property; unless due to the negligence of or misconduct by either party.
20. **Miscellaneous:** Upon execution of the lease, Tenant shall be entitled to a banner in the window of premises that says, "Future Home of ABC Realty."

(Continued)

After this Proposal is fully executed and all contingencies are removed, the executed Proposal is to be used for drafting a Lease and is not binding on either party until the Lease is executed by Tenant and Landlord. Any conflicts between the executed Proposal and the Lease shall be controlled by the Lease.

Agreed by Tenant:
ABC Realty

_____

President/CEO   Date

Agreed by Landlord:
John Doe, et al.

_____

Landlord   Date

_____

Attachments: Exhibit A—Floor plan of space

Using a space planner may add two to four weeks to the leasing process, but its well worth it because planners may be aware of space usage issues that can save a broker countless headaches after the lease is signed and the broker moves into the space. Often, the commercial leasing agent representing the landlord or owner will have a good referral for a space planner or designer.

THE LEASE

After obtaining an accepted letter of intent, it is generally the responsibility of the landlord or the landlord's leasing agent to create a draft lease for review. It is recommended that a broker have any lease reviewed by an attorney before signing it. From the time a letter of intent is submitted, it typically takes one to two weeks before a draft lease is available for review. Figure 6.6 indicates some provisions that should be carefully examined in a lease, though it is by no means complete. Legal counsel can provide a much more extensive list.

Lease Forms

There are a couple of standardized form providers for commercial-investment real estate that a residential broker may not be familiar with. These forms

FIGURE 6.6   Provisions to Pay Attention To in a Lease

- **Net usable versus net rentable space.** This provision reveals what additional rent will be charged for common area space (hallways, bathrooms, etc.). Typically, an office building will have a "load" of an additional 10 to 15 percent in net rental space. So a 2,000-square-foot space (usable) might have rent based upon 2,300 square feet (representing a "load" of 15 percent).
- **Common area maintenance (CAM) charges.** This provision explains the anticipated monthly amount of shared expenses that will be paid for maintaining common areas of the property. A CAM charge might typically fall in the 15 to 50 cents per square foot range, depending upon the amenities of the property. Expenses covered under a CAM charge might include janitorial services, landscaping, parking lot cleaning, and so forth.
- **Emergency cancellation for unusability of the premises.** This relates to a tenant's unilateral right to cancel or terminate a lease in the event of an unforeseen natural disaster or a problem that renders the space unusable, through no fault of the tenant, such as an earthquake, tornado, or flood. Most leases contain an emergency release provision that allows termination of the lease if a landlord cannot restore the property within 90 days. This is too long a period of time and should be limited to a 30- to 45-day maximum. Landlords will resist the shorter time frame, but the broker is faced with major customer retention challenges if the company has no functional office location for more than 30 to 45 days.

are widely used across the United States and have provisions appropriate to local marketplaces contained within them. As an educational process, it might be prudent for a broker to review a few standardized forms prior to actually leasing a space. Two standardized form providers are:

- Professional Publishing Company (ProfPub.com)
- AIR Commercial Real Estate Association (AIREA.com)

Types of Leases

There are a couple of primary types of leases which may be encountered during this process. These are:

- **Gross lease.** In a gross lease, the rental rate that is set forth in the lease is the total rental rate, that is, there are no additional monthly charges. For most start-up offices, this is the most common type of lease you will see.

- **Net lease.** This type of lease is typically seen when an office space is located within a larger complex of other tenants. In a net lease, a base rent will have an additional amount to be paid, either monthly or quarterly, for common area maintenance costs (CAM charge, or "load" on your lease). Furthermore, a net lease may contain provisions in which the tenant is responsible for paying a prorated portion of property taxes, insurance, or capital repairs. A broker should be careful when taking on a net lease because the CAM charges can be a significant amount, catching the broker off guard.

COACHING CORNER

BE CONSERVATIVE

Avoid the common mistake of leasing a space that is too large for your needs. You will be tempted to think about your growth, confident in your abilities to recruit numerous agents in a short time frame, and that confidence can translate into a trend to take on the responsibility of too much space. If your company grows quickly and is highly successful, you can always relocate your office or secure additional space close by. Conserve your start-up capital.

TENANT IMPROVEMENTS

Depending on the space selected for the new office, a broker may have to negotiate with the landlord over the issue of tenant improvements, commonly referred to as *TI*. In some cases, the would-be office is already laid out with an existing floor plan, phone and power outlets, and network cabling and merely needs new carpet and painting. In other cases, the space is nothing more than a vacant shell, requiring all these items to be built into the space before occupancy by the new brokerage.

The amount of cooperation and participation from a landlord will depend on the type of space being leased. If the space is an office-type space, such as in an office park, the landlord will most likely be willing to install, or pay for, walls and doors to create individual offices, conference rooms or kitchen areas, any electrical outlets, network cabling, and phone line outlets. However, if the chosen space is a ground floor retail-type space in a shopping center, the landlord will typically be willing to provide only an empty space with white walls, often referred to as a *vanilla shell*.

Sometimes, a retail-space landlord may offer some TI allowance (discussed later), but don't count on it.

There are three primary methods to pay for desired improvements in the new office. The first is that the broker/tenant pays cash for all physical improvements. This assumes that the broker has the cash available but causes an immediate drain on the broker's precious start-up capital. In a very high-end real estate office these improvements could cost $100,000 to $300,000 to complete.

The second method of paying for tenant improvements is by financing them through a lender. For most start-up brokers, this takes on the form of borrowing equity from their home using an equity line of credit. Sometimes financing is available through a small business loan or a line of credit for the business obtained from a local bank. Between these two financing options, a home equity line of credit will most likely have the lower interest rate.

The final method of paying for tenant improvements is to have the landlord actually do the physical improvements at his or her cost and either pay for the entire build-out or to share in the cost through a TI allowance. Some landlords will allocate a certain amount of money per square foot of rentable space that they are willing to spend on upgrading or building out the property for a tenant (e.g., $15 per foot for a 2,000-square-foot office would mean a budget of $30,000 for tenant improvements, with no additional cost being passed on to the tenant). It's important to know that a TI allowance is often received in the form of a reimbursement, so the initial outlay of capital to pay for the improvements is on the tenant, who is then reimbursed once the improvements have been installed in the space. If asking for improvements that exceed the TI allowance, then the tenant may pay the balance due for improvements or elect to forgo the additional improvements.

OTHER CONSIDERATIONS

There are other considerations with respect to the facility that are also important.

Light

Natural light in a space is extremely important. Numerous studies have demonstrated the importance of exposure to natural sunlight as an element

---

| Tales from the Real World |

A FLOODED OFFICE

In December 2005, Marin County, California, experienced record-breaking rainfall. As a result, the sewer and drainage systems of small towns throughout the county were taxed beyond their capacities. A nine-person brokerage office located on the ground floor of a building in one of these areas experienced a backflow of sewage from restrooms in a neighboring common hallway. This resulted in the office being covered in one to two inches of raw sewage, an environmental hazard to be sure. While the landlord was quick to act, the environmental issue required the involvement of specialty cleaning and mold companies, as well as the county health department. The broker, in an effort to keep the company working, set up a temporary office in his house, where all nine people were set up at temporary tables among the broker's household furnishings. The broker's lease gave the landlord 90 days to restore the property, or the broker could terminate the lease and relocate the company permanently. It was on the 89th day that the broker received word that the space was ready for reoccupancy. This experience caused enormous emotional tension among the crowded agents, not to mention between the broker and his spouse. While the story had a happy ending because the brokerage stayed together and returned to its office space, this could have been a real disaster if the broker had 45 agents.

---

in maintaining a positive, upbeat attitude. This issue is so important for some people that they become emotionally depressed and stressed if they do not experience sunlight, or UV rays, on a daily basis. There is an entire industry of UV-ray–generating machines that has arisen in the last few years because of this issue. Because natural light is so essential to the well-being of agents and staff, a broker should think about this when selecting an office space.

Acoustics

Acoustics are critical to a business, as anyone who has ever been to a noisy restaurant can tell you. The acoustical impact of using "hard" reflective surfaces (e.g., glass, teak, concrete, and brick) as wall or other interior surfaces should be considered when decorating an office. Hard surfaces may make private conversations difficult without speaking in low tones. Sales associates need an office where they can have confidential conversations while sitting at their desks. They also need to be able to hear people on the phone without straining or having to plug their other ear with their finger. Consider using soft wall decorations, such as tapestries or oil paintings and padded cubicle dividers, in any open bullpen area.

KEY POINTS

- Select the location for an office based upon market performance and statistics. Use multiple listing service data to obtain market information and performance history.
- In selecting the street location of the office, consider visibility, foot traffic, signage, parking, accessibility, and the broker's personal preferences.
- Focus the office search and save valuable time by determining the square footage range needed for the office *prior* to looking at spaces.
- Use commercial Web sites, the local MLS, and networking with commercial brokers to find potential office locations.
- Use the questions provided in this chapter to gather information prior to writing a letter of intent.
- Use a letter of intent containing the essential terms and conditions of a future lease to indicate interest in a potential office location.
- Have an office lease reviewed by legal counsel prior to signing it.
- Tenant improvements (TI) and the cost thereof should be addressed in a lease.
- Create a more functional and comfortable office environment by considering lighting and acoustics in the office design and layout.

COMMUNICATIONS AND TECHNOLOGY SYSTEMS

Opportunity is missed by most people because it is dressed in overalls and looks like work.

—THOMAS EDISON

Communication and technology systems in a real estate office are critical to the company's ability to communicate with and among its agents and customers. In this chapter, we take a look at the important technologies present in a real estate office. While some of these systems are common sense, it's easy for a broker to forget a simple piece of machinery that is vital to his or her agents' productivity and the company's daily functionality. The anticipated costs of systems and equipment are also discussed, since this area is one of the largest uses of initial capitalization.

TELEPHONE AND VOICE COMMUNICATIONS

Selection of a telephone system begins with a determination of how many inbound telephone lines a company will need. Start by counting the number of telephone workstations that are going to be in the office; for example, an office with 25 desks, a conference room, and 3 staff people would have a total of 29 telephone stations. Having 29 phone stations does not mean, however, that a company will need 29 inbound phone lines because not everyone in the office is using the phone all at the same time. A rule of thumb in determining how many phone lines will be needed is to apply a ratio of 30 to 40 percent to the total phone stations. So, an office with 29 phone stations would need 9 to 12 phone lines ($29 \times 30\text{--}40\%$). Furthermore, additional phone lines should be provided for fax machines. It is recommended that a company provide one fax line for agents to use and a private fax line for the company transaction coordinator and/or the broker.

Consideration should also be given to the style or model of the company because it may in fact affect the number of phone lines used in the office; for example, a high-density model brokerage with hundreds of agents and only a minimal office facility may only have four to five phone lines for the staff, a couple of conference rooms, the broker, and a couple of extra stations for agents. Home office, or satellite, agents do not need inbound phone lines, although they may need a voice-mail box within the company phone system, which is discussed later in this chapter.

There are two types of vendors that are used in setting up voice and data communications: (1) a telephone-line service provider and (2) a telephone equipment provider. The telephone-line service provider is the "phone company" that will bring phone lines to the office and to whom the monthly phone bill will be paid. While most phone companies will offer wiring installation services, the cost of having them do so is prohibitive and a waste of money. A telephone equipment provider sells phone equipment and systems and will be a more cost-effective solution for installing all the telephone and network wiring within the office.

Telephone-Line Service Providers

A phone call to the local phone company is where most brokers start when they're thinking about opening an office and looking for phone lines. These are companies such as AT&T, Verizon, or SBC. Local major phone companies have two primary options for the small-business person. The first option is normal business telephone lines, which are the least expensive option available from a major phone company. With normal business lines, the broker may need an internal phone system and/or a voice-mail system that is capable of providing additional features like conference calling, call forwarding, do not disturb, messaging, and so forth.

The next option available from a major phone company is electronic business lines. On the West Coast this type of business line was once referred to as a CENTREX line. A special EBS (electronic business set) type of phone is used with electronic business lines. An EBS phone set is powered from a low-voltage signal on the actual phone line. Electronic business lines and EBS phones are a good phone solution for brokers with smaller offices (i.e., under 10 agents) because they provide most of the features found in a professional phone system without the broker having to make the capital expenditure of a costly telephone system and voice mail. The drawback to electronic business lines is that they may be as much as double the cost of normal business telephone lines. In spite of this additional monthly cost, the thousands of dollars in savings by not having to buy an in-house phone system makes electronic business lines a viable option for most start-up brokers.

While major telephone companies are a reliable source for business telephone lines, they may not offer the best value. Typically, within each regional market, there are also alternative telephone service providers. On the West Coast, companies like Tele Pacific or Echelon provide phone lines at a significantly lower rate than that of the local major telephone company. A broker will save hundreds of dollars monthly by taking the time to properly investigate phone company options.

T1 or Fractional T1 Service

A *T1 trunk line* is a large clump of fiber optical communication lines that is capable of handling an enormous volume of both voice and data communication. A T1 line is an ultrafast broadband connection that is often used by large companies with hundreds of employees to handle their communication needs. A T1 line that is dedicated to one company is extremely costly and is overkill for a start-up company. However, in recent years, alternative telephone companies have begun to provide T1 access on a shared basis, known as a *fractional T1*. A fractional T1 offers an ideal solution for small to medium-sized brokerages because it consolidates voice and data services into one provider and offers a significant discount on overall telephony rates. It is recommended that brokers inquire into the availability of fractional T1 service as part of their phone service selection process.

KEEP YOUR EYE ON THE BILL!

A broker acquired an established firm in a major metropolitan marketplace and decided to acquire a new telephone system at a cost of over $25,000. When the broker explained this idea to his business coach, the coach let out an audible gasp and recommended that the broker search for refurbished or used equipment as a cost-saving measure. The broker took the recommendation and found a comparable used system for only $15,000.

This prompted the broker to look at the company's phone bills, and he discovered that the company's telephone bills were $9,000+ per month with a major local phone company. The broker shopped for better pricing for phone service and ultimately reduced the monthly phone bill to $2,500, representing a savings of over $6,500 per month or $78,000 per year!

Telephone System and Equipment

Having determined the phone line service provider, a broker will need to select the actual phone equipment (or phone system) that will be used by the company. Small company telephone systems will have two key elements, the first of which is the "PBX" or "switch" or "KSU" (key switching unit). These are three names for essentially the same piece of equipment. They are the "box" that hangs on the wall in the phone room and controls the flow of incoming and outgoing calls. It is the heart of the phone system, and all telephone handsets are connected to this box via wiring in the wall. The box is where the external phone line lines are actually connected to the phone system. A new phone system will cost in the range of $4,500 to $15,000, depending on features and capabilities, plus an additional $150 to $250 per telephone handset.

The second element of the phone system is the *voice-mail server* (a computer with voice-mail software on it). Some newer digital telephone systems have both of these elements contained within one machine, but the cost of such a two-in-one system will typically be higher. The voice-mail computer system will generally sit in the phone room of the office, near the phone system box. It's recommended that the broker and/or a key staff member be trained in how to add, remove, or modify voice-mail boxes in the voice-mail system. Features in voice-mail systems will vary with the cost of the system, and a broker can expect to pay in the range of $3,500 to $8,500 for most independent voice-mail systems.

FIGURE 7.1   Sample Cost Comparison of a New versus a Used Phone System

	New	Used
Telephone system	$8,000	$4,000
20 telephones	$5,000	$4,000
Voice-mail server and software	$5,500	$2,750
Costs to install 10 phone lines	$1,200	$1,200
Costs to install 20 phone stations	$3,000	$3,000
Total costs	**$22,700**	**$14,950**
Capital savings		**$7,750**

When purchasing the company's first phone system, you should consider the option of buying a used system instead of a new system. A new phone system, like a new automobile, is immediately worth about one-half of its original price tag the minute it is used. A one- or two-year-old used (or refurbished) telephone system offers a strong value at a reasonable cost. Figure 7.1 provides an example of a comparison between new and used phone systems. When buying a used or refurbished phone system, make sure that the phone handsets can still be purchased and that there is a reasonable belief that they will be available over the next two to three years. (Companies that sell phone systems generally won't bring up the fact that they also have used or refurbished phone systems available in their warehouse, so it important to ask about them.)

An alternative to buying a complete phone system is to get special phones lines called *electronic business lines* from the service provider. This type of phone line carries a minimal electric signal that, in combination with special EBS lines, allows special features to be used remotely over the phone lines so that the broker doesn't need to spend vital start-up capital on phone or voice-mail systems. EBS lines/phones will feel as if there is a phone and voice-mail system in the office, giving access to virtually all the same features. The drawback to EBS lines/phones is that the actual phone handsets are more expensive ($250 to $450) than standard handsets and the monthly phone line fees are more costly, sometimes costing twice as much monthly for the basic line fee. See Figure 7.2 for a breakdown of the initial costs of installing electronic business lines and phones.

On the surface, the EBS lines/phones appear to be more cost-effective than normal phone systems until a comparison is made with the typical monthly phone bill. (See Figure 7.3.)

FIGURE 7.2   Sample Initial Cost of Electronic Business Lines and Phones

Telephone system PBX/KSU:	N/A
20 telephones @ $250/phone:	$ 5,000
Voice-mail box setup costs @$50/box:	1,000
Costs to install phone lines (10):	2,000
Costs to activate 20 phone jacks at stations:	3,500
Total	$11,500

FIGURE 7.3   Sample Monthly Phone Bill Comparison

Description	Normal Lines via a "T1"	Electronic Business Lines
Basic phone/data service	$475	$550
Voice mail	$0 (server in-house)	$350
Local minute rates (voice)	$0.04–$0.06	$0.06–$0.10
Local minute rates (data)	$0	$0.06+
The bottom line	$475+ minutes rate	$900+ higher minutes rate
So…	$425+ per month cheaper	

COACHING CORNER

WATCH PHONE EXPENSES CAREFULLY

The waste of money on telephones and telephone services is phenomenal in our industry. When working with brokers around the world to increase profitability, one of the first places we look for cost savings is the broker's monthly telephone and Internet bills. Frequently, we are able to save brokers 30 to 40 percent on their phone bills by changing service providers or negotiating with their current providers for better deals. I recommend that brokers look at their telephone expense at least once every two years to explore how they could reduce it. Phone company programs change and improve periodically, but the phone company isn't going to call you to tell you how you can spend less.

A new option coming soon is Internet-based telephone lines and systems. While the Internet-based phone line is already available in some areas, I am hearing mixed reviews from some brokers who are currently using it, stating spotty reliability as an issue.

EBS lines/phones are a great short-term (one to two years) solution for a small start-up office because the company will be growing rapidly, and it is wise to wait until the company has proven that it will survive before spending money on an in-house phone system and voice mail.

Figure 7.4 is a list of "must haves" for any phone system. These features will accommodate company growth without your having to replace the phone system within a year or two. (See Personal Exercise 22.)

FIGURE 7.4   Phone and Voice-Mail System "Must Haves"

1. Phone system must be able to be integrated with in-house voice mail.
2. Phone system should be expandable to increase inbound phone line capability (often accomplished by the purchase and insertion of a computer card).
3. Caller ID system at each extension.
4. "Hands-free" speakerphone capability at the phone sets.
5. Call rollover into voice mail when the station handset is in use.
6. Voice mail assigned to each telephone set with voice-mail lamp indicator.
7. A "backdoor" phone line linked directly into voice mail (so agents can call into voice mail).
8. Easy to use voice-mail box assignment and editing to allow staff to make changes.
9. Available voice-mail boxes that do not require a phone station (for satellite agents).
10. Easy-to-use and easy-to-read handsets.

PERSONAL EXERCISE 22

PHONES

1. Determine the number of phone stations and handsets that you will need in your office.
2. Make contact with at least one major phone company and one alternative phone service provider and get estimates for installing phone lines in your office. Compare the estimates.
3. Obtain an estimate from a phone company for EBS lines/phones, if available in your area.
4. Obtain at least two to three bids from phone system vendors.

INTERNET COMMUNICATIONS

Most start-up companies will handle their Internet communications by getting DSL (digital subscriber line) for the office. DSL is fine for a small office or as an initial start-up solution and will most likely be able to handle the usage needs of the brokerage. Eventually, as the company grows, the DSL will experience a slowdown. Think of DSL like a freeway; as more cars get on the freeway, traffic slows down. When photo-intense multiple listing services, large graphic files, and large text files are all being viewed and sent back-and-forth over the Internet simultaneously by the agents, imagine the traffic jam.

As discussed above, a broker may want to consider fractional T1 voice/data lines instead of DSL. Lower overall costs will be the benefit.

COPIERS

Copiers are a vital lifeline in a real estate company and are also extremely expensive, which means a mistake can be costly to a broker. Consider the following options:

- **Buying a new copier.** This is the most enjoyable of the options. Who doesn't love a new copier with all the newest features? It is also the most costly option. A new copier costs from $4,500 to $15,000 depending upon the features of the machine. Spending valuable start-up capital on a new copier is not recommended. However, if you elect to get a new copier, you can temporarily conserve cash by financing the copier purchase. Interest rates for equipment financing typically run in excess of 7 percent annually, with terms from 36 to 60 months. A downside to buying a new copier is that, depending on the usage and maintenance, it may be worn out within five to seven years and outdated within three to four years.

- **Leasing a new copier.** Leasing should be considered a superior option to buying because it gives you the ability to get new equipment without the initial cash expenditure of purchasing and will typically have lower payments than financing a purchase. In addition, the copier can be replaced at the end of the lease for a newer machine. The desired features of two-sided copying, reducing capabilities, and sorting and stapling capabilities are essential to a real estate office. A copier with these features will typically lease for $250 to $475 per month, with a

FIGURE 7.5   Comparison: Buying versus Leasing a Copier

Description	Buying Cash	Financing Purchase	Leasing
Initial cash expense	$7,500	$1,425 (3 mos. payments)	$1,350 (3 mos. payments)
Monthly fee	$0	$475 for 48 months	$450 plus copies
Service contract*	$125	$125	$0 (included)
Buyout at end		$750	$0 (you wouldn't)

* A *service contract* is an agreement in which you pay a monthly fee to cover potential repairs and servicing of the machine. You can avoid paying this when you own the machine, meaning that you will simply have to pay an hourly rate for repairs and parts, but most financing contracts will require a service contract for maintenance of the machine. It is typically included in the lease payment when you're leasing.

minimum commitment of 36 months. Additionally, the base monthly payment covers only the machine rental and not the number of copies made during the month; expect an additional charge of $0.05–$0.07 per copy. Monthly lease payments should be kept as low as possible by the higher lease-end residual value of the copier (i.e., the estimated value of the machine at lease end). The residual value of the copier is not relevant, since the machine is most likely not being purchased at lease end. (See Figure 7.5.)

- **Buying a used copier.**   Where a new copier will depreciate to half its value the minute the first copy is produced, a used copier will offer a better overall value because of its reduced initial cost. Because copier companies receive numerous used machines turned in at the end of leases, they frequently have an ongoing inventory of used machines that have been serviced on a regular basis. If you are unable to find used copiers in your local area, another possible source for a used copier is craigslist.org, a Web site that has become an invaluable resource for everything from used telephone equipment to personal dating connections.

- **Renting a used copier.**   This option is often forgotten or not thoroughly investigated by most brokers because they don't know that renting is an available option. While copier vendors prefer to lease or sell machines, the reality is that they typically have an inventory of used machines sitting in their warehouse and would prefer to be receiving some monthly payment on a good used machine rather than have it collecting dust. Renting is different from leasing because the commitment is month-to-month, and a rental can be canceled with 30 days' notice. Initially, a broker can expect a minimum of a 90-day rental

FIGURE 7.6   Copier "Must Haves"

Required features:

1. Auto-feed tray
2. Tray sorter for up to 20 groups of documents
3. Letter-sized and legal- sized paper drawers
4. Automatic stapler
5. Zoom and reduce capabilities

Nice, but not required features:

• Networking capability (allows use as a mass-printer)
• Scanner capability

period. Payments can be as low as $100 per month, and copying charges may or may not apply. Furthermore, after renting a machine for a while, the copier vendor may be willing to sell the machine at a deep discount, thus costing the broker as little as $500 to $1,000 to own the machine.

Given the above options, the need to protect initial capital, and the desire to maintain as much flexibility as possible, renting a copier is truly the best option available to a start-up broker. If renting is not possible in the broker's local marketplace, then using craigslist.org to buy a used machine offers the next best solution. Figure 7.6 is a list of "must haves" to consider when choosing your office copier.

FAX MACHINES

Because of the important role a fax machine plays in the real estate business, a broker should buy the best machine available. Since it will be used dozens of times per day, it is vital to get a heavy-duty machine that is extremely reliable. A good fax machine will cost between $350 and $1,200 and should be network-capable (i.e., have the ability to be connected to the company local area network) thus allowing the sending of outbound faxes directly from a computer. The machine should also have the capability of scanning to convert documents into PDF (portable document format) files.

Electronic Fax (E-fax)

E-faxing means that the company subscribes to an online service that provides a direct fax number that converts inbound faxes into PDFs and then e-mails the documents to a designated e-mail address. E-faxes have grown in popularity with the increased mobility of customers and agents. Especially when there is no immediate access to a fax machine, the PDF version of the fax sits in an e-mail awaiting download or viewing.

An e-fax online service typically costs $10 to $20 per month for each e-fax phone number. A variety of e-fax providers can be found by simply typing the term *e-fax* into a search engine. Two of the more popular providers are efax.com and myfax.com. A broker who is part of a major franchise system should check to find out whether special discount rates have already been negotiated by the franchisor with specific e-fax providers.

It is not recommended that a broker provide (i.e., pay the cost of) e-fax service for all company agents. However, by contacting an e-fax provider, the broker can often establish a discount if multiple agents within the office pay for and use the service.

LOCAL AREA NETWORK (LAN)

There are three types of networks that a broker can set up in the office. These are:

- **Peer-to-peer local area network.** In this type of network, the broker simply provides a local area network connection at the agent's workstation, allowing the agent to connect a desktop or laptop computer via an Ethernet cable into the network. This connection is wired into a hub (a small electronic box that is connected to all the local area network stations and to the outbound Internet connection). This is the most cost-effective method of networking a start-up company's computers. A hub will cost only $35 to $100 and can easily be purchased in sizes to accommodate four to twenty or more connections. Additional connections can be handled with additional hubs.

    With a peer-to-peer network, it is essential that the broker has an internal policy requiring virus protection software and spyware protection software on that computer, prior to connecting to the network. This is because a virus-contaminated computer will contaminate every computer on the network within minutes of connecting to the network. It's not uncommon that multiple computers are infected and even permanently damaged by a network-received virus.

- **In-house network server.** An in-house network server is a single computer system that has direct access to the Internet and connects to agent workstations via network Ethernet cabling. There is no hub required, as in a peer-to-peer network, because all computers are simply connected directly to the network server. In-house network servers have become more reasonably priced in the last few years, with a typical cost of $3,000 to $7,500 for a small company.

  An additional firewall device or software for a network server is absolutely essential because the server will have an open connection to the Internet. If unprotected, it will be vulnerable to intrusion from the outside. A firewall device does not eliminate the need to have antivirus and spyware software on the server, but it increases security, further protecting confidential data on the server.

- **Wireless network.** A great number of agents will use laptops because of the mobility it offers them. A broker should be supportive of this mobility and provide wireless networking within the office. For most offices, a wireless router (similar to a hub, but it broadcasts the data signal wirelessly) that will serve most start-up offices will cost around $50 to $75. When the wireless router is installed, a password security system should be set up to prevent access from noncompany users. A wireless router is an easy solution for network connectivity in the office because it also eliminates the need for hard-wired workstations, thereby saving the broker money.

COMPUTER WORKSTATIONS

While a brokerage is expected to provide network capability in the office, a start-up broker should not buy computers for individual agent use. However, the company will be expected to provide one to three computers for general or "public" use by agents. Typically, these computers are placed in such areas as a common workroom or in a conference room. These public computer workstations will often be used by home-office or satellite agents as well as by visiting agents. These computers should be purchased from a major "big-box" retailer, such as BestBuy, CompUSA, Staples, and so on. A broker doesn't need to buy the most expensive machines but rather should purchase computers that will be good workhorses under heavy use by agents. The cost of such computers will be in the $600 to $800 range per machine. In addition, the broker will want to install Microsoft Office on these machines to give agents access to MS Word, MS Excel, and MS PowerPoint.

PRINTERS

Depending upon the size of the office, a broker will need between two and four printers attached to the local area network for use by all agents and staff. At least one or two of these printers should be color laser printers, while the remaining printers can be simple black laser printers. A broker can expect to spend $350 to $850 for a color laser printer that is heavy-duty enough to handle the load of a real estate office, with simple black laser printers costing $200 to $300 each.

A broker should avoid a color printer that uses wax ink color sticks for printing. Wax ink printers produce exceptionally high-quality documents, but they are *very* costly to operate, and documents generated by these machines will not pass through copier document feeders, so copies of these documents can't be made quickly. Also, a broker should avoid leasing printers because printer leases are costly and typically run for two to three years, locking a broker into machines that may be outdated or worn out in only one to two years.

BINDING SYSTEM

A brokerage will need to have a binding system to assemble listing presentation materials. There are three primary binding systems on the market today that can be easily acquired and supplies purchased at stores such as Office Depot or Staples. These are Unibind, Velobind, and Ibico binding. The costs of these systems are about $50 to $150 each, with the added requirement that the actual plastic spiral bindings and presentation covers will have to be purchased and kept supplied at the office. Each of the systems has its advantages and disadvantages, and a broker should evaluate them based upon the way in which the agents will use the binding system.

THE TECHNOLOGY PLAN

The final step in thinking about equipment for the office is to develop a technology plan. A technology plan is a carefully thought out list of the

FIGURE 7.7   Sample Technology Plan

Description	Cost
Phones and voice mail	
• Purchase used or refurbished phone system	$3,500
• Purchase 20 phone sets for workstations @$225 ea	$4,500
• Installation of phone system with network and phone at each workstation [$75/workstation (20 workstations) + 6 hr @$60/hr]	$1,860
• Purchase used or refurbished voice-mail system	$2,500
• Installation of voice-mail system (2 hr @ $60/hr)	$120
• Phone lines + data lines (fractional T1) installation	$1,250
Total Phone and voice mail	**$13,730**
Computer workstations and printers	
• 2 general computer workstations @$800 ea	$1,600
• 2 color Laser printers @$450 ea	$900
• 2 noncolor laser printers @$350 ea	$700
Total computers and printers	**$3,200**
Other office equipment	
• Copier, rented on a monthly basis (3 mos. rent @ $150/mo)	$450
• Fax machine (2 @ $350 ea)	$700
• Ibico binding system + plastic spines and covers	$250
Total other office equipment	**$1,400**
Projected total technology and equipment cost	**$18,330**

technologies and equipment that will be needed in the office, along with the anticipated budget for purchase and installation of those items. See Figure 7.7 for a sample technology plan.

KEY POINTS

- In order to reduce the likelihood of overbuying or overpaying, determine the phone system size and desired features before shopping.
- A broker should investigate phone companies thoroughly, including local alternative vendors.
- Consideration should be given to buying used and/or refurbished equipment as a cost-saving measure.

- A fractional T1 line for telephone and data service can save hundreds of dollars monthly.
- Renting a copier will provide the best value for a start-up company.
- When purchasing a fax machine, buy only new fax machines because they are too important and too heavily used to take a chance with used equipment.
- A broker should consider using an e-fax system whenever possible, allowing easy electronic transfer and storage of documents.
- A peer-to-peer system with a hub will be the most cost-effective networking system for the start-up company.
- When connecting agent computers to the company network, require the use of virus protection and spyware software on the agent computers.
- Wireless capability for a network should be provided by a broker.
- A broker should acquire two to three computers for general agent use. These computers should be of average quality and contain Microsoft Office software, along with antivirus and spyware software.
- When purchasing printers, be sure to buy at least one color laser printer to be used in printing listing presentations.
- A binding system to be used by agents in assembling presentations should be on the list of initial equipment purchased by a start-up broker.
- A technology plan, including a budget, should be created before the broker starts to buy equipment.

A POLICIES AND PROCEDURES MANUAL

Incidents should not govern policy, but policy, incidents.

—NAPOLEON BONAPARTE

A policies and procedures manual describes overall firm policies or the procedural steps to be followed in conducting the day-to-day business of the company. It also gives guidelines as to what agents and/or employees are to do when confronted with the various situations that will arise during the operation of the real estate company. A real estate brokerage needs minimum procedures and guidelines for its agents for two reasons: (1) so it doesn't get sued because an agent wasn't given a procedure on how to do something correctly, and (2) as evidence that an agent was told the correct way to do something, in case an agent's omission of an act leads to a lawsuit. (See Personal Exercise 23 at the end of this chapter.)

TEMPLATES FOR POLICIES AND PROCEDURES MANUALS

Most start-up real estate companies do not have a policies and procedures manual because the broker is unaware of its importance, or the broker doesn't want to invest the time required to complete one. Most brokers believe that they have to create a policies and procedures manual from scratch, and they have no idea where to begin. By searching the Internet, numerous prewritten policies and procedures manual templates can be found for purchase that will save hundreds of hours. This is a good place to start for some of the more regulatory general issues of a typical business, yet there are several important areas that should be covered in this manual that are unique to the real estate industry. Note that a manual that is specific to the real estate brokerage industry is offered by the Council of Real Estate Brokerage Managers, which can be found at www.CRB.com.

SUBJECTS TO COVER IN A POLICIES AND PROCEDURES MANUAL

The rest of this chapter addresses the subject areas that should be covered in a policies and procedures manual and is fairly comprehensive. However, because marketplaces differ in both traditions and laws, a broker may need to enhance what is provided with relevant local topics or procedures. Once a draft of a policies and procedures manual has been written, it should be reviewed by the broker's legal counsel prior to its being disseminated to the company agents and employees.

Introduction

A policies manual should open with a letter from the broker to all company salespeople and employees, in which the broker explains the purpose of the policies manual and how it is to be used.

About the Company

For people who have just joined the company, the "about the company" portion of the policies manual provides background on the firm and informs readers of the company's vision and purpose, including:

- Company core values
- Company core ideology
- Company vision statement
- Background of the company
- Structure of the company's ownership and leadership
- Affiliates or alliances of the company

Agent Hiring Process and Documents

There should be a section that contains an explanation of the hiring process for new or experienced agents and what documents will be required at the time of hiring.

A COUPLE OF DAYS VERSUS THOUSANDS OF DOLLARS

Even if you start with a template, it's still going to take you two to three days to properly complete a policies and procedures manual. This is time well spent because it will save you thousands of dollars in three simple ways:

1. You may have a defense against one of your agents doing something stupid if your policies manual has set forth guidelines that the agent didn't follow.
2. You may save money on your annual errors and omissions insurance premium because you *have* a policies and procedures manual.
3. You may find it easier to fire an agent who fails to follow the protocols set forth in the manual.

Training

The training portion of the manual should set forth the company training philosophy, discussing and outlining the company's new licensee and experienced agent training program. If the broker has a training reimbursement program, this is the section of the manual that should contain details concerning how company agents can participate in the program and obtain reimbursement.

Listings

The portion of a policies manual that discusses listings should explain:

- Types of listings the company's agents may take
- Commissions the agents are expected to charge for listings
- Criteria for accepting listings
- Requirements for entering listings in the local MLS
- Samples of forms to be used in taking listings
- Desired listing period for new listings
- Procedures to follow when turning in listings to the company
- How to reserve a buyer exception in a listing
- How to cancel or withdraw a listing
- Procedures to order "for sale" signs or to place ads for a listing
- How to co-list with another agent or with another company

Agency Disclosure

In the agency disclosure section of a policies manual, the state's agency laws should be explained, and guidelines should be given to agents so that they can comply with state laws and agency policies.

Buyer Representation

In the buyer representation section of the manual, company procedures for its agents to follow when representing buyers should be covered, including a sample of a buyer-broker agreement form, if one is used by the company.

Showing Property

An outline of the procedures to follow when showing property to prospective buyers should be covered, including how to set showing appointments, procedures for driving buyers around, and guidelines for following up with listing agents or sellers.

Open Houses

The subject of open houses should cover the procedures for agents to follow when holding open houses, including how to place the open house ad, steps for communicating with sellers, and how to follow up with open house prospects.

Writing Offers

In the section on writing offers, the broker will need to include information on what purchase agreement form should be used by the company, how agents are to handle earnest money deposits, requirements for obtaining buyer signatures on offers, and how agents are to present offers on behalf of their buyers.

Handling Incoming Offers

The section of the policies manual on handling incoming offers should discuss the procedures to follow when an offer is received by a company listing agent on one of his or her listings, including live offer presentations with a seller and what to do when offers are faxed into the office or dropped off in sealed envelopes. It is important to include guidelines concerning what to do with offers that are not accepted. Multiple offers and how to handle them should also be discussed in this section.

Counteroffers

The procedures to be followed in writing, or in responding to, counteroffers should be specific and clearly laid out for the company agents. If multiple counteroffer forms are allowed in the broker's marketplace, the use of appropriate forms should be covered with extreme care.

Accepting Offers

A broker's agents will need to know the procedures to follow when clients accept offers, including how to open an escrow, who opens an escrow, how to handle an earnest money deposit, how to turn in an accepted offer at the real estate company, and what steps to follow in the first few days of an escrow.

Disclosures

A policies manual should list the disclosures to be collected from sellers or buyers during transactions, as well as the disclosures to be made by the agents themselves.

Escrow Procedures

A broker needs to establish policies and procedures pertaining to the escrow process in a real estate transaction, including opening escrow, handling earnest money, contract contingencies, conducting physical inspections, vendor/inspector recommendations, the role of an agent in helping a buyer obtain financing, settlement procedures, handling deposit increases, early possession by a buyer or "rent-back" by the seller, attending the closing, and finally working with attorneys.

Commissions

The policies and procedures regarding commissions should include:

- Modifying commissions during a transaction
- The company commission rates for transactions
- When a commission becomes due and is payable to the agent
- Requirements that agents must complete before receiving commissions
- Referral fees to licensed individuals
- Finders' fees to nonlicensed individuals
- What happens when earnest money deposits are forfeited
- Commissions when an agent is a principal in the transaction
- Commission disputes with clients
- Commission disputes between agents in the company
- Commission disputes with outside brokers

Claims and Insurance Coverage

Company agents should be informed of what is or is not covered in the company errors and omissions insurance policy. This section of the policies and procedures manual should also include the procedures to be followed when a dispute, claim letter, or volatile issue arises. Agents should be instructed to notify the broker or manager at the earliest possible hint of a potential claim. Failure to do so may result in limited or no coverage by some errors and omissions (E&O) carriers.

Conditions of Association with the Company

In the section relating to conditions of association with the company, a broker should establish the parameters and conditions to be met for an agent to

---

Tales from the Real World

TIMING IS EVERYTHING

An agent of ABC Realty received a letter on November 1 from an unhappy client who had recently purchased a home through the agent. In this letter, the client said, "If you don't resolve this to my satisfaction, I will have to pursue other remedies available to me." The agent unsuccessfully attempted to try to resolve the issue and didn't deliver the initial letter to the broker, believing that it wouldn't matter because the broker would know soon enough about the problem.

On December 1, the broker's errors and omissions insurance policy with insurance carrier A expired, and the broker obtained a new E&O policy from insurance carrier B.

On December 10, the broker was served with a lawsuit from the unhappy client, and the broker immediately notified insurance carrier B of the claim. On December 20, insurance carrier B notified the broker that it would not cover the claim because the claim arose prior to its policy going into effect, and insurance carrier A refused to cover the claim because the broker failed to notify it within 30 days of the original claim, which was November 1. This was the date the broker's agent first received the letter from the unhappy client—a letter which the broker never knew existed until the insurance carrier denied the claim.

As a result the company found itself unprotected because of the agent's failure to notify the broker immediately when the unhappy client letter was received on November 1.

---

maintain association with the company; for example, minimum acceptable performance standards, minimum automobile insurance coverage, and dress code requirements. The termination process should also be discussed in this section.

Sales Associate Conduct

Given the highly litigious nature of today's society, a broker should set forth the minimum standards of conduct expected from sales agents. This may cover such areas as:

- Greeting clients
- Answering company telephones
- Harassment policy

- Complaint procedures
- Conduct toward other sales associates within the company
- Conduct toward outside agents with other companies
- Conduct toward staff members

Expenses

The policies manual should touch on the issue of the expenses that typically occur during the listing and selling of real estate and who is responsible for those specific expenses. For example, will the company or the agent pay for the agent's automobile insurance? How about auto fuel? How about property flyers? This list could be endless, so a broker should focus this section on the most common areas of concern.

Alliances and Affiliates

If a company has alliances with other firms or affiliations with specific vendors, the company's agents should know about them, especially if the company has expectations concerning working with members of these alliances and or with the affiliates.

Telephone Policies

To prevent misuse, a broker should include a brief paragraph about the policies regarding use of company telephones for noncompany business, including long-distance phone calls. If a company has a bullpen area, the broker may wish to include information about the use of appropriate and inappropriate language and its impact when overheard by other agents or clients.

Internet Policies

A broker needs to provide some minimum guidelines and expectations when it comes to using the Internet and/or e-mail communications. This should include company branding requirements for agent Web sites, guidelines regarding e-mail content, and use of company computers to surf the Internet on personal business.

Advertising Policies

The company's advertising policies should be set forth, making sure that they address all forms of advertising that are reasonably used on a regular basis. This includes classified ads (how to place them, how big they should be, what the company pays for, and the company approval process); Internet advertising (appropriate/inappropriate Web site links, use of lead generation sites, requirements for agent Web sites); television advertising (who pays for it, quality guidelines, preapproval of script).

Relocation Services

If a real estate brokerage works with a relocation company or service, the broker will need to include guidelines for agents when they are working with the relocation company. It's important to include information on how inbound relocation referrals are assigned within the brokerage and procedures to be followed by the agents when sending an outbound relocation referral. If the company has a requirement for relocation certification for its agents, this section should include information about how agents can become certified.

Broker-to-Broker Referral Procedures

Referrals are an important part of the real estate business. As a result, a broker should make an attempt to encourage outbound referrals and the solicitation of inbound referrals. The procedures to follow when placing/receiving referrals should be covered in this section.

PERSONAL EXERCISE 23

POLICIES AND PROCEDURES

Review each of the subject areas to be covered in a policies and procedure manual. Write a minimum of one paragraph on each of these subject areas for your company. Include these paragraphs in your company policies and procedures manual.

KEY POINTS

- A broker should invest the necessary time to create a proper policies and procedures manual because this document may become important to the company's legal defense against a future claim.
- Adapting a prewritten policies and procedures manual template will save time.
- A policies and procedures manual should be reviewed by legal counsel prior to its being implemented.
- At a minimum, a broker's policies and procedures manual should address all the issues discussed in this chapter.

CHAPTER 9

PAPERWORK

*Employers are frustrated because there is so much paperwork
and oftentimes you don't know if things are real or not.*

—JOHN GAY

The dreaded paperwork. It plays an enormous role in the real estate industry. As the owner of a company and the real estate license upon which all responsibility falls, it will be up to the broker to establish paperwork requirements for his or her company. While most brokers have had prior experience as agents using checklists to ensure complete and accurate escrow files, a few others have had their commission checks actually withheld until a transaction file is complete with all required documents. As the person who will require proper paperwork procedures, there are times when a broker will lose popularity with an agent or two.

However, popularity should be the least of a broker's concerns where paperwork is the issue because there are legal requirements to be met and liability prevention to be considered. A broker will want to create a paperwork system or process in order to establish a "standard of care" or "standards of practice" within the firm. A standard operating procedure in the processing of paperwork may be central to a defense against claims made by unhappy customers.

PERSONNEL FILES

All files relating to people who work for the company—sales associates and salaried employees—should be handled with care. Each kind of file should contain specific forms and papers which are discussed below.

Sales Associates

A broker should maintain personnel files on each of the agents that work for the company. These files should be treated with the highest of confidentiality, and it is recommended that they be kept secured in a locking file cabinet in the broker's office. If a broker has more than one office location, these files should be kept at the location where the broker actually sits, allowing the broker immediate access to any agent's file when needed.

Agent files should be clearly identifiable by simply looking at the type of file folder being used; for example, if yellow file folders are used for agent personnel files, don't use yellow file folders for any other purpose in the company. This way should a personnel file folder be inappropriately sitting out on someone's desk, the broker and/or staff members know immediately that such a file folder should be secured. Generic employment folders work perfectly for this purpose, and they can be purchased easily from major office supply stores.

Sales associate personnel files should contain the following documents:

- A checklist to be initialed by a key staff member (such as an administrative assistant) as documents are added to the file
- Emergency contact information sheet
- Agent's independent contractor agreement
- Commission addendum to agent's independent contractor agreement

- W–9 form (providing tax identification number for reporting purposes)
- The sales associate's real estate license
- I–9 form (for naturalization verification), if appropriate
- Copy of agent's driver's license
- Copy of agent's automobile insurance coverage showing company as additionally insured
- Signed receipt for the company policies and procedures manual
- Copy of transfer documents required by the department of real estate, local association of Realtors, or local multiple listing service

COACHING CORNER

FIND THE QUIET TIME

You are going to need to review countless files. In order to develop efficiency and not totally dread the task of reviewing files, I encourage you do this chore at the quietest time of your typical day. Some brokers arrive early at work and complete file work before the agents or staff arrive, while other brokers prefer the early evening or late afternoon. Either way, you need to close your office door and get to it, not taking phone calls until after you have completed reviewing all the files on your desk. Also, don't have more than one file open at a time. Nothing is more upsetting than losing a piece of paper from file A by inadvertently putting it into file B. (You may never find that piece of paper again.) By doing file work during a quiet time of the day and putting on some calming music in the background, the task will pass quickly and you will have the proper mindset for the job at hand.

Employees

As with sales associate personnel files, the kind or color of file folders used for employee personnel files should be distinctive and not be used for any other purpose. Employee personnel files should contain the following documents:

- A checklist to be initialed by the broker's administrative assistant as documents are added to the file
- Emergency contact information sheet
- Employment application completed and signed by employee

- Copy of employee résumé, as originally received
- Employment or hiring letter (or other document used to hire the employee)
- W–4 tax withholding form
- I–9 form (for naturalization verification), if appropriate
- Copy of employee's driver's license
- Signed receipt for the company's employee handbook (See Chapter 11 for information about the employee handbook.)
- Signed receipt for the company policies and procedures manual
- Copy of medical insurance application, when and if applicable

The papers listed above should be in each employee's initial file setup. Thereafter, the employee's personnel file will grow with employee reviews, records of disciplinary warnings or actions, or copies of commendations.

Security of Personal Information

As employers, brokers must take careful steps to prevent the theft or unauthorized reproducing of their agents' or employees' personal information. Personnel files should be secured, and a sign-out sheet should be required to allow access to such files.

LISTING FILES

We move now to the day-to-day business of taking listings and the paperwork to be collected as a minimum standard with each listing. One of the problems with real estate paperwork is that a broker rarely understands its importance until it is too late. Inevitably, when a claim is made against a broker's company or one of the broker's agents, it is some missing piece of paper that could have exonerated one or both. This is why a broker should use file checklists which help to ensure that the most common litigious issues are covered by the paperwork in each file. Figure 9.1 is a list of documents to include with each listing.

TRANSACTION FILES

There is no greater risk reduction tool than a complete and thorough transaction file. As previously mentioned, there are many times when proper documentation of a transaction can serve as a strong defense against

FIGURE 9.1   Sample Listing Checklist

Property address: _____ List price: $_____
Sales associate: _____ Expiration date: _____

Owner 1 name: _____	Owner 2 name: _____
Address: _____	Address: _____
City/state/zip: _____	City/state/zip: _____
Work phone: _____	Work phone: _____
Home phone: _____	Home phone: _____
Mobile phone: _____	Mobile phone: _____
E-mail: _____	E-mail: _____

Forms Required for Listing File

_____Agency disclosure form

_____Listing agreement signed by all owners

_____Copy of MLS input sheet

_____Property entered into MLS (copy of MLS detail printout)

_____Seller Foreign Investment in Real Property Tax Act (FIRPTA)
statement

_____Copy of property brochure or flyer

_____Copy of initial CMA given to seller

_____If applicable, order home warranty.

Company: _____ Policy no.: _____

_____Yard sign request form

_____Classified ads (2) for the property

_____JPEG photos (2) mailed to marketing assistant or transaction
coordinator

_____Lockbox installed at property (lockbox no.:_____)

_____Copy of inspection reports

For Office Use Only

_____Photos received by staff

_____Verify sign installed

_____Listing entered into Lucero (back-end software program)

_____Just listed cards ordered and mailed

_____Listing announced at office meeting

_____Remove sign and lockbox

_____Update seller contact information in database

potential legal claims. On the other hand, the opposite is also true; poor documentation can cost money.

The documents required in a transaction file are often quite extensive. Figure 9.2 is a sample escrow checklist.

FIGURE 9.2   Sample Escrow Checklist

Property: _____ We Represent: ☐ Buyer   ☐ Seller   ☐ Both
Acceptance Date:_____ COE Date:_____ Sales Associate(s):_____
Sale Price: $ _____ Contingent?:   ☐ Yes   ☐ No   _____

Approved   *Document*
_____   1   Open Escrow Memo
_____   2   Escrow Time Line
_____   3   Escrow Commission Demand
_____   4   Escrow Closing Papers and copy of all
_____   5   Company Commission Check
_____   6   Agency Disclosure
_____   7   All Contracts, Counteroffers, Addenda
_____   8   Insurance Contingency Addendum
_____   9   Copy of Initial Deposit Check
_____ 10   Copy of Trust Fund Log Entry for Initial Deposit
_____ 11   Receipt for Initial Deposit from Title Company
_____ 12   Copy of Increase of Deposit Check
_____ 13   Copy of Trust Fund Log Entry for Increased Deposit
_____ 14   Receipt for Increase of Deposit
_____ 15   Liquidated Damages Ratification
_____ 16   Real Estate Transfer Disclosure Statement (RETDS)
_____ 17   Supplement to RETDS
_____ 18   Home Warranty $_____max.
                      Waived?_____ or Company:_____
_____ 19   Standard Disclosures
_____ 20   Lead-Based Paint Disclosure (req'd. on property built before 1978)
_____ 21   Environmental Hazards and Earthquake Safety Booklet Receipt
_____ 22   Earthquake Hazards Report
_____ 23   Smoke Detector and Water Heater Certification
_____ 24   Property Natural Hazard Zone Disclosure Report
_____ 25   Property Tax Bill
_____ 26   Preliminary Title Report w/Covenants, Conditions, and Restrictions
                      (CC&Rs); Easements; etc.—Buyer's Approval
_____ 27   Nonforeign Seller Affidavit (FIRPTA)
_____ 28   Appraisal Contingency Removal (California Association of Realtors *only*)
_____ 29   Financing Contingency Removal   Due Date:_____
_____ 30   Inspection Contingency Removal   Due Date:_____
_____ 31   Copies of Inspection Reports   With:_____
_____ 32   City/Town Inspection Report and Contingency Release

Common Interest Documents and Contingency Release:

_____ 33 Common Interest Development (CID) Disclosure Supplement
_____ 34 Request for CID Documents
_____   a. Articles of Incorporation/Association
_____   b. Bylaws
_____   c. Declaration of CC&Rs w/amendments
_____   d. Rules and Regulations
_____   e. Last 12 months Homeowners Association (HOA) Meeting Minutes
_____   f. Pro Forma Budget
_____   g. Financial Statements
_____   h. Year-End Audit/Review
_____   i. HOA Collection Policy
_____   j. Insurance Summary
_____ 35 Copy of Multiple Listing Service (MLS) Printout and Flyer

REVIEWING FILES

The broker of record for a company has the responsibility to review all transaction files and paperwork for completeness and compliance with state laws. The use of checklists, such as the samples provided, will help speed up the file review process. (See Personal Exercise 24.) Here are the steps to an efficient file review system for a broker:

Step 1. Agent turns in initial file.   An agent turns in the listing or transaction file to a member of the broker's staff, who then creates the file folder for the property, attaches the appropriate checklist, and clips all the initial paperwork on top of the empty file folder. This transaction file folder, with the paperwork attached on top, is then placed in the broker's inbox for review.

Step 2. Broker reviews new documents as they are added to file. By using this simple visual cue of having new paperwork clipped to the outside of the file, the broker can quickly see the documents that need to be reviewed without wasting time looking through the entire file each time it arrives on the desk for review. Once the broker has reviewed the new documents, they are placed within the file. The broker then returns the file to a staff member, who files it with other listing or transaction files.

Step 3. Agent adds new paperwork to the file.   During the course of the transaction, the company agent will add documents to the file. Periodically, a staff member pulls the file out for the broker to review and clips all file paperwork additions to the exterior of the file and puts the file in the broker's inbox.

Step 4. Broker periodically reviews the file.   As before, the broker reviews only the new documents that have been added to the file, puts the papers into the file, initials the escrow checklist indicating that the paperwork has been placed into the file, and returns the file to a staff member. This process of back-and-forth file review is typically done three to four times during a normal transaction, with a broker spending only five to ten minutes examining the paperwork each time.

Step 5. Final file review.   About three to five days prior to escrow closing, a staff member brings the file to the broker for final review. This step will ensure that the agent will have time to obtain any missing documents prior to the close of escrow.

PERSONAL EXERCISE 24

CHECKLISTS

Use the examples given and other sources available to create the following files and checklists for your company:

1. Agent personnel file checklist
2. Employee file checklist
3. A master personnel file for agents with blank versions of required documents
4. A master personnel file for employees with blank versions of required documents
5. A listing file checklist
6. An escrow file checklist

SECURING AND SAVING TRANSACTION FILES

Transaction files are ultimately the final record for what has transpired between buyers, sellers, and the brokerage firms involved. These files, which may be subpoenaed in any future claim, must be stored in a secure environment for a significant period of time. Typically, a broker will want to keep the files for the year immediately following the date of the transaction on site at the company, as the company periodically needs access to these files for a few months. After two years, transaction files should be removed to a secure off-site storage facility and retained for a minimum of three to five additional years (speak with legal counsel about the desired period of time for storing files). With the advent of electronic storage, there are companies that will convert hundreds of transaction files into a few CDs, which allows for easier storage of these files. Converting paper files into electronic files may seem expensive at first, but not when compared to the cost of renting a storage facility large enough for three to five years' worth of transaction files.

Agents should never be allowed unattended access to a closed transaction file. If an agent feels that he or she has made a mistake on a particular document, especially one that the broker has already reviewed and placed in the file, that document may mysteriously disappear if the agent has access to the file too easily. Brokers are encouraged to maintain a level of file security that is appropriate, given the important nature of transaction files. If a company uses a transaction coordinator, the most appropriate place for the transaction files might be in the transaction coordinator's office. This

---

Tales from the Real World

A PICTURE IS WORTH THOU$ANDS

A brokerage had a policy requiring its agents to take photographs of each interior room and the front and back of the property exterior at the start of each listing. These photographs were turned in to the company and placed in the listing file to document the original condition of the listing.

An agent at this brokerage took photographs in accordance with this company policy. Months went by, and the property was sold to a buyer who was a major local real estate litigation attorney and his wife. The buyers were given adequate time to inspect the property, but citing their experience in real estate, declined to have any inspections performed on the property. The agent had the buyers sign a waiver stating that the agent had recommended that the buyers get inspections on the property by a third-party professional inspector. The buyers signed the waiver, and escrow closed.

Six months later, the broker received a letter from the buyers claiming that the seller had misrepresented the condition of the property and that the agent had not properly recommended further inspections of the property.

The brokerage declined to settle the claim, and an arbitration ensued. During the arbitration hearing, the transaction file was subpoenaed, which contained the property photographs (substantiating the seller's defense as to the condition of the property) and the inspection waiver signed by the buyers (substantiating the brokerage defense).

In spite of a favorable arbitration decision, the broker paid legal fees in excess of $3,000. However, imagine what the cost would have been had the transaction file not been as thorough and complete as it was.

office can be locked in the evening, providing a certain level of security, but left open during the day when the transaction coordinator is present. It then becomes natural for agents to turn their paperwork in to the transaction coordinator, who then accesses the file and passes it on to the broker for review at the appropriate times. This is just one idea for file security; a broker will need to find a system that works for his or her company.

SOURCES FOR STANDARDIZED FORMS

Standardized employee forms are available in software that can be purchased at an office supply store for as little as $25. Also, by entering the phrase "personnel forms" into your Internet search engine, you will find a number of sites that sell personnel form templates.

Standardized residential real estate forms can be typically found at the local association of Realtors, or from software such as True Forms, software containing a variety of real estate forms. True Forms can be found at www.trueforms.com. Similar sources for commercial real estate forms can easily be located on the Internet.

KEY POINTS

- Proper documentation is essential to real estate brokerage operations and a very real part of risk management.
- The use of checklists and systems for reviewing and maintaining all paperwork will help in establishing and maintaining standard operating procedures for a company.
- Using a back-and-forth approach to reviewing transaction files will help save time and ensure completed file work at the close of escrow.
- A broker should save company files for a minimum of three years, or as directed by legal counsel.
- Converting paper files into electronic files will save space and allow the broker to store files indefinitely.

10

AGENT COMPENSATION PLANS

The art is not in making money, but in keeping it.

—PROVERB

Agent compensation plans, or commission splits, are one of the most strategic issues of running a real estate company. No matter how long a broker is in the business, he or she is always looking for the perfect commission structure that will help to retain agents, while increasing the profitability of the company.

COMMISSION FROM AN AGENT'S PERSPECTIVE

Agents working for a broker view their commission split from the perspective of individuals needing to financially survive and provide for their families. The last thing agents think about is the survival of the company within which they work. Agents assume that the company is doing well as long as *they* are doing well. Agents want to get the highest commission split possible, and they view the commission split level as a sign of their success. This perspective is not unique. In fact, this mindset is so prevalent that entire companies have been created around the idea of giving the agent more and more of the overall commission. In today's competitive environment for retaining agents, some brokerages are giving 95 to 100 percent of the commission to their agents.

An extreme example of this is the brokerage that charges a monthly fee of only $100 to $200 to its agents, provides minimal or no services for its agents, and lets the agents retain 100 percent of their commissions. The brokerage makes its profits by retaining hundreds, and in some cases thousands, of agents. Under this brokerage model the goal is to collect as many agents as possible, resulting in greater monthly fees collected.

Over the last 25 years, this trend to continually surrender to ever-increasing agent demand has given rise to a major dilemma for real estate brokerages: the company dollar continues to erode while operational expenses increase. As a broker, a former agent finds himself or herself on the other side of the table, needing to adopt the mentality and framework of "the company side" of the issue. A broker wants to be generous and benevolent with the sales associates but is not sure how generous to be given the need to protect the brokerage's profitability and survival.

When creating commission plans, a broker can base the plans on one of three factors: (1) gross commission income (referred to as GCI), (2) agent net income, or (3) company dollar. It doesn't matter which system is used; it's more a matter of personal preference and competitive trends in the local marketplace.

The commission plans shown here are samples only; they are not intended for use in any particular marketplace. While each of these commission plans has in fact been used as shown, it is impossible to evaluate whether any of these plans would be appropriate or competitive in a particular marketplace.

IT'S NOT JUST ABOUT SPLITS

You should know that different types of commission plans attract different types of agents. Some commission plans will attract high-producing "lone wolf" agents, while other plans will attract more average-producing "groupie" agents. Your commission plan will be a reflection of the type of agent you want to attract. To encourage a good mix of agents, you may want to consider offering multiple commission plans, in a sense creating a menu of commission options for your agents.

Don't forget, agents won't come to your company just because you have the best commission splits. Agents are looking for leadership from their broker, not just higher splits. If a broker has a bad reputation, a generous commission split will not help recruit agents. Conversely, if a broker has a reputation as a dynamo that helps agents achieve higher production levels, the commission split can be less generous to the agent because the broker's *value proposition* is so strong and offers a more important benefit than just a higher split.

The key to keeping more company dollar is your total *value proposition*.

THE STANDARD PLAN

The *standard commission plan* used to be called a *graduated commission plan*. It was given this name because an agent graduated from a lower commission split to a higher commission split at several tiers. Figure 10.1 is a sample of the standard plan:

FIGURE 10.1   Sample Standard Plan

Agent Earnings	Commission Split (Percent to Agent)	Maintenance Threshold
$0–$20,000	50%	N/A
$20,001–$30,000	55%	$25,000
$30,001–$50,000	60%	$40,000
$50,001–$75,000	65%	$60,000
$75,001–$100,000	70%	$85,000
$100,001–$125,000	75%	$115,000
$125,000–$150,000	80%	$135,000
$150,001+	85%	N/A (always resets to 80%)

Note: This is a sample plan only and is designed to provide an example, not to be used in a broker's office.

Considerations for Using the Standard Plan

Before electing to use a standard commission plan, a broker should consider the following:

- In Figure 10.1, notice the column on the right called the *maintenance threshold*. This column contains the minimum level that must be achieved by an agent in order to *retain* the commission split level at each tier. For example, if an agent working under the standard plan shown in Figure 10.1 made $55,000 during the production year, that agent would have achieved a minimum commission split of 65 percent during the year but would *not* have made the required $60,000 to retain that 65 percent split level going into the next year. Instead, the agent would have made enough commission income to retain only a 60 percent split level, which shows a maintenance threshold of $40,000. A maintenance threshold will help create balance and equity in a standard commission plan by ensuring that an agent who produces slightly less than he or she normally would in a year receives a correction in the commission split.
- A broker may wish to modify the standard commission plan by using a training plan, which initially reduces the commission split for a new licensee who joins the firm, but gives the broker the ability to have a higher tier agent act as a mentor (see training plan below).
- If a broker offers other commission plans, as shown below, the standard plan will most likely be the least favored by the broker's agents because it offers the slowest increase in the agent's split. However, this plan does attract those agents who are coming from large corporate and brokerage firms because this is the sort of plan that they are used to seeing and offers a minimum amount of downside risk for the agent.

Strengths of the Standard Plan

The strengths of the standard plan include the following:

- Because of the multiple tiers, agents can receive incremental increases that keep them motivated toward ever-increasing production.
- Agents enjoy the opportunity to maintain their current commission split without reverting all the way back to a 50–50 split.
- If a broker's top producers are on high tiers, this helps to act as a retention tool because the agents might be afraid that changing companies would result in lower earnings.

Weaknesses of the Standard Plan

The weaknesses of the standard plan include the following:

- If a marketplace softens quickly and a majority of a broker's agents are at higher commission splits, the company could be left with a diminishing company dollar and increasing operational expenses. This phenomenon is a major contributor to the financial challenges of a real estate brokerage.
- If adjustments are needed to the tier level thresholds in order to keep pace with rising expenses, the company could be vulnerable to losing agents.
- Agents are creatures of habit, and they get used to a certain commission split. It is difficult to roll them back, even if only requiring a one-tier rollback in this plan.

Tales from the Real World

THE SHOPPER

A broker went on a recruiting push and was able to obtain a key agent interview with an experienced agent. During the first interview with this agent, she revealed to the broker that she was at a 70 percent split with her current company and would move to a new company only if that company offered a better split. The broker was eager to explain his superior commission plans and gave the agent a copy of the commission options to review so that the agent could select the most appropriate plan to meet her needs. The broker gave her assurances that a minimum commission split of 75 percent would be hers if she joined his firm.

The agent then returned to her current company, telling the broker that she had been offered a higher split and would stay only if the company would give her an 80 percent split, which it did. The agent was ecstatic because she now was receiving a full 10 percent more than before and, as a thank you, she gave the copy of the competitor's commission plans to her broker.

Beware the shopper.

THE SCRATCH PLAN

Scratch commission plans have become increasingly popular in recent years. In the scratch plan, there are typically only two tiers of commission split levels. This plan is designed so that the brokerage receives a large

FIGURE 10.2   Sample Scratch Plan

Company Dollar Received	Commission Split (Percent to Agent)
$0–$25,000	50%
$25,001+	100%

Note: This is a sample plan only and is designed to provide an example, not to be used in a broker's office.

amount of the agent's gross commissions early in the agent's production year, until the company has received enough gross profit (company dollar) from the agent's activities to cover the operational expenses and target profit percentage for that agent. After the company has received the target company dollar, the agent is then given the lion's portion of the commission. Figure 10.2 is a sample scratch plan.

Considerations for Using the Scratch Plan

Prior to creating and implementing a scratch commission plan, a broker should consider the following:

- A broker must first determine the minimum amount of revenue needed from each agent to cover the costs associated with the average agent in the broker's office, *plus* the amount of profit desired from the broker's average agent. The method to determine desk costs and costs per agent is discussed later in Chapter 16. As an example, if a broker's operational costs per agent were $15,000 and the broker determined a target profit percentage of 20 percent, the minimum breakpoint for the second tier under a scratch plan would be that amount of company dollar revenue which generated $18,000 ($15,000 costs + $3,000 profit) to the company. If an agent achieves this level of production, the broker has covered company expenses and received the target profit.
- For a scratch schedule to be effective for the company, the agent must be reset back to zero dollars each year. This allows the company to receive the required target company dollar each year.
- A broker must be cautious when determining the tier breakpoint under a scratch plan. If this number is set too low, the broker will be setting the company up for a financial loss on each agent. If the number is set too high, the broker will discourage agents from joining or remaining with the company.

- Using a scratch plan, in combination with an "off the top" administrative fee, will allow a broker to receive some minimal level of continuing income from agents who reach the highest tier on the scratch plan. The administrative fee is discussed later in this chapter.

- A broker should consider using the agent's hire date as the agent's anniversary date under the scratch plan system. This way, the company will always have a mix of agents at lower and higher commission splits throughout the entire year, as opposed to having all the agents adjust on January 1, which means that all the agents would be on high commission split levels during the last couple of months in the year (a time when broker's typically are in need of cash flow).

Strengths of the Scratch Plan

The strengths of the scratch plan include the following:

- The company receives its company dollar and profit early in the agent's production year.

- The company will retain a higher average company dollar overall. Most agents are average producers who will be enticed by the promise of achieving the higher commission split despite the lower commission split on the first tier of the scratch plan.

- This plan can be a great retention tool because agents who achieve the highest tier early in their production year will be unlikely to leave the firm over a commission split issue.

- From a financial perspective, a scratch plan establishes the "value" of an agent to the company and really makes all agents of equal value to the firm; for example, if the most company dollar a broker is going to achieve is only $18,000 from each agent, then that is the financial value of each and every agent, regardless of the gross commissions generated by an agent. This really reduces the control that a top producer might otherwise have over a broker.

Weaknesses of the Scratch Plan

The weaknesses of the scratch plan include the following:

- A broker essentially puts a cap on the profit received from each agent.
- A company will make less money on big producers.

- If the broker has all the agents with the same anniversary date (e.g., December 31), then the last part of the year (e.g., November and December) would hold very little company dollar. In addition, the company would be vulnerable to recruiting efforts of its competitors during the month of January, when all the company's agents are reset to the lowest commission level.

PERSONAL EXERCISE 25

COMMISSION PLANS

Use the format shown in earlier examples to create the following:

- A standard commission plan for your company
- A scratch plan for your company

HOME AGENT PLAN

A broker may wish to modify either of the above commission plans for agents who elect to have no desk space in the office, preferring to work from their home. A *home agent plan* recognizes the fact that an agent who works from home costs the company less money. Figures 10.3 and 10.4 are two examples of home agent plans that have been generated by modifying the previously provided samples of a standard commission plan and a scratch commission plan.

FIGURE 10.3   Sample Home Agent Standard Plan

Agent Earnings	Commission Split (Percent to Agent)	Maintenance Threshold
$0–$20,000	60%	N/A
$20,001–$30,000	65%	$25,000
$30,001–$50,000	70%	$40,000
$50,001–$75,000	75%	$60,000
$75,001–$100,000	80%	$85,000
$100,001–$125,000	85%	$115,000
$125,001–$150,000	90%	N/A (always resets to 85%)

Note: This is a sample plan only and is designed to provide an example, not to be used in a broker's office.

FIGURE 10.4   Sample Home Agent Scratch Plan

Company Dollar Received	Commission Split (Percent to Agent)
$0–$19,000	50%
$19,001+	100%

Note: This is a sample plan only and is designed to provide an example, not to be used in a broker's office.

Notice that each of the plans offers the agent a lower breakpoint between tiers. This is the company's way of acknowledging the fact that the agent who works from his or her home costs the company less than an agent who works at a desk in the office.

Strengths of the Home Agent Plan

The strengths of the home agent plan include the following:

- Since home agents present very little cost to a real estate brokerage, greater company profit per agent is received from agents using a home agent plan.
- The company can hire more agents than it has desk facilities to accommodate.
- Home agent plans are a good way to phase out retiring agents from a firm.

Weaknesses of the Home Agent Plan

The weaknesses of the home agent plan include the following:

- Reduced contact with the agent. While this may be a good thing in some cases, a broker should not underestimate the importance of consistent office presence to agent motivation in the company.

DESK FEE PLAN

Under a *desk fee plan,* the agent pays a monthly fee to the brokerage firm in exchange for a higher commission split. With this arrangement, the brokerage firm achieves a more consistent monthly income stream and attempts to share the financial risk of the business with the agents in the company. Entire franchises have been established based on the concept of desk fee plans.

In order to determine the proper desk fees to charge an agent, a broker must determine the company's annual desk cost plus target profit percentage. Then the broker would divide this annual amount into monthly installments, which results in the monthly desk fee to be charged to the agent. If working with a major franchise, the franchisor will help by providing a formula to help the broker determine the appropriate desk fees to use for the company.

Figures 10.5 and 10.6 are a couple of sample desk fee plans. Notice the difference in fees to the agent and the services provided for those fees.

When using desk fees, the broker will have to decide what services or expenses the agent is to be billed for and what will be covered by the company. For example, will the agent be charged for each copy that is made on the copier? (Companies that use desk fees often have agent coding devices attached to their copiers to allow agent billing for copies made.) The same issues apply to telephone usage, property brochures, and so forth.

FIGURE 10.5   Sample Desk Fee Plan 1

Monthly Desk Fee	Commission Split (Percent to Agent)	Provided to Agent
$1,250	100%	Private office, desk, phone, voice mail, Internet access, use of office facilities

Note: This is a sample plan only and is designed to provide an example, not to be used in a broker's office.

FIGURE 10.6   Sample Desk Fee Plan 2

Monthly Desk Fee	Commission Split (Percent to Agent)	Provided to Agent
$500	80%	Desk in bullpen area, phone, voice mail, Internet access, use of office facilities

Note: This is a sample plan only and is designed to provide an example, not to be used in a broker's office.

Strengths of the Desk Fee Plan

The strengths of the desk fee plan include the following:

- The brokerage can receive consistent monthly income from its agents. This helps the cash flow of the office and allows the broker to pay its own bills on a monthly basis.
- Top producers are attracted to desk fee plans because the plan creates a perception of a maximum cost of being at the company.
- A small company, based upon a desk fee plan concept, will feel more like a small cooperative brokerage, in that the agents may want to be involved in cost-reducing measures to help control their own desk costs.

Weaknesses of the Desk Fee Plan

The weaknesses of the desk fee plan include the following:

- This plan often attracts a specific type of agent personality that is very control- or ego-oriented, that is, the "lone wolf," who sees the brokerage only as a necessary evil, often not desiring to contribute to the spirit of the company through participation in company sales meetings and/or events.
- The company must maintain extremely tight controls over its agent payables; that is, the broker has to be good at collecting bills from agents. If a broker is confrontation-averse, doesn't like acting like a bill collector, or simply doesn't keep good accounting records, desk fee plans could be perilous for the company.
- A broker can end up left "holding the bag" if an agent fails to pay desk fees and then leaves the company.
- Because of the differences in agent personalities, a broker may find it difficult to offer a desk fee plan option along with other commission plans.

VIRTUAL OFFICE COMMISSION PLAN

The *virtual office commission plan* is generally only used by a virtual office company. A virtual office company hires all its agents as home agents, providing no desk facilities whatsoever, but maintaining a company office that offers only conference rooms, "hotel" (i.e., temporary) workstations for agents, desk space for support staff, and an office for the broker. In

FIGURE 10.7   Sample Virtual Office Commission Plan

Monthly Desk Fee	Commission Split (Percent to Agent)	Provided to Agent
$150	95%	A broker and allowed use of the company name

Note: This is a sample plan only and is designed to provide an example, not to be used in a broker's office.

a virtual office commission plan, the monthly fee paid by the agent is minimal, and the brokerage survives by maintaining a large numbers of agents.

Figure 10.7 illustrates an example of a virtual office commission plan.

Strengths of a Virtual Office Commission Plan

The strengths of a virtual office commission plan include the following:

- This plan provides consistent monthly revenue to the broker.
- This plan will attract agents quickly, rapidly creating significant market share for the company.

PERSONAL EXERCISE 26

MORE COMMISSION PLANS

Using the format shown in the examples, create the following:

- A home agent commission plan for your company
- A desk fee plan for your company

Weaknesses of a Virtual Office Commission Plan

The weaknesses of a virtual office commission plan include the following:

- The company must have dozens, if not hundreds, of agents in order to receive a desired level of profitability.
- This type of commission structure usually attracts lower-producing agents who typically close a minimal number of transactions per year.

This can lead to a company developing a reputation for having only mediocre-producing agents, making it potentially more difficult to recruit higher-producing agents.

DETERMINING ANNIVERSARY DATES

When working with agent commissions, a broker will need to establish the agent's anniversary date. This is the annual date when the agent's production performance is evaluated, and the commission level is adjusted based upon the agent's production during the prior 12 months. There are two common options used for establishing agent anniversary dates.

Calendar Year Method

Under the calendar year method, agents are evaluated and adjusted on January 1 of each year. Any changes to the commission plans would be announced during the month of December, taking effect on January 1 of the upcoming year. Several national companies use the calendar year method. This method can create a lot of uncertainty and fear for a broker. If annual adjustments to commission plans are unpopular with the agents, there is a potential that all of the agents may leave the company. This can create anxiety for the broker, particularly if the company's production year has not been very good and a majority of agents are facing commission split rollbacks. Another downside to the calendar year method is that high-producing agents will typically be on higher commission splits during the last portion of the calendar year, which is a time when a broker might need a higher company dollar to cover costs during a normal seasonal slowdown of sales activity.

Hiring Date Method

An agent's date of hire can serve as the anniversary date. Under this system method, the anniversary dates of a company's agents will be spread throughout the year, so there won't be a particular time of the year when all the agents are on higher commission splits, and there is also less likelihood of a mass exodus of agents occurring based upon commission rollbacks because the agents are not experiencing these changes at the same time. However, this also means that changes to commission plans will not fully be felt by a company until the entire agent roster has passed through a complete cycle of anniversary dates.

Using a Rolling Period

An alternative to using anniversary dates is to use a rolling period for determining agent commission rollbacks or adjustments. Under a rolling period system, agent performance is evaluated on a rolling three- to six-month period. If the agent's performance falls below the required pace of production for the period, the agent would be rolled back automatically at the end of each three- to six-month period. The primary benefit of using the rolling period method is that it quickly adjusts to changing market conditions, allowing the company better timing in retaining its company dollar when it needs it most. The drawback to using this system is that it is more complicated than other systems to administer and agents may be attracted to a longer-term commission commitment offered by a competitor.

THE COMMISSION ADDENDUM

Because commission plans will change more frequently than the contract used for hiring agents, commission plans are best set forth in a separate commission addendum, not in the actual body of the agent's independent contractor agreement. Such an addendum would be referenced in the independent contractor agreement. This allows the use of a standardized independent contractor agreement, such as a form available from a local association of Realtors. If changes, modifications, or removal of a commission plan occurs, agents would sign the new commission addendum in their annual review with the broker. (See the Appendix for a sample commission addendum.)

ADJUSTING OR CHANGING COMMISSION PLANS

Inevitably, a broker will want to amend or change commission plans if for no other reason than to keep up with inflationary increases of operational expenses or changing competition. Instituting commission plan changes is a sensitive issue, requiring careful thought and implementation by a broker. For example, calling a mass meeting of the agents to announce a minor change in a commission plan would be a mistake because such an announcement would create great panic and anxiety among the agents; a surefire way to create a rebellion in a company.

When making commission plan changes, a broker should consider modifying the commission addendum in December and gradually introducing changes to the agents as individual anniversary date performance reviews are conducted. This will help avoid mass anxiety that otherwise might occur among the agents. Furthermore, this gives the broker the ability to make individual compromises with specific agents without discussing such special arrangements in an open meeting.

ADMINISTRATIVE OR OFF-THE-TOP FEE

National franchise offices pay a franchise fee on each and every transaction that they close. This fee typically ranges from 5 to 8 percent and is taken off the top of the commission before determining an agent's commission split. This franchise fee is paid regardless of the type of commission plan used by the brokerage. Agents are familiar with paying such off-the-top franchise fees. So if agents are willing to give up this portion of their commission to a franchise in exchange for the perception of increased marketing exposure, why shouldn't a nonfranchise company charge this same percentage fee to its agents as an "administrative fee"? In fact, the trend to charge an "admin fee" is becoming more and more popular across the United States as a means of brokerages recovering marketing expenditures, legal defense costs, or other expenses.

The use of an administrative fee effectively increases company dollar and helps to protect and maintain profitability. When introducing an administrative fee to the agents, a broker should clearly explain the purpose of such a fee, highlighting the benefit that the agents will receive from paying such an admin fee. A broker could explain that the fee is a "risk management" fee, helping to overcome the increasing cost of errors and omissions insurance; or a "marketing" fee to help the broker with companywide marketing programs; or simply a companywide fee to protect the brokerage's profitability and to ensure its survival.

Use of an administrative fee is recommended for a nonfranchise office because it helps maintain company profitability in an environment of ever-diminishing gross profits or company dollar. The sample commission addendum in the Appendix contains a paragraph specifically mentioning an administrative fee.

MINIMUM ACCEPTABLE PERFORMANCE STANDARDS

It is recommended that a brokerage maintains minimum acceptable performance standards (referred to as MAPS) from all agents in the company.
This could be expressed as a minimum number of transactions (e.g., 10
transactions per year per agent) or as minimum company dollar contribution to the company (e.g., $19,000 per year per agent). A company's MAPS
should reflect the minimum amount of money needed from each agent
so that the operating costs of the business, plus the profit percentage
targeted by the broker, will be covered. The method to determine a company's MAPS is discussed in Chapter 16. Having, maintaining, and enforcing MAPS are critical to a productive, profitable company. A company's
MAPS will also act like a recruiting beacon, attracting agents who produce
at, or above, the minimum standard of the company.

KEY POINTS

- A broker should use a commission addendum that contains commission plan options instead of including commission plan(s) in the actual
body of the company's independent contractor agreements.
- Initially, a broker should offer a limited number of commission plans
from which agents can select because of the impact on the personality
of the company.
- A broker should consider the use of the home agent plan to increase the
number of the agents that can be recruited, especially if company desk
space is limited.
- A broker should select a commission plan that is appropriate to the
company's culture and is competitive within the market. A commission
plan should not be selected simply because of the novelty it may offer
the company.
- The use of an agent's hiring date as the anniversary date for that agent's
commission adjustments and evaluation is recommended.
- An administrative or admin fee at the outset of a brokerage can help
increase company dollar and offer an opportunity for greater profits to
the company.

11

OH MY, EMPLOYEES!

Start with good people, lay out the rules, communicate with your employees, motivate them and reward them. If you do all those things effectively, you can't miss.

—LEE IACOCCA

Real estate brokers focus an enormous amount of resources on their real estate agents, developing training programs and spending thousands of dollars in marketing and countless hours providing physical and emotional support so the agents can be as productive as possible. However, these same brokers often overlook the importance of the company's staff employees in accomplishing its mission. The employees within the company are a direct extension of the real estate broker's influence in the office. When the broker is not available, agents will seek advice and assistance from staff employees. When customers arrive at the office, they are typically greeted by an employee. And finally, administrative support for the broker is typically provided by an employee. So it is only appropriate that we include a discussion of employee-related issues in this book.

In the formative stages of a brokerage, the broker has the ability to be relatively flexible in working with staff employees and agents. As the organization grows, the broker will have to raise the bar of professionalism for handling employee-related issues. There are increasing legal requirements as a brokerage grows in size, and it is simply a matter of time before an organization faces challenges concerning its employees.

EMPLOYEES OR FRIENDS

When a broker hires employees, it's almost a given that the broker genuinely likes them as people. And, during the course of weeks, months, or even years of employment, the broker will often socialize with these employees. The boundary between employer and friend can easily become blurred, especially when the elements of late work hours, regular social events, and alcoholic beverages are added into the mix. Crossing the boundaries from employer to a friend, social acquaintance, or even personal relationship is a serious mistake for a broker and can potentially make the company vulnerable to claims of harassment or the perception of favoritism among agents and other staff members.

While it is important for a broker to have and attend company social events and to be supportive of employees, a broker needs to keep strong boundary lines, avoid excessive drinking at these events, and prevent ending up alone with an employee or agent of the opposite sex in a nonbusiness environment. While this sounds paranoid, one only has to turn on the news to find some high-ranking executive that has been brought to ruin by some employee claiming harassment. A broker shouldn't make the mistake of thinking that harassment occurs only from a male employer and a female employee; this pendulum swings both ways. A broker's best line of defense is common sense.

THE EMPLOYEE HANDBOOK

A brokerage will need an employee handbook to establish rules of conduct and performance expectations for its employees. The following is a

---

Tales from the Real World

BLURRED BOUNDARIES

A broker at a real estate office got his boundaries blurred. In spite of the fact that he was married, he began working late-night hours with an agent in the office. These late-night working sessions turned into an after-work drink at a local bar, followed by several more of these "innocent" drinking evenings. Eventually this broker had an affair with his agent. No one knew that it had happened; they were very discreet. That is until one day when the broker made a decision and took action on behalf of the brokerage, but in a matter that was not in the interest of this agent. The agent, now very upset and angry with the broker, elected to telephone the spouse of the broker and reveal the affair that had been going on between the agent and the broker.

Soon after this revealing phone call, the broker had a surprise visit from his wife in the middle of the busy workday. The broker came out of his office to meet his charming wife, who then slapped him in the face, accused him of adultery, and said she wanted a divorce. This drama occurred in front of the employees and agents of the office. Years later, the event is still being talked about.

Need we say it? Perhaps this broker needed to remember boundaries.

---

minimum list of topics that should be included in an employee handbook. Complete Personal Exercise 27 at the end of the list.

- **Introduction.**   Explain the purpose of the manual, why it was written, and how employees should use it.

- **About the company.**   Include an overview of the company and its structure. This should include the company's core values, core ideology, company vision, structure, and background of the firm and any affiliate or alliance relationships that the company may have in place.

- **Hiring process and required paperwork.**   An employee handbook should explain a company's hiring process and the required paperwork to be included in each employee's personnel file.

- **At-will employment.**   A broker may want to consider an "at-will" employment policy for employees. This means that the term of employment is for no definite period and that the employment relationship may be terminated by the employee or the company at any time and for any reason, with or without cause or advance notice. This may help avoid a claim for unlawful discharge of an employee. Discuss the benefits and drawbacks of "at-will" employment agreements with an attorney before attempting to use one; they may not be appropriate for all companies.

- **Equal employment opportunity.** A broker should include a statement advising employees that the company has a policy that provides equal employment opportunity for all applicants and employees. A statement should be included that the company does not unlawfully discriminate on the basis of race, color, religion, sex (including pregnancy, childbirth, or related medical conditions), national origin, ancestry, age, physical disability, mental disability, medical condition, family care status, veteran status, marital status, or sexual orientation. A company may also wish to include a statement about making reasonable accommodations for disabled employees.

- **Policy against harassment.** An employee handbook should include a declaration about the company's commitment to provide a workplace free of harassment, including harassment based on gender, pregnancy, childbirth, or related medical conditions, race, color, religion, national origin, ancestry, age, physical disability, mental disability, medical condition, marital status, sexual orientation, family care or medical leave status, or veteran status. A harassment definition should include verbal, physical, and visual conduct that creates an intimidating, offensive, or hostile working environment or that interferes with work performance. Harassment should also include unwelcome conduct such as requests for sexual favors, conversation containing sexual comments, and unwelcome sexual advances.

- **Internal complaint procedure.** A company's internal complaint procedure should include (1) how to file a complaint, (2) how a complaint is investigated, (3) how to appeal a decision, and (4) a nonretaliation policy.

- **Regular hours of work.** The company should define its regular work hours, for example, 8 a.m. to 5 p.m., and so forth, and explain when lunch hours and breaks are to be taken by employees.

- **Pay days.** Employees will need to know how pay periods are defined and when the paychecks will be available for each pay period.

- **Overtime pay.** A definition of overtime is essential—when it is allowed, the pay rate for overtime, and whether or not preapproval is required for overtime.

- **Pay advances.** If the company allows pay advances, the process for an employee obtaining such an advance should be explained.

- **Payment on resignation or termination.** An explanation of how and when an employee gets paid upon termination should be discussed.

A broker may have different processes if the employee resigns or is terminated.

- **Performance reviews.** It's a good idea to include an explanation of any performance reviews that the company will be conducting with employees, including how frequently these performance reviews will be held.

- **Employee benefits.** An employee handbook should contain an explanation of the company's employee benefit programs, including but not limited to liability insurance, worker's compensation insurance, medical and dental insurance, educational assistance, holiday and vacation leave, leaves of absence, family and/or medical leave, pregnancy leave, legally required leaves of absence (e.g., military service, jury duty, etc.), and sick days. The handbook should specify who is eligible for which benefits.

- **Workplace rules and procedures.** In establishing workplace rules and procedures, a company should address the following areas, at a minimum:
  - Rules of conduct and discipline policy
  - Job performance
  - Misconduct, such as:
    Insubordination
    Dishonesty or theft
    Discourtesy
    Misusing or destroying company property
    Disclosing confidential information without authorization
    Falsifying or altering company records
    Harassing, including sexually harassing employees or customers
    Being under the influence of, using, or possessing alcohol or illegal or controlled substances while conducting company business
    Leaving the job without authorization
    Possessing a firearm or other weapon while conducting company business
    Being convicted of a crime that indicates unfitness for the job
  - Attendance and tardiness
  - Personnel records

- **Conflicts of interest.** A broker's employee handbook should comment on potential conflicts of interest for the employees. The most innocent of situations can create the impression of a conflict of interest, and employees should make every effort to avoid such impressions. Potential conflicts to address are accepting personal gifts from competitors, working for a competitor, using confidential company information for personal gain, having a personal relationship with a subordinate, and making personal use of company assets.

- **Solicitation, distribution, and bulletin boards.** A broker may wish to have rules for employees regarding solicitation for noncompany-related activities on the company premises. Should the company allow employees to distribute noncompany written materials while at work? What rules does the broker have regarding the use of company bulletin boards that are intended primarily for the purpose of communication with employees?

- **Security and confidential information.** Real estate companies possess and control confidential and sensitive communications and information about employees, agents, and customers. Consequently, there is a need to maintain the security and confidentiality of this information. A broker's employee handbook should include specific recommendations for information security, including a comment that all employees share in the responsibility to ensure that proper security is maintained. Confidential information includes such items as customer lists and files, personnel files, computer records, financial and marketing data, process descriptions, research plans, formulas, and franchise trade secrets.

- **Use of company technology resources.** An employee handbook should include guidelines for the use of company computers, software, Internet access, e-mail, phones, copiers, fax machines, and any other technology resource that the company makes available to employees. The broker should include an advisement that all information or communications placed on company computers have no right to privacy and may be reviewed by the company. A broker may also wish to include a provision that advises employees that the company may monitor computer usage. And finally, a provision prohibiting the downloading of unauthorized programs/software needs to be included in the company employee handbook.

- **Drug-free workplace guidelines.** An employee handbook should address the company's intent to maintain a workplace that is free of drugs and alcohol, if for no other reason than to maintain employee safety. It should address what disciplinary actions may result from violation of the company's drug-free workplace guidelines. If a company desires the right to conduct drug testing of its employees, the guidelines for such testing should be included in the employee handbook.

┤ **Tales from the Real World** ├

YOU'VE GOT TO SEE THIS!

A broker was sitting at his desk when his receptionist came into his office and said, "You've got to see this—*now*." She led the broker to the office of his recently hired transaction coordinator, where he saw the transaction coordinator slouched in her desk chair, completely passed out from intoxication at 10:15 a.m. Her clothes were disheveled, and her shoes had fallen off her feet. The broker, unable to awaken the sleeping transaction coordinator, called an ambulance.

The broker met the ambulance at the hospital, only to discover that the admitting nurse recognized the employee from several prior similar events. The broker, on the basis of a written policy against intoxication on the job, terminated the employee, who was sent off to a rehab program.

- **Termination.** An employee handbook should contain an explanation of employment termination, both voluntary and involuntary. If the company is an "at-will" employment company, the company will want to reserve the right to discharge with or without cause and with or without prior notice. (A broker should check with legal counsel on this subject.)

- **Workplace safety.** As a matter of common sense and good business practice, a broker's employee handbook should explain the company's injury and illness prevention program.

- **Travel and expense reimbursement.** In compliance with federal employment laws, a broker's employee handbook should include a summary of what travel and other expenses will be reimbursed to the employee by the company. This is particularly important if the broker is having staff members travel to the office supply store, making deliveries, and so forth. A broker may want to require a standard expense reimbursement form to be signed and turned in by the employee to comply with tax reporting requirements. A broker should be prepared to reimburse automobile mileage at the official IRS rate.

- **Arbitration.** A broker may want to include a provision that requires employees to sign a separate arbitration agreement requiring that they submit to arbitration in the event of an employment dispute. Again, a broker should seek advice of legal counsel on this issue.

YOUR EMPLOYEE HANDBOOK

For each of the areas discussed, write your ideas on how to address the issue in your company. Expedite assembly through pasting and copying functions of a computer.

TEMPLATES FOR AN EMPLOYEE HANDBOOK

As a time-saving measure, a broker can quickly start creating an employee handbook by using a ready-to-use template, which can be found on the Internet by researching the term "employee handbook." Such templates are available for a nominal fee.

HANDLING EMPLOYEE PAYROLL

The minute a broker brings employees into the company, the broker will have to comply with state and federal laws, including employee tax withholding requirements. This is one area of a broker's business operation that must adhere to the strictest standards and compliance measures. Failing to pay required payroll taxes will result in an unexpected visit from a representative from the state taxation board. Payroll tax violations can result in seizure of business or personal assets and closure of the business.

There are two ways to address and handle the processing of a company's payroll taxes. The first method is to process and handle the payroll internally. This means that the company bookkeeper refers to the tax laws and tax tables to determine withholding amounts from employees' payroll checks and then sends in the required tax funds to the various tax agencies. This do-it-yourself method of handling payroll is often used by start-up businesses because of their desire to save money. However, improper filing of payroll taxes or the inappropriate use of an employer's payroll tax funds is one of the most common problem areas for small businesses.

The second method for processing payroll is to use an outsourced payroll service, such as Automatic Data Processing (ADP), Paychex, or Accuchex Corp. By using these companies, an authorized employee can simply "phone in" payroll each payroll period. The payroll processing company then creates all the payroll checks (branded with the company information), determines the necessary withholding requirements, and withdraws required tax funds from the company's bank account on payday. These funds will automatically be forwarded to the appropriate tax agencies, along with the required reporting documents. A broker can expect to pay $50 to $100 per payroll period for the services provided by a payroll processing company. There may also be a minimal charge of $100 to $200 to set up a payroll processing account. By outsourcing payroll processing, a broker will ultimately save an enormous amount of time and money as well as reduce risk.

SOME THOUGHTS ABOUT MEDICAL BENEFITS

In order for a company to provide small group medical benefits to its employees, the broker may have to have a minimum of three employees covered under the policy. This is typically the smallest group that most insurance companies will consider covering. The owner of the company is considered an employee, leaving the broker with a minimum of two other employees in order to obtain a group rate under a medical insurance plan.

The issue of medical insurance costs is always a sensitive one. Employees would prefer that the company pay entirely for their medical insurance. Given the financial challenges of a start-up firm, a broker may wish to initially cover only the minimum 50 percent of the medical insurance premium for each employee alone (no dependents). This means that the employees themselves will have to make up the other 50 percent. Also, at the start of the company, the broker may want to pay only for the cost of the employee, with any spouse or dependent costs being paid for 100 percent by the employee.

A broker should be concerned about providing medical insurance benefits to all employees the minute they join the company. What if employees are terminated 30 days later because they are unreliable or a complete mismatch for the firm? If employees are covered from their first day of employment, the broker could end up paying for medical insurance premiums for employees whom the broker has no intention of retaining. In some states, a company has no choice but to offer medical insurance benefits the moment it hires someone. If that is not the case, the broker may wish to take a more fiscally responsible path by offering medical benefits only to employees who pass a 90-day probationary period.

INCENTIVE PLANS FOR KEY EMPLOYEES

As a brokerage grows, the broker may wish to offer some sort of incentive plans for those key employees who are truly helpful to the operation. Other than employee stock option plans (ESOPs) or 401(k) plans which are complex to establish and administer, incentive-based compensation is a good way to help secure employee loyalty and performance. Some ideas for such programs include:

- **Recruiting bonus.**   Giving an employee 5 to 15 percent of the company dollar received from the first three closed transactions by an agent the employee helped to recruit to the company.
- **Goal/objective bonus.**   Offering a $100 to $500 bonus for specific objectives related to that employee's job, if accomplished within a mutually agreed-upon target time frame.
- **Production bonus.**   Offering a bonus to employees when the company closes transactions in excess of a target number of closings for a particular month; for example, providing employees with a bonus if the company targets closing 50 transactions in a month, but actually closes 60 transactions in the month.
- **Profit-sharing bonus.**   Offering a bonus directly from company dollar for every transaction closed; for example, a broker might offer a bonus of 5 percent of company dollar on all closings. A broker needs to be careful with this concept because this could become an excessive amount of money.

DISCIPLINING EMPLOYEES

There will inevitably be a time when you will have to discipline an employee. There are some basic rules to follow when doing so:

1. Never discipline an employee in the open office area. Rather, bring the individual into your office or conference room and close the door.
2. Never discipline an employee of the opposite sex without having a second individual present in your office with you. This can be an assistant manager or your administrative assistant. This is a critical precautionary measure for avoiding any harassment claims by the employee.
3. Make use of written warnings after giving one to two verbal warnings to an employee. This provides documentation of the warning. The employee should sign and date one copy of the written warning, which should be placed in the employee's personnel file.
4. If an employee breaks the law in the performance of his or her duties with your company, you must act swiftly to terminate this individual. A failure to comply with the law cannot be overlooked or tolerated.
5. Do not compromise your standards of performance and expectation where your employees are concerned, no matter how much you like an employee. Doing so only compromises the integrity of your organization and will be viewed as incongruent by your agents and other employees.

EMPLOYEE STRUCTURE OF THE OFFICE

Before hiring employees, a broker should give some thought to the overall employee structure of the office or company. To define an office structure, a broker should use a flowchart in conjunction with accurate job descriptions. These should be included in the company's employee handbook and given to all employees prior to their joining the firm. When thinking about an employee flowchart that sets forth the overall structure or chain of command in the company, a broker may want to consider various models that are used in today's real estate market. Figures 11.1, 11.2, and 11.3 are examples of these models.

JOB DESCRIPTIONS FOR KEY EMPLOYEES

Figures 11.4 through 11.7 are sample job descriptions for the key positions in a real estate office. (Also included are examples of compensation packages, which should *not* be included in any general job description area of a company's employee handbook.)

FIGURE 11.1   Small Real Estate Office Structure

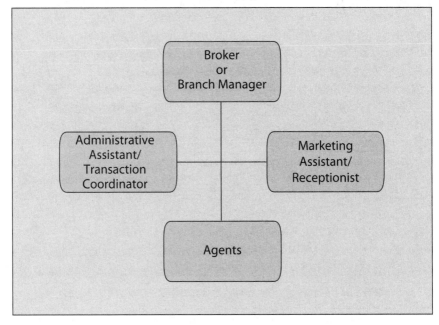

FIGURE 11.2   Medium-Sized Real Estate Office Structure

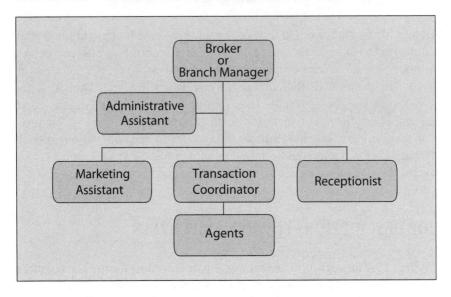

FIGURE 11.3   Large Real Estate Office Structure

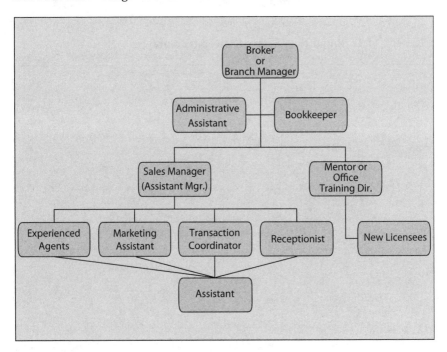

FIGURE 11.4   Sample Job Description

SELLING BRANCH MANAGER OR BROKER JOB DESCRIPTION

Purpose of the Branch Manager

The primary purpose of a branch manager is to (1) assist broker/owner in the development of the branch vision and business plan, (2) carry out and implement the branch business plan, (3) provide feedback to the broker/owner on the results of branch activities, (4) implement any modifications to the branch business plan as deemed appropriate and necessary by the broker/owner, (5) generate and maintain a profitable branch office, (6) provide leadership and training for branch sales associates, and (7) recruit additional sales associates to the branch.

Duties of the Selling Branch Manager or Broker

The selling branch manager or broker shall have the following responsibilities in the office:

1. Conduct personal real estate sales to provide the branch manager/broker with additional revenue as needed.
2. Oversee all planning and operational aspects of the office/company.
3. Recruit sales associates for the company, both new licensees and experienced agents.
4. Act as the primary source of management and leadership for all licensees hired by the company.
5. Create and implement company leadership development program.

Performance Expectations for a Selling Branch Manager or Broker

The following is a list of performance expectations for a selling branch manager or broker with the company:

1. Recruit an annual net minimum of six new licensee sales associates to the company.
2. Annually recruit a minimum of six experienced sales associates to the company. An experienced sales associate is defined as a licensed sales associate with more than one year of licensed experience and a minimum annual production of $3 million in sales volume.
3. Supervise all listing and sales transactions of all licensed sales associates in the office. Any area of concern that arises in such transactions, and for which the selling branch manager has no prior experience handling, should be discussed with the broker/owner prior to implementation of any solution.
4. Be available to act as a back-up general manager to the broker/owner for all offices in the event that the broker/owner is unavailable for any reason.
5. Achieve a 40 percent market share in the Lake Lure market area.
6. Take appropriate actions to maintain branch profitability.
7. Implement and monitor an in-house referral program for company-generated leads.
8. Oversee and implement the company training program for all new licensees.

(Continued)

FIGURE 11.4   Sample Job Description (Continued)

Independent Contractor

A selling branch manager or broker in our company shall be an independent contractor for purposes of income tax responsibility. Nothing herein shall be interpreted to create an employer-employee relationship. The selling branch manager or broker shall be responsible for all of his or her own personal income tax reporting and payment.

License and Experience Requirements

A selling branch manager or broker must possess and maintain an active real estate broker's license.

Compensation

The selling branch manager or broker shall receive the following compensation:

1. Annual salary of $30,000, paid in biweekly installments
2. An override of 10 percent of the company dollar portion of gross commission income received by the branch office

---

FIGURE 11.5   Sample Job Description

ASSISTANT MANAGER JOB DESCRIPTION

Purpose of the Assistant Manager

The primary purpose of an assistant manager in the company is to (1) provide support for the broker/owner, (2) help propel the company to its growth objectives, (3) give the company additional recruiting presence in the marketplace, and (4) provide increased training support and structure for new licensee sales associates in the company.

Duties of the Assistant Manager

The assistant manager shall have the following responsibilities in the company:

1. Act as a salesperson, listing and selling real estate properties.
2. Recruit sales associates for the company, both new licensees and experienced agents.
3. Act as the primary source of management and leadership for all new licensees hired by the company.
4. Act as the secondary source (back-up) for management and leadership for all experienced sales associates in the office.
5. Train new licensees, including the following elements:
   - Complete basic skills videos
   - Mentor new licensees
   - Conduct weekly group training meetings
6. Complete the company leadership development program.

Performance Expectations for an Assistant Manager

The following is a list of performance expectations for an assistant manager with the company:

1. Achieve a personal sales production of $4 million to $5 million in annual gross sales volume.
2. Recruit an annual net of three to five new licensee sales associates for the company.
3. Annually recruit a minimum of three experienced sales associates to the company. An experienced sales associate is defined as a licensed sales associate with more than one year of licensed experience and a minimum annual production of $3 million in sales volume.
4. Supervise all listing and sales transactions of all new licensee sales associates in the office. Any area of concern that arises in such transactions, and for which the assistant manager has no prior experience handling, should be discussed with the broker/owner prior to implementation of any solution.
5. Be available to act as a back-up manager for the broker/owner for all office sales associates and staff in the event that the broker/owner is unavailable for any reason.
6. Oversee and implement the company training program for all new licensees.

Independent Contractor

An assistant manager in the company shall be an independent contractor for purposes of income tax responsibility. Nothing herein shall be interpreted to create an employer-employee relationship. The assistant manager shall be responsible for all of his or her own personal income tax reporting and payment.

License and Experience Requirements

An assistant manager must have an active real estate salesperson license, which should have been active for a minimum of two years prior to his or her appointment as an assistant manager.

Compensation

The assistant manager shall receive the following compensation:

1. A monthly stipend of $1,200, paid on the first of each month
2. An override of 5 percent of company dollar for the first year of production from each new licensee or agent recruited* by the assistant manager
3. An override of 10 percent of company dollar for the first year of production from each experienced licensee or agent recruited* by the assistant manager.

---

* The final hiring decision for all recruits shall be made by the broker/owner. Company dollar is defined as gross commission income minus sales associate commission. Experienced licensee or agent shall be defined as a minimum annual production of $2 million in sales volume for the 12 months prior to recruitment to the company.

FIGURE 11.6   Sample Job Description

SAMPLE MENTOR/OFFICE TRAINING DIRECTOR JOB DESCRIPTION

Purpose of the Mentor/Office Training Director

The primary purpose of a mentor/office training director in the company is to (1) take primary responsibility for recruiting and training new licensees, (2) help the company achieve its growth objectives through recruitment efforts, and (3) act as a back-up leader to the broker/selling branch manager and assistant manager.

Duties of the Mentor/Office Training Director

The mentor/office training director shall have the following responsibilities in the company:

1. Act as a salesperson, listing and selling real estate properties.
2. Recruit new licensee sales associates for the company.
3. Act as the primary source of management and leadership for all new licensees hired by the company.
4. Act as the secondary source (back-up) for management and leadership for all experienced sales associates in the office, in the absence of the selling branch manager or assistant manager.
5. Train new licensees, including the following elements:
   - Complete basic skills videos
   - Mentor new licensees including:
     a. Actively participate in listing presentations and buyer interviews.
     b. Assist the new licensees with all written offers.
     c. Act as a second agent in the new licensee's first three closed transactions.
   - Conduct weekly group training meetings, including the following:
     a. Lead 1.5 hour sessions.
     b. Hold new licensees accountable for production activities.
     c. Provide ongoing training of needed subject areas.
6. Complete the company leadership development program:
   - CRB (Certified Real Estate Brokerage Manager) designation and complete manager's development record

Performance Expectations of the Mentor/Office Training Director

The following is a list of performance expectations for a mentor/office training director with the company:

1. Achieve a personal sales production of $4 million to $5 million in annual gross sales volume.
2. Recruit an annual net of 10 to 12 new licensee sales associates for the company.
3. Supervise and participate in the first three listing/sales transactions of new licensee agents in the office. Any area of concern that arises in such transactions, and for which the mentor/office training director has no prior experience

handling, should be discussed with the selling branch manager or assistant manager prior to implementation of any solution.

4. Be available to act as a back-up manager for the selling branch manager and assistant manager for all office agents and staff in the event that they are unavailable.

5. Oversee and implement the company training program for all new licensees.

Independent Contractor

A mentor/office training director in the company shall be an independent contractor for purposes of income tax responsibility. Nothing herein shall be interpreted to create an employer-employee relationship. The mentor/office training director shall be responsible for all of his or her own personal income tax reporting and payment.

License and Experience Requirements

A mentor/office training director must have an active real estate salesperson license, which should have been active for a minimum of one year prior and had a minimum of 24 closed escrows prior to an appointment as mentor/office training director.

Compensation

The mentor/office training director compensation is set forth as follows. The company may modify this program at any time.

1. *Commission split.* 80 percent fixed commission rate on all real estate transactions.

2. *Mentor fees.* 25 percent portion of the gross commission income (GCI) of the first three closed escrows (sale transactions) for any new licensee sales associates working with the mentor/office training director. This mentor fee is subject to the commission split set forth in item 1 above.

3. *Training completion bonus.* A bonus of $1,000 for each new licensee under the company's training program who closes three transactions within twelve months of his or her affiliation with the company.

4. *CRB program.* The company will pay for the tuition portion of CRB classes taken.

FIGURE 11.7   Sample Job Description

ADMINISTRATIVE ASSISTANT JOB DESCRIPTION

Purpose of the Administrative Assistant

The primary purpose of an administrative assistant in the company is to (1) provide support for the broker/owner, (2) oversee the working condition of all office systems, (3) ensure a pleasant experience for our customers; and (4) provide support to our sales associates.

(Continued)

FIGURE 11.7   Sample Job Description (Continued)

Duties of the Administrative Assistant

The administrative assistant shall have the following general office responsibilities in the company:

1. Open the office and turn on all office lights, heating or air-conditioning, and office machines. Unlock office front doors. Make coffee (regular and decaf) in the workroom area. Do a walk-through of the office and tidy up the common areas, conference room(s), and waiting areas.
2. Answer phones and greet customers.
3. Advise broker/owner when office machines are not working properly and arrange for repairs as needed.
4. Supervise temporary or part-time staff employees.
5. At the end of the workday, turn off computer; empty coffee pots; put visible dirty dishes into dishwasher; do a walk-through of the office and tidy up common areas, conference room(s), and waiting areas; turn off office lights and machines; reduce heating and air-conditioning settings; lock front doors upon departure.
6. Maintain an accurate, up-to-date roster of sales associates and distribute the roster to everyone in the company.
7. Initially set up and deliver to broker/owner all sales associate personnel files.
8. Perform other duties as assigned by the broker/owner.

Performance Expectations of the Administrative Assistant

The following is a list of performance expectations for an administrative assistant with the company:

1. Maintain the assigned work hours (i.e., arrive on time, leave on time).
2. Maintain a professional appearance at all times.
3. Maintain a pleasant demeanor and positive attitude at work.
4. Perform the duties indicated above in a professional and efficient manner.
5. Bring to the attention of the broker/owner any irregularities or potential problems that appear to be occurring in the office workplace.
6. Maintain confidentiality of all company information.
7. Use company equipment, files, personnel, and time at work for work-related business only.
8. Strive for excellence in the performance of the administrative assistant position.

Employee Status

The administrative assistant is a full-time employee of the company. There is a 90-day probationary status for all employees, including the administrative assistant.

Work Hours and Location

The administrative assistant works Monday through Friday, 8:30 a.m. to 5:30 p.m. at our main office at 123 A Street.

Compensation

The administrative assistant position has a starting salary of between $25,000 and $36,000 annually.

Benefits

After the initial probationary period, the administrative assistant receives the following benefits:

- Up to ten paid vacation days per year
- Up to five sick days per year
- Paid holidays (see employee handbook for specific days)
- Participation in medical, dental, and vision plans, if available

Direct Supervisor

The broker/owner is the direct supervisor of the administrative assistant.

PERSONAL EXERCISE 28

COMPANY STRUCTURE

Think about your new company. Using your own ideas plus those provided in this chapter, do the following:

- Write out your company's ideal leadership structure.
- Create a flowchart that clearly shows company or office responsibilities.
- Create job descriptions for each key position.

KEY POINTS

- A broker should maintain a professional working relationship with employees, avoiding the perception of compromising situations.
- A company should have an employee handbook that addresses the areas discussed in this chapter, and then have it reviewed by legal counsel.
- A broker/owner should consider using an outsourced company (such as ADP, Accuchex Corp., or Paychex) for processing payroll; it will save time and money.
- A company should consider a 90-day probationary period for all employees.
- The use of incentive plans or bonuses will keep employees motivated as active contributors to the company.

- A broker/owner should take the time to determine overall office structure, or chain of command, for employees and agents to help them understand where they fit in the big picture.
- The broker/owner should have written job descriptions to define employee staff positions or licensed independent contractor positions.

12

IDENTIFYING AND RECRUITING AGENTS

Your mental attitude gives your entire personality a drawing power that attracts the circumstances, things and people you think about most!

—NAPOLEON HILL

Nothing energizes a company more than the addition of new agents. Agents are excited to be part of a growing company, and they are inspired by the broker's leadership team. When other agents see the value of being at the company, they are positive about joining the company. In this way, the acquisition of additional recruits validates the broker's current agents' decisions to join the firm. This constant mixing of recruiting energy and the addition of agents improves the overall esprit de corps of the company, increases market share and agent productivity, and improves the broker's chances of recruiting more agents.

Recruiting is the single most important activity that a broker or manager does on a daily basis. A real estate company is either in a state of expansion (growing its agent base and market share) or contraction (losing agents and/or listings to competitors), so a broker needs to be vigilant in pursuing growth in the form of recruiting. It can be a challenge for a broker to recruit agents to a new company that has no track record or established market share, but it is not impossible. The journey of building an office that is filled with productive agents starts with an understanding of the company's current value proposition and a broker's commitment to a clearly defined vision. (See Personal Exercise 29.)

PERSONAL EXERCISE 29

YOUR RECRUITING STARTING POINT

Complete an initial assessment of your company by answering the following questions:

1. Why do you need to recruit?
2. How many agents do you currently have in your office?
3. How many agents do you want to recruit? Why? How did you arrive at this number?
4. What recruiting efforts have you made before?
5. What are the top three things a potential recruit wants to know from you in a recruiting discussion?
6. What reasons have potential recruits given as to why they will *not* come to your company?
7. Why do *you* think potential recruits may not want to come to your company?
8. Why would agents want to come to your company?
9. What does your company offer that agents cannot find at other companies?
10. How many recruiting contacts do you make per week? And how do you make these contacts?
11. On a scale of 1 (lowest) to 10 (highest), how would you rate the following items in your company?

    Visual appearance of the office   _____
    Location of the office   _____
    Parking facilities   _____
    Quality of agent desk space   _____
    Size of agent desk space   _____
    Office equipment quality   _____
    Training programs   _____
    Company reputation   _____

Quality of your current agents   _____
Listing presentation materials   _____
Advertising presence   _____
Quality of image (signs, logo, etc.) _____
Market share/position   _____
Vision statement   _____
Business plan   _____
Average of the above items   _____

12. How do you personally feel about recruiting?
13. What is your company's average per person productivity (PPP), that is, how many closed transactions per year do your agents average?
14. What is your company's average company dollar percentage?
15. From where did you get your current agents?
16. What has been your most successful recruiting effort? Why?

Review your answers to the above questions. Write down any thoughts that come to mind.

BIRDS OF A FEATHER

When a broker goes out into the marketplace and begins attempting to recruit agents, the broker will quickly learn about the power of attraction, meaning that agents are attracted to other agents and organizations that are similar to themselves. We've all heard that "birds of a feather flock together." If a broker has an office of well-liked, highly productive agents with great attitudes, the broker will find it easier to attract agents who are similar to those already in the firm. Conversely, if a broker has an office filled with lazy, slow, nonproductive agents, then the office will attract similar agents and the broker may become discouraged with recruiting efforts, finding it difficult to bring in highly productive agents because they won't want to be associated with the broker's current agents.

The power of attraction is important to remember not only when a broker is recruiting, but also with each agent hired. A broker should be constantly thinking about the quality factor of the company's agents and how it will help or hurt the broker's recruiting efforts. This is true even if the brokerage is initially a one-agent company; the broker's individual reputation and production record will be acting as an attractant to potential agents. Hopefully, the broker has developed a reputation of excellence and integrity in the marketplace. If so, these will help in getting potential recruiting appointments and actually attracting agents to the company.

| Tales from the Real World |

PROTECTING YOUR CULTURE

A broker/manager worked at a prestigious, high-end Beverly Hills real estate company that had an average list price in the multimillion dollar range. The company had multiple offices and over 1,500 agents.

A local competitor with over 1,000 agents had exploded into existence in the neighboring San Fernando Valley within a very few years. This competitor had a significantly lower average price and had developed a reputation of hiring any agent that could "fog a mirror." A significant portion of this company's agents were part-timers. The leader of this company was a very charismatic, energetic, and aggressive individual who developed extremely loyal agents. The offices of this company were located at large supermarket areas that had been vacated. A photograph of this broker, standing in front of a sea of desks in a former grocery store location, was displayed in the Chicago Art Institute and titled, "Real Estate, California style."

This young upstart crow of a broker ended up having to close his brokerage. He immediately affiliated with the high-end real estate company and assisted it in recruiting his 1,000+ agents. Seeing this as an opportunity, the prestigious real estate company hired as many of this broker's agents as it could bring aboard.

Within a couple of days, the entire culture of the prestigious real estate company had changed, and within a few years this company had lost its dominance over the real estate marketplace and was sold to a national franchise.

DEFINING THE PROFILE OF YOUR POTENTIAL AGENTS

In an effort to start with clarity and reduce wasted time, a broker should spend some time determining the ideal agent that the broker would like to have work with the company. This profile should include the agent's production, personality, longevity in the business, attitude, and so forth because it all becomes important in creating a company's culture, which is a compilation of the agents within the company and the style of the company leader. A broker should develop a profile for targeting experienced agents and a profile for new licensees. (See Personal Exercise 30.)

DEVELOPING YOUR RECRUITING PLAN

With clarity concerning the target agent to recruit, a broker is ready to develop and implement a recruiting plan. A recruiting plan is a step-by-step

---

PERSONAL EXERCISE 30

PROFILING THE TARGET RECRUIT

For experienced agents:
1. What marketplace should your agents serve?
2. What is the minimum amount of experience that you would like in an experienced agent?
3. What is the maximum amount of experience that you would like in an experienced agent?
4. How long should your ideal agent have lived in your marketplace?
5. What sort of minimum production history would you like to see from your target agent?
6. What sort of attitude would you like in the agents in your company?
7. Describe the energy level you would like to see in your potential agents.
8. What sort of attitude toward education and training should your agents have?

For new licensees:
1. What marketplace should your new agents live within or be familiar with?
2. What are some specific qualities you want in your new licensees?
3. What sort of work experience should your new licensees have?
4. What sort of financial reserves should your new licensees have?
5. What sort of attitude would you like in the new licensees that join your company?
6. Describe the energy level you would like to see in your new licensee agents.
7. What sort of attitude toward education and training should your new licensee agents have?

---

process that the broker intends to follow over the next year in an effort to recruit agents to the company. There are only a few specific activities that a broker can do to recruit agents, but it is the combination of these activities, coupled with the broker's focus and attitude at the time, that allows the broker to carry out the plan that will determine the level of success achieved in recruiting.

A broker will need to make a minimum of five interactive contacts, within a reasonably condensed period of time (typically four to eight weeks), with each potential recruit. It takes this minimum of five contacts before agents will even consider a new company as a viable alternative to their current companies. This does not mean that prospective agents will immediately run to the recruiting broker's company; it simply means they will *consider* the company as an option when they are thinking about changing firms. This five-step process is like a staircase that must be

FIGURE 12.1   Five-Step Recruiting Plan

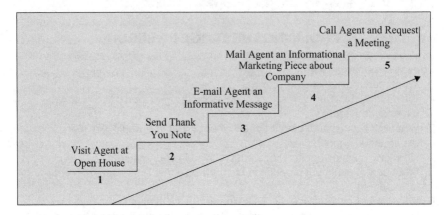

climbed in order to get to the door labeled "Recruiting Opportunity" in a prospective agent's mind.

The sample recruiting plan in Figure 12.1 includes a face-to-face visit at an open house, a handwritten thank you note, an e-mail message, a marketing piece sent in the mail, and a telephone call. This plan takes advantage of using a variety of media to communicate the message that the broker is a caring individual who pays attention to this agent.

RECRUITING ACTIVITIES

Below is a list of recruiting activities that a broker could perform within the company's own recruiting plan. A broker should include each of these activities in the recruiting plan, personalized to accommodate his or her own style.

- **Visit agent open houses.**   Each and every week, a broker should visit the broker tour open houses of 5 to 10 experienced agents who work for other companies. It's not too important to screen the open houses for a particular agent type, because the broker never knows who is thinking of changing companies, or who might know of an agent who is thinking of changing companies. The broker should just get out there and meet agents. Upon arriving at the open house, a broker should walk proactively up to the agent and introduce himself or herself. Explaining to the agent that the broker is looking for a few select experienced agents for the company, the broker should ask the agent if he or she might know of anyone who is thinking of changing companies. Regardless of the response, the broker should thank the agent for his or her time and take a quick look around the listing (to be respectful). It is critically important to this meeting that the broker be positive and assertive in attitude, without being arrogant. Some agents will be surprised at the presence of a broker walking into their open house and approaching them; it's probably been weeks, if not months or years, since the agent last heard of a broker/manager walking into an open house to meet him or her.

- **Create an e-mail newsletter.** A broker should create a monthly e-mail newsletter that could be distributed to potential recruit targets, as well as to current agents in the company. As a time-saving measure the broker may consider using the services of an online Internet newsletter provider. The newsletter should talk about upcoming events at the company, successful closes of escrow, training programs coming up, information on legal changes that may affect the agents, and anything else that might be of interest. A broker can help create buzz about the company by including some information about agents or staff who have recently joined the company. The primary purpose of this newsletter is to create a sense of movement and a feeling of a dynamic environment at the company.

- **Create a recruiting marketing brochure.** Every company should develop a marketing brochure that talks about the benefits of being an agent at the company. This could be a professional-looking one-page handout or a beautiful folded brochure. One company used a recruiting brochure called "The Edge," so named because it gave the top 20 reasons why being at the company gave an agent "the edge" in getting listings and closing transactions. Whatever the format, the message contained in this recruiting marketing piece is far more important than its overall visual quality. This does not mean that a broker can simply make photocopies of a brochure, but it also doesn't have to cost a small fortune either. This recruiting brochure can be handed out at open houses or can be mailed to agents.

- **Create a postcard campaign.** A broker could create a six- to eight-week postcard campaign using four-by-six full-color postcards. This type of campaign should be inspirational or humorous in its nature in order to attract attention and stand out in the minds of the agent who receives the postcards. On the backside of the postcards, the broker could have a personal photograph and contact information, along with some sort of direct solicitation, such as, "We're currently looking for a few good agents who are interested in being part of an exceptional

organization." Sending out these postcards once a week to all the
agents in the target marketplace will create awareness about your
recruiting mission. The most cost-effective solution for postcard printing can be found online. Some online printers will allow the broker
to create an entire campaign in one sitting, specifying the mailing date
that each new postcard is to be mailed. Then on the specified date, the
postcards will go out to the broker's mailing list without the broker
having to think about it.

- **Teach at a local licensing school.** By becoming a teacher at a local
real estate licensing school, a broker will get exposure to new licensees
as they enter the business. This will enable the broker to see these
potential new licensees in a completely different environment and
allow the broker to evaluate their competency and production potential.
Students will know that the broker runs a company, so there is no need
to solicit their interest. They will simply come up to the broker after
class and ask if the broker is looking for any new agents.

- **Use handwritten personal note cards.** Each and every time a
broker meets an agent from another company, the broker should follow
up that meeting with a handwritten personal note card. Typically, 200
customized personal note cards cost between $200 and $300. If trying
to save money, a broker may simply use a quality note card purchased
from a high-quality stationery supply store. The key here is quality; the
texture of this note card and the hand addressing of the envelope will
demonstrate the level of respect for the recipient. These details also
speak to the quality of the broker's organization. These note cards can
also be used as thank you notes. One broker went so far as to use a
wax seal when sending out personal handwritten note cards, virtually
guaranteeing that the note card would be opened and remembered.

- **Write a short series of testimonial recruiting letters.** A broker's
own agents are a secret weapon. Their comments about the brokerage
will mean more to potential recruits than anything the broker says.
A broker can create a short four- to six-letter series of informational
letters that are testimonials by some of the company's own agents about
the experience of working at the company. A picture of the individual
agent should be included. This sort of campaign serves to remind
potential recruits that the broker's company has many happy agents
who are willing to help build their own company. A theme in each
letter could be considered, talking about some specific service that the
company provides. These letters should be sent out at least once a week
until the series is completed.

- **Hold an open-house event at your office.** This is the perfect recruiting event when a broker initially opens a new office or a second office location, or announces the affiliation of a new agent with the company. This open house should be held immediately after the broker open houses conclude in a particular week. This event could have a theme, such as a spring barbecue, and should be catered. The broker can either mail invitations in advance or have flyers distributed at all of the agents' open houses to announce the event (do this during the week prior to broker open houses). The broker should also invite all the company agents and encourage them to invite agents from other companies. Conducting some sort of drawing at this event, requiring all attendees to put their business cards into some sort of drawing bowl, is an easy way to know who attended and will allow the broker to follow up with agent attendees from other companies.

- **Make telephone calls to agents.** Yes, personal telephone calls. Nothing means more to an agent at another company than to receive a telephone call from the manager or broker of another firm asking if that agent would consider changing companies. It's flattering and says, "I think you're important enough to take the personal time to call." When a broker calls these agents, the broker shouldn't just call them and ask if they want to move to the broker's company. That will result in a guaranteed no. Instead, the broker should explain that he or she is attempting to build a quality organization that is composed of quality individuals. The broker should then acknowledge that the agent has been brought to the attention of the broker through the agent's own production, or through the recommendation of an agent in the broker's office. Given the agent's position of respect, the broker could ask who he or she might know who is a high-quality individual and might be thinking of changing companies or might be interested in hearing about the programs that the broker's company can offer. This soft sell will result in a very pleasant conversation that will leave a positive feeling about the broker and the company with this agent. A broker should make 5 to 10 of these phone calls per week, remembering to follow up each call with a handwritten personal note card.

- **Acknowledge and congratulate all co-op agents.** When a transaction closes in a broker's office, the broker should send a congratulatory gift and handwritten personal note card to the co-op agent (agent from the other company). This gift can be as simple as a small bouquet of flowers, a potted plant, or a balloon attached to a big candy bar. The specific gift doesn't matter, but the act of giving it does. This simple thank you will truly be appreciated and cause the co-op agent to ask, "Why isn't my company doing this?"

- **Invite outside agents to your training programs.** If a broker is holding a training class on a specific subject, the broker could have company agents invite agents from other companies to attend. This should be a "no strings attached" offer. The idea is to simply create the opportunity for outside agents to experience the culture of the broker's firm. Who knows? Maybe the agent will be impressed with the training program, the agents in the company, or the mere fact that the broker invited him or her to attend. The broker should be sure to follow up with a handwritten personal note card.

These are just a few of the activities that a broker might consider in creating a recruiting action plan. Now develop your own recruiting plan using Personal Exercise 31.

PERSONAL EXERCISE 31

CREATE A RECRUITING PLAN

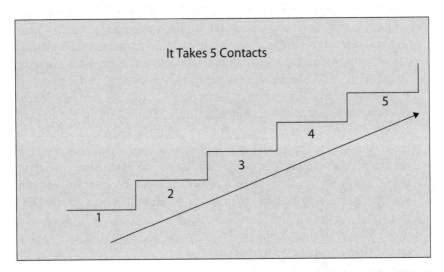

It Takes 5 Contacts

Create your own five-step plan for recruiting experienced agents. Be sure to include two to three of the ideas discussed in this chapter, plus a few of your own. Elaborate fully on each step. For example, if a step calls for a specific e-mail to be sent, write out the content of the e-mail. Finally, make sure that you include the specific dates when these activities will be performed.

The One-on-One Agent Interview

It's a common mistake for a broker to begin an interview by just spewing forth a list of reasons why an agent should join the company. This demonstrates a mindset that is company-centric, not agent-centric. A broker should keep one-on-one agent interviews focused on the agent, not on the broker or the company. The agent is looking for leadership, not a laundry list of features of the company. Leaders demonstrate real caring about their agents, so a broker should think about the 85/15 rule—keep the agent talking 85 percent of the time in the interview, while the broker limits comments to only 15 percent of the conversation. This is accomplished by continually asking questions. Here are some questions that a broker may ask in an agent interview:

- Why are you meeting with me?
- What's working well for you at your current company?
- What's not working well for you at your current company?
- What is causing you to investigate other companies at this time?
- What have you heard about our company?
- Why do you think you might be a good fit at our company?
- What are the top three priorities for you in considering a brokerage with which to affiliate?
- In considering coming to our company, what are your major concerns?
- What would you most like to know?
- Tell me about yourself. What did you do before real estate? What sort of hobbies or interests do you have?
- If you were to make a move to another company, what time frame are you thinking about?

The Best Recruiting Weapon

An important secret weapon to include in any recruiting campaign is the current agent base in the company. A broker does this by talking about the recruiting strategy in a sales meeting and asking the agents for their help. A broker should explain to the agents that they can help the company in a few key ways:

1. **Give recommendations.**   The agents can give the broker names of agents at other companies that they would like to see at the company.

WHAT'S REALLY IMPORTANT?

Whenever I talk about recruiting with a group of managers, I like to ask them what they think is the single most important reason an agent changes companies. Invariably, a majority of these managers will tell me that agents change companies because of commission splits, that is, if a new company offers the agent a superior commission split level, then the agent would simply leave the current company and head for the new company. This response tells me a lot about the way these managers perceive their job. While commission splits certainly need to be in a comparable range for an agent to consider a change, it is *not* the primary reason why an agent changes companies.

Agents change companies because of leadership. Let me say that again. *Agents change companies because of leadership.* Real estate agents, like any other person who works for any company, want to be inspired, motivated, appreciated, respected, and supported by the leadership of their company. Agents also need to respect their company leaders; if they lose the respect for the broker, it won't be long before the agent leaves, regardless of the agent's commission split level.

When a broker tells me that commission split is the most important thing to an agent, it tells me that the main importance that an agent has to that particular manager is the generation of money; the agent is merely reflecting the manager's priorities. I would encourage you in your interviews to be genuinely concerned about the agent's career path, emotional well-being, and desire for improvement. By focusing on these areas, you will demonstrate to the agent that you are a leader of people, not just a manager of commissions.

The agents can also keep their ears to the ground, letting the broker know of any agents who are rumored to be unhappy or looking to change companies.

2. **Speak positively of the company.**   Agents can demonstrate support for the broker's recruiting efforts by simply speaking positively about the company whenever they are asked about it. A broker really needs to emphasize this point to agents because it is extremely important. For example, if a broker had an interview with agent Phil from a competing company, Phil will want to verify the satisfaction of the broker's own agents before considering moving to the firm. He does this by asking the broker's agents questions about the broker and the firm, while attending open houses or at local board events when the broker is not around. If Phil gets negative reports from the broker's agents, any recruiting opportunity with Phil will be destroyed.

3. **Report any inquiries about the company.** When an agent asks one of the broker's agents for information about the company, even an innocent inquiry can mean that the agent has some interest in the broker's firm or is considering changing companies. A broker needs to ask all company agents to report any inquiries immediately to the broker, allowing follow-up with the agent to answer any questions he or she might have.

Recruiting New Licensees

Generally, it is much easier to recruit new licensees than it is to recruit experienced agents. This is primarily because new licensees do not have any existing business to risk by changing companies. Furthermore, the sheer number of available new licensees gives the broker better odds at being able to attract a few of them. Regardless, a broker still needs a carefully thought out plan of attack for recruiting new licensees. Agents just entering the business have different needs from experienced agents. They are more interested in the training programs, lead generation systems, and marketing support that a company will offer them as they launch their career.

In the last few years, the number of new licensees entering the real estate industry has exploded in the United States. In California alone, there has been an increase of over 60 percent in the number of new agents. As a company owner with limited resources and a desire to protect the quality of the company, a broker has to be careful about how much time is spent on recruiting new licensees and about who is selected to join the company. Statistically, we know that as many as 50 percent of new licensees who enter the real estate business will leave the industry within one year. Furthermore, half of the remaining 50 percent will end up leaving the business within the following two years. This means that on average, only an estimated 25 percent of the agents who become licensed will in fact remain practicing salespeople or brokers. The importance of this is that if a broker were to simply hire any new licensee who is willing to join the firm, the broker would statistically waste a lot of time because as many as 75 percent of those agents would end up leaving the business. When a broker factors in the costs of lost time, a trainer's lost time, the costs of training materials, and the carrying costs of a typical new agent, it's not uncommon to discover that the costs of training an agent is somewhere between $15,000 and $25,000; a broker simply cannot afford to waste this kind of money and resources on potentially unproductive agents. This means that a broker will need a streamlined but effective method of screening potential new licensees so that the broker selects only the absolute best candidates from the available pool.

The Group Interview

A broker typically spends 30 to 40 minutes interviewing every new licensee candidate. This could result in a huge waste of time for the broker. As an alternative, a broker could use a technique called a group interview. Using a group interview process, a broker will be able to effectively screen as many as 50 candidates within one and a half hours. This is an enormous saving of time. Following are the specific steps to follow for conducting a group interview.

Step 1: Place Ads for "An Introduction to Real Estate" Night

Shown in Figure 12.2 is a sample advertisement that a broker would place in the classified employment section of a local newspaper. A broker should also place the same advertisement on craigslist (www.craigslist.org). Notice that this ad does not contain any phone numbers, but instead refers the reader to a Web site. By requiring the candidates to go to a Web site in order to sign up for the seminar evening, a broker is creating a threshold test of technology competency. If the candidate does not have computer or Internet access or the intelligence to pick up the phone and call directory assistance to ask for the company phone number, then such a candidate would most likely not show up anyway.

FIGURE 12.2   Sample Ad for a Seminar on Starting Your Career in Real Estate

---

AN INTRODUCTION TO REAL ESTATE

ABC Realtors would like to invite you to attend an evening seminar to discuss a career in real estate. You'll learn about:

- The benefits and challenges of real estate
- Your first 90 days
- The cost of entering real estate
- Training programs
- How to select a company
- And more!

  To reserve your seat register online at www.ABCrealtors.com.

Step 2: Construct a Response Web Page on the Company Web Site

Having directed people to the company Web site in the ad, the broker will need to have prepared either a sign-up Web page on the company Web site or a Web page that contains instructions for potential candidates concerning how they can reserve a seat at the seminar event. If the broker cannot create a sign-up page, then candidates should reserve a seat by faxing their résumé to the office or calling the broker's administrative assistant directly. (Note: The broker should not handle any ad responses directly. This compromises the process and diminishes the impact of the broker's presence at the group interview evening.) If the broker is able to create a sign-up page, a résumé from all attendees should be requested. The company is creating two threshold tests, in that (1) people who are not seriously interested in a real estate career will not be willing to send a résumé, and (2) people who are unwilling or unable to follow simple instructions are not necessarily people the broker would want as real estate agents in the company. Additionally, if attendees do send in a résumé, the broker will have them available to review for spelling errors, thoroughness, and organizational skills.

Once potential candidates have responded to the company's online request to attend, they should receive an automated response from the Web site that tells them that their seat has been reserved and that contains an Internet link to an online personality assessment tool.

Step 3: Personality Assessment Tools

The use of electronic assessment tests is an essential step in the evaluation process for job candidates. These tests will provide the broker with objective information about potential candidates. A broker should not read these evaluations and assessments prior to the group interview evening because the assessment may create a bias. The time to read these assessments thoroughly is when and if the candidate is selected for an individual interview. This way, if candidates do not make it past the group interview, the broker has not wasted time reading assessments.

Step 4: Confirmation E-mail or Call

Either the day before or the morning of the group interview, a staff member from the company should confirm the attendance of those people who have signed up for the group interview by sending a confirmation e-mail to them or by calling them to confirm their attendance. It is not uncommon that people forget that they have made the appointment to attend a group interview, and this phone call or e-mail could be a memory jog that ensures their attendance.

Step 5: Preparing Handouts

In preparing for a group interview, a broker will need to spend some time creating handouts that will be given to attendees as they enter the room. These handouts do not need to be super-quality printed brochures; they can be produced through a word processor and a color printer. The purpose of these handouts is not to impress the attendees, but rather to simply give them a takeaway that they can later review at home. At a minimum, a broker may want to create handouts for the following:

1. **Registration sheet.** This sheet should include space for the attendee's name, address, phone number, and e-mail address, as well as a place where the attendee can check a box indicating whether or not he or she is interested in a follow-up interview with the broker. This sheet is handed in at the end of the evening.
2. **"20 Questions to Ask before Joining a Real Estate Broker."** A company should create a sheet that provides attendees with several questions to ask any real estate broker. These questions will be helpful to attendees as they are interviewed at various real estate companies and should be constructed in such a way that the company's responses to these questions will appear favorable.
3. **Company brochure.** This brochure could simply be a one-page handout with the benefits of joining the organization listed. Or it could be an elaborate high-quality glossy brochure that is professionally printed. However, a company needs to remember the audience; keep it simple.

Step 6: Setting Up the Room

The room setup for a group interview is significantly different from that of a typical career night. On a career night, attendees are encouraged to meander through the office and meet other agents from the company; they are given a brief presentation about the career opportunities at the company. In the case of a group interview, however, the room is set up for a more formal presentation. The broker or manager giving a presentation is at the front

FIGURE 12.3   Group Interview Setup

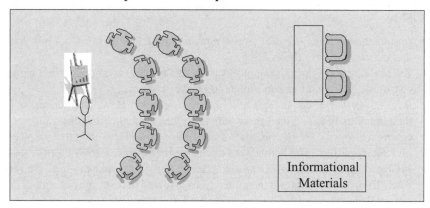

Informational Materials

of the room, while attendees are seated in formal rows, all facing the presenter. There is a flipchart or possibly a whiteboard at the head of the room, giving the feeling of a classroom rather than an entertaining evening about real estate. Seated behind the attendees at a table should be two to three hand-selected individuals from the company who will serve to evaluate and rate the quality of the attendees. Figure 12.3 shows the correct room setup for a group interview.

Step 7: Greeting Attendees

As attendees arrive for the group interview, they should be greeted by a staff member at the door, who checks them in on an attendance roster and gives them the informational handouts. Attendees should also have name tags available for them to use. Preparing the name tags in advance gives the attendee a sense of importance and elevates the appearance of the professionalism of the company.

Step 8: The Presentation and Agenda

The presentation should begin on time, with the entrance of the broker, following a predetermined agenda that may or may not be posted on a flipchart or whiteboard. The broker proceeds to cover a series of topics as if teaching an informational program. As part of the program, the broker may wish to use a PowerPoint presentation. Figure 12.4 is a sample agenda for a group interview, along with a brief explanation of the subjects to be covered.

FIGURE 12.4   Sample Agenda for a Group Interview

AGENDA

- *Introduction of presenter and present company staff.* Briefly introduce everyone and the assistants for the evening.
- *Tell us about you.* Have the attendees individually stand up and give their name, city of residence, and reason for attending the program.
- *Advantages and disadvantages of a real estate career.* Have the attendees give their opinions first, and then share with them the advantages and disadvantages.
- *Characteristics of successful real estate salespeople.* First have the attendees give their opinions, and then affirm or correct their perceptions.
- *Information on getting a real estate license.* Give an explanation of the real estate licensing process and the time frames involved in case some attendees are not yet licensed.
- *Training programs for success.* This discussion should be an overview of training programs that are typically available in the industry from companies. It should not be focused only on the training programs in the broker's company.
- *Your company's new licensee training programs.* Specifically discuss how new licensees are trained in your company.
- *Your company's ongoing training.* This part of the discussion should focus on what ongoing training new agents could expect to receive if they join the firm.
- *Start-up costs.* Discuss the total costs to enter and get started in the real estate business.
- *Financial commitment.* Prepare the attendees for the extent to which they can expect to spend money in their first six months of the business. Be sure to include marketing expenses, training expenses, and survival costs.
- *Selecting the* right *broker.* Direct the attendees to the "20 Questions to Ask before Joining a Real Estate Broker" handout that was given to attendees as they entered the room. Pick two or three key issues to focus on, and discuss them with the attendees.
- *Your company's philosophy.* Turn the focus of the presentation to your company. Touch on the company's response to a few of the questions from the prior discussion. Remember, this should not be a sales pitch, but more of an informative discussion educating the attendees about the company.
- *What you need to know.* Pick two to three key points that are important for the attendees to know about your company. Much like a 60-second elevator pitch, get to the heart of what makes the company great.
- *Your hiring process.* Explain the hiring process if the attendees are interested in working for your company. Convey the impression that there are only one to two openings, even if there are far more than that in reality. This makes the attendee feel more exclusive—lucky to be considered by the firm.
- *Thank attendees for coming.* Close the presentation and send the attendees on their way.

Attendee responses and participation in the group interview should be evaluated by the broker's assistants, who should evaluate attendees in the categories of on-time arrival, appearance, attitude, participation, and overall impression. Ratings can be on a scale from 1 to 10, or simply from "poor" to "excellent."

Step 9: Closed Session Review of Attendees

Once the attendees leave the group interview, the broker should then meet with the assistants in a closed session and discuss which of the attendees should be considered for hire. By writing the names of the top three candidates down independently, then comparing the results, the broker will get a reduced list of the best candidates from the evening. It is not uncommon for the same candidates to be selected by everyone.

Step 10: Interview Invites

Either after the conclusion of the group interview or first thing the next morning, the broker's staff should contact the chosen candidates by e-mail or telephone and schedule an appointment for a meeting with the broker in a one-on-one interview.

Step 11: The Interviews

Assuming that all goes well in the first interview, a broker should schedule the candidate for a second interview with an assistant manager or an administrative assistant. This second interview will help eliminate favoritism or verify the broker's observations about the candidate.

Step 12: The Hiring Decision

Finally, the broker decides whether or not to hire the candidate. Notice that this decision does not occur during the evening of the group interview or at any time prior to the conclusion of the second one-on-one interview. A candidate who goes through this entire screening process will most likely be a higher-quality agent than someone who was simply picked up off of the street. By now, candidates have demonstrated their intention and seriousness around the real estate business, as well as their ability to speak in public, dress professionally, arrive on time for meetings, and ask intelligent questions. A broker shouldn't take these simple skills for granted.

PERSONALITY ASSESSMENT TOOLS

Earlier, the use of personality assessment tools in evaluating new licensees was recommended. There are two specific personality assessment tools that are commonly used when hiring potential agents. These are (1) The Real Estate Simulator and (2) The DISC Personal Concept.

- **The Real Estate Simulator.** The Real Estate Simulator can be found at www.realestatesimulator.com. A company subscribes to this service by paying a monthly fee. Depending upon the program selected, the broker may have unlimited potential recruits participate in the simulation provided during the period of membership. Recruits are sent a link to the simulation, and the results are sent to the broker. The simulation takes about 40 minutes to complete each time and should be done over a broadband connection. The recruit plays the role of an agent, interacting with several virtual clients who are interested in buying or selling property. During the simulation, the recruit will be taken through the entire sales cycle, from client introduction to closing escrow. Recruits will be given the opportunity to demonstrate their ability to handle objections, negotiate price, understand client needs, deal with personality clashes, and even handle periodic rejection. The resulting report on the recruit is easy to read and provides some insightful information into the candidate's personality and his or her potential for success in the real estate industry.
- **The DISC Personal Concept.** The DISC Personal Concept has been around for many years and is more applicable to business in general than the real estate simulator. There are several online services that handle the assessment, which costs between $15 and $25 per assessment. The assessment is taken online, and the results are immediately available to the broker. The assessment consists of the candidates selecting from among groups of words, those words that they feel are most like them and those that they feel are least like them. The results are calculated, and the candidate's personality traits are assigned to one of four quadrants of personality types. The DISC Personal Concept will provide a superior psychological evaluation of a potential recruit, but to properly evaluate the results, the broker will have to take a seminar on how to interpret the results accurately. This seminar is relatively costly, but will provide

significant benefit to the broker who elects to use the DISC Personal Concept.

DETERMINING RECRUITING NEEDS

Now that we've discussed recruiting both experienced agents and new licensees, it is appropriate to talk about the steps a broker should consider in determining how many agents to recruit in order to achieve the company's growth objectives. Here is a step-by-step process:

Step 1. Determine walking vacancies. *Walking vacancies* are the agents currently in the company who are not generating enough income to meet the broker's minimum acceptable performance standard (MAPS), that is, not making enough money to cover the cost of their own desk. If a broker is just starting an office, there won't be any walking vacancies—yet. However, if the broker is starting with a few existing agents, then the walking vacancies are those agents who (1) do not generate enough company dollar to cover their desk cost, (2) have toxic personalities and are causing problems within the firm, or (3) are new licensees who have been with your company in excess of six months and who have failed to close an escrow or obtain a listing. (A new licensee who is energetic, productive, and a positive influence on the organization may be given a reprieve for an additional six months, but under no circumstances should a broker keep a nonproducing new licensee longer than one year from the agent's original start date.)

Step 2. Determine anticipated attrition. If the company has been around for a least one year, the broker should look back and determine the number of sales associates lost to other companies. This should be expressed as a percentage of the original agent count. For example, if a broker started last year with ten agents, but lost two agents to other companies, the company suffered a 20 percent attrition rate. Apply this rate to the current number of agents to anticipate a reasonable number of agents who will be lost to attrition during the next year. In order to maintain the number of agents currently in the company, the broker should recruit at least the number expected to be lost through attrition. If a broker is starting with no agents, the broker should expect a minimum attrition of one agent.

Step 3. Determine target growth needs. If a broker currently has 10 agents, and wishes to increase this number to 40 agents, the target growth need is 30 agents.

Step 4. Determine total number of recruits. To determine the total number of recruits that a company will need, add the walking vacancies (step 1), the number of agents expected to be lost to attrition (step 2), and the number of agents needed to meet the target growth (step 3).

Step 5. Determine the ratio of new licensees to experienced agents. Having determined the total number of agents a broker will need to achieve the target growth, the broker will have to make a decision concerning what percentage of new hires will be new licensees and what percentage will be experienced agents. If a broker has an existing firm, then a mix of 20 percent new licensee to 80 percent experienced agent is a ratio that keeps a firm fresh and energetic, while providing enough experience. If however the company is a start-up, the broker may have to recruit a higher percentage of new licensees in the first year of business, typically targeting 50 to 60 percent of recruits as new licensees. This higher ratio of new licensees for a start-up office occurs because it is more difficult to attract experienced agents to a company with no track record in the marketplace, while new licensees are more receptive to the higher level of personal attention that they will receive at a smaller start-up office.

PERSONAL EXERCISE 32

DETERMINE RECRUITING NEEDS

Step 1: Determine your walking vacancies
How many agents do you have in your company or office who are not producing enough company dollar to pay for their desk cost?   _____

Step 2: Determine anticipated attrition
How many agents do you anticipate losing to attrition in the next year *(minimum attrition expectation equals one sales associate)*?   +_____

Step 3: Determine target growth needs
Given the number of your current agents, how many additional agents will you need to achieve your target company size in the next year?   +_____

Step 4: Determine total number of recruits
Add the numbers from steps 1 through 3.   _____

Step 5: Determine your ratio of new licensees to experienced agents
If you are an existing firm, 20 percent of recruits should be
new licensees.   _____
If you are a new firm, 50 to 60 percent of recruits should be
new licensees.   _____

KEY POINTS

- Before launching into a recruiting program, a broker should first determine the starting point.

- A company will attract the type of agents who are currently in the company or agents similar to the broker, if the company is just starting out.

- A broker should define the profile of the ideal agent for the company before making recruiting contacts.

- A recruiting plan that consists of at least five steps should be developed when targeting experienced agents. These five steps should be taken within two to three months in order for the recruiting program to build momentum.

- Agents change companies because of leadership, not because of commission splits.

- The company's current agents can be the broker's best secret weapon for recruiting, or they can quickly destroy recruiting efforts by what they say or, in some cases, by what they don't say.

- Using a group interview process for recruiting new licensees will save a broker significant time in weeding out unqualified candidates.

- Personality assessment tools such as The Real Estate Simulator or The DISC Personal Concept can be valuable aids in providing insight into the true character and potential of job candidates.

- In determining a company's total recruiting needs, the broker must be sure to include walking vacancies, anticipated attrition, and target growth need.

13

TRAINING

*People will perform under stress in the same manner in which
they have trained and practiced.*

—CLIFF PEROTTI

Training and education are an important part of a company's culture. They are the lifeblood that brings rejuvenation and freshness to a company. This chapter focuses on (1) the nature and types of training programs that should be developed or implemented by a broker for agents and (2) sources of training to improve the skills and abilities of the broker/manager.

TRAINING FOR EXPERIENCED AGENTS

There are several sources of training to assist a broker's experienced agents in improving their skills and their net income. A company should consider incorporating each of the following areas into its training programs.

Sales Meetings

A broker's sales meetings offer the perfect opportunity to provide ongoing training for experienced agents, as well as new licensees. The broker should make a point to provide a 10- to 15-minute highly informative training session in the weekly sales meeting. These training sessions should be on topics that are immediately relevant to the agents. To help brokers and managers who have difficulty in creating interesting sales meetings, author John Mayfield has written a great book called *5 Minutes to a Great Sales Meeting*. A broker can use Mayfield's book to help create an energized sales meeting, especially if the broker has otherwise been too busy to prepare adequately (i.e., the broker forgot to prepare anything) for the weekly meeting.

Monthly In-House Training

Brokers often overlook the fact that, as veterans of this industry, they have personal knowledge and experience that should be shared with their agents on a regular basis. By developing a regimen of teaching at least one training program targeted at experienced agents per month for the company, the broker will be increasing company spirit and making a direct contribution to the agents' knowledge base. This type of program should be one to one and a half hours in length and targeted at a level where experienced agents would find it beneficial and rewarding. The subjects taught in these programs should be timely with respect to the current market conditions and needs of the agents. If a broker is at a loss for subject ideas for training classes, the broker can always asks the agents for ideas in a sales meeting.

A broker should also consider training programs that are provided by the various title companies or home warranty companies, so long as these training programs are not just veiled commercials for product sales. The broker can avoid the embarrassment and negative impact on credibility by investigating a proposed program thoroughly. Informative program offerings should be offered at least once per month.

COACHING CORNER

PROTECT YOUR SALES MEETINGS

Weekly sales meetings often become viewed as an obligatory task rather than an opportunity to inspire. As a result, brokers often fail to prepare for the meeting, or they rely on outside speakers or vendors (e.g., title companies, home warranty companies, or property inspection firms) to provide food, education, and/or entertainment. This ultimately delivers a negative message to your agents and could create an agent response such as: "If you are too busy to spend 30 to 40 minutes preparing for this meeting, then I'm too busy to give you the 45 to 60 minutes you're asking of me to attend your meeting."

If sales meetings are not being attended by at least 90 percent of your agents, you need to "take it up a notch." Here's a list of ingredients that can help create a successful sales meeting:

1. Play energized music before the meeting as agents arrive.
2. Start meetings on time and keep to 35 to 45 minutes in length. (No longer than 60 minutes.)
3. Acknowledge weekly production and successes.
4. Discuss an aspect of your company's business plan that you have achieved.
5. Discuss upcoming exciting programs.
6. Conduct a 10- to 15-minute training session.
7. Do a "haves and wants" session.

And finally, close the sales meetings to outside vendors. The weekly sales meeting should be a broker's one-on-one time with the agents. It should be treated like a confidential family meeting, in which outsiders are not welcome, unless they are potential recruits to your company. This will elevate the importance of your sales meetings in the minds of your agents and will allow you to openly discuss the company's vision, direction, and challenges with your agents.

Designation Training Programs

There are several statewide or national designation programs offered by state associations of Realtors or the National Association of Realtors that offer an element of prestige and differentiation for the broker's agents. There is documented proof that agents who possess a particular designation have significantly greater earnings than agents without the designation. Many agents are not aware of these programs, so a broker may want to provide some information for agents. Some of the most popular designations are:

- CRB—Certified Real Estate Brokerage Manager (for brokers, managers, and team leaders)
- CRS—Certified Residential Specialist (for residential real estate agents)
- CCIM—Certified Commercial Investment Member (for commercial-investment real estate agents and others with commercial-investment focus)
- CPM—Certified Property Manager (for those specializing in property management)
- LTG—Leadership Training Graduate (leadership development program)
- GRI—Graduate of the Realtors Institute (for residential real estate agents)
- SRES—Senior Real Estate Specialist (for residential agents specializing in working with seniors)
- E-PRO—Certificate for Internet Professionalism (for agents to further their Internet skills)

Supporting designation programs is a great way for a broker to enhance the training of experienced agents. A broker could encourage agents to participate in these advanced training programs by providing a reimbursement program, for example, a reimbursement out of the agent's next closing up to $500 per year toward designation tuition.

Seminar Programs

There are numerous seminar speakers in the marketplace that have developed various programs focusing on prospecting, lead management, Web site development, and a variety of other topics that can be very helpful to a broker's agents. Screening and selecting a few seminar programs to support can benefit both agent and company alike.

Coaching

Coaching programs have become extremely popular over the last few years, primarily because of their highly individual approach toward increasing an agent's production and in helping the agent lead a balanced life. In the early stages of an agent's career, the broker may act in the capacity of a coach. However, more seasoned agents may respond better to an outside coaching program, because it is often easier for an agent to trust a third-party independent coach. A good coaching program can help agents achieve higher production levels, greater levels of happiness in their personal lives, and emotional retracking when the agent has hit an emotional low. A broker should investigate a few different coaching options and select one or two programs to which agents can be referred.

Remediation Program

When a broker has underperforming agents in the company, the broker may want to consider offering some sort of remediation program that is a high-intensity 8- to 12-week program in which the agents meet in a small group at least once or twice a week. These meetings are typically one to one and a half hours in length and are focused on tracking the activities of the agents, holding them accountable, moving prospects along to the next stage, and increasing productivity. The concept behind a remediation program is that it is the last ditch effort to salvage a nonproductive agent. This type of program can also be used to move a broker's C producers into the B producer category, so a broker may want to call the program something motivating, such as "Taking It to the Next Level" or "Production Dynamics."

By offering a combination of the above training programs, a broker could effectively create a comprehensive approach to training of experienced agents, without incurring too great a cost.

PERSONAL EXERCISE 33

YOUR EXPERIENCED AGENT TRAINING

1. What training programs will you provide in-house for experienced agents?
2. What outside designation programs will you endorse, and how will you encourage your agents to participate in these programs?
3. Who are the seminar speakers or trainers who you believe will help your agents be more productive?
4. How will your company encourage your agents to attend the programs offered by these speakers?
5. What are the options for coaching programs for your agents? (If you don't know, use an Internet search engine to investigate a couple of options.)
6. How will your company encourage your agents to participate in a coaching program?
7. If you were to have a remediation program, what would that look like?

TRAINING FOR NEW LICENSEES

There are three primary steps of training that a broker should consider implementing for training new licensees.

Step 1: Basic Skills Program

A basic skills program consists of 40 to 80 hours of classroom instruction that covers everything from prospecting to the escrow paperwork. If a company is part of a major franchise, such programs are typically offered regionally by the franchisor, allowing the franchisee to send new licensees to the program for a fee. If the brokerage is an independent firm, then the broker will have to design and implement some sort of basic skills program for the firm. Developing such a program is extremely time-consuming and is not necessarily the wisest use of the broker's time.

An independent brokerage may consider buying a basic skills training program that has already been prepared and produced on DVD. There are several of these quality programs available in the market today. They typically include a student workbook and facilitator handbook for the broker to use along with the program. By using such a DVD program, the agents can participate in the training program at their own pace by watching the DVDs in the office.

A basic skills program acts as a "fast start" program by providing the new agent with all the basics of prospecting for clients, showing property to buyers, making listing presentations, and much more. This means that the agents receive an enormous amount of information in a very short period of time. The consequence of this is that retention may be very low. A broker should reinforce subjects taught in the basic skills program through an ongoing program of group coaching.

Step 2: Group Coaching

The next step for training new licensees requires them to participate in a weekly or biweekly coaching class with the broker, a sales manager, or other mentor. Group coaching sessions typically have four to six new licensees in attendance and are basically training classes that last for one to one and a half hours. Each week, the leader/trainer should review the agents' production activities and discuss one training subject area in depth. The trainer should also emphasize debriefing the weekly "war stories" of the agents during the sessions because this will allow the trainer to address a specific real example with one agent, while all the other agents in attendance are learning from the same lesson as they listen in. This process escalates the learning curve of the new licensees, because they each hear the experience and the recommended solution without having to encounter the experience; they can learn from the mistakes of the other agents in the room.

Step 3: The Mentor

When some companies think of implementing a mentorship program, they simply go to their active agent roster and ask who among their existing agents might be interested in working with a newbie agent. This can result in the wrong agent being appointed as a mentor. Trainees working under the wrong mentor will typically complain about being used as a slave or a gofer for the mentor. This is a serious problem, because the company has spent an enormous amount of time and energy in developing this new licensee only to have this person's motivation destroyed by an ego-driven "mentor." Careful thought should be given by the broker as to who is qualified to be a mentor in the company. A mentor should be someone who has demonstrated a willingness to help other agents and answer questions for new agents in the office.

New licensees should be expected to work with an assigned mentor for a minimum of six months *and* three closed sales transactions. By using both a minimum time requirement and the production requirement before releasing a new licensee from the mentor program, a broker is ensuring that most of the commonplace transactional situations will have been encountered by a new licensee. The mentor should assist the new licensee with listing presentations, buyer interviews, and escrow transactions. In addition, the mentor should work with the new licensee on developing a business plan, a marketing strategy, time management issues, and maintaining productivity.

A broker can compensate a mentor through revenue-sharing, by giving a portion of the new licensee's production to the mentor. For example, a broker could give 25 to 30 percent of the gross commissions generated from the new licensee's first three transactions, or a lower percentage of 5 to 10 percent on the entire first year's production of the new licensee. By paying the mentor on an incentive basis for closings, the broker is encouraging the mentor to assist the trainees throughout the entire transaction, not just at the outset of listing or escrow.

PERSONAL EXERCISE 34

YOUR NEW LICENSEE TRAINING

1. What steps would you include in your new licensee training program?
2. How will you accomplish providing a basic skills program for your new licensees?
3. Who will be responsible for teaching or facilitating your basic skills program?
4. If you are considering a group coaching program for your new licensees, who will be the individual responsible for developing and implementing this program? What will the structure of this program be?
5. If you are going to have a mentor program, what are the criteria you will look for in a mentor candidate?
6. Write down the names of at least three mentor candidates that come to mind.

A company should produce a monthly one-page training calendar that can be given out in a sales meeting, placed into the agents' mailboxes, and tacked up on the company bulletin board. This training calendar should include all scheduled training classes, dates and times of sales meetings, and any special office functions that will be occurring during the next month. Typically, a company would issue this monthly training calendar in the last week of each month, covering the next monthly period.

TRAINING FOR THE BROKER

While the resources for education specific to real estate brokerage management are limited and less commonly available than those for sales associates, here are three management-specific recommendations.

1. **Council of Real Estate Brokerage Managers.** The programs offered by the Council of Real Estate Brokerage Managers (CRB) are designed for real estate brokers and managers; they focus on strategic planning, financial planning, increasing agent performance, marketing, and recruiting. The core CRB programs are currently offered either via live presentation or on CD-ROM. While it is a major inconvenience for a broker to be absent from the office to attend a course in person, there is great value to be obtained by attending a live presentation program because of the opportunity to hear ideas from other marketplaces. Also, one of the strongest elements of the CRB affiliation is the networking that occurs among the brokers.

2. **Coaching/consulting programs.** If a broker is part of a franchise, the franchisor may have regional business consultants who meet periodically with the broker to discuss the progress of the company and to offer assistance and support. For brokers who are not part of a franchise system, there are private coaching or consulting firms that work with brokers, either individually or in small groups. A broker can expect the costs of a coaching relationship to be in the range of $650 to $750 per month. The costs of consulting services vary based on the experience level of the consultant and the task required. Typically, a cost of $2,500 to $5,000 per day would not be out of the norm. Given the pace

---

Tales from the Real World

YOU GET WHAT YOU EXPECT

A broker had six new licensees, none of whom had completed a sale or taken a listing in their first six months of the business. The broker had invested an enormous amount of time in training these new licensees.

"What's wrong with these people?" thought the frustrated broker. "They seem to be doing all the right things. I've put every one of them through a three-week training program and given them all my best scripts and marketing ideas. I just don't get it."

He held a meeting with the new licensees to discuss their lack of production. One of the agents said, "We're doing everything we can. Sellers won't give us a listing because we're new, and no buyer wants to work with us once they find out we're new to the business."

The broker decided to go out with these agents on a few presentations and buyer interviews to assess their performance. He quickly learned that all the agents made a strong point of mentioning to the prospects that they were new to the real estate business. One agent, a former hairdresser, felt more comfortable discussing the seller's hairstyle than giving real estate advice. In all the cases, the agents apologized to the prospects in their first meeting for their lack of experience and knowledge. The agents' insecurity with their own experience level created insecurity in the potential clients; the prospects never really had a chance to feel okay about working with the agent.

The broker called another meeting with these new licensees and had one new licensee give a listing presentation in front of the others, which the broker videotaped. The agents were mortified at their blatant mistake.

Regardless of the great training programs provided to agents, they will get a result that corresponds to what they expect.

at which a real estate broker must solve problems, a coach or consultant quickly proves his or her value.

3. **NAR annual expo or national franchise annual convention.** It is recommended that a broker attend either the National Association of Realtors Expo or, if a broker is part of a franchise system, the franchise's national annual convention. During either of these three- to five-day events, a broker will have an opportunity to see cutting-edge products and attend educational and informative sessions. Additionally, a broker will have the opportunity to meet other real estate brokers throughout the United States, thus expanding his or her referral network.

A broker needs to stay atop the most current trends and contemporary thinking on all aspects of the brokerage industry. This means attending new programs on a regular basis. Brokers should consider attending at least three to four major training programs per year, gathering at least one pearl of wisdom from each program attended that will help them improve their business, their awareness, or their ability to help those around them. This mindset will have a compounding effect on the broker, helping the broker to improve the quality of his or her life and business exponentially.

KEY POINTS

- A broker should develop training programs for new licensees as well as for experienced agents in the company.
- A mixture of in-house programs, outsourced seminars, and other multimedia programs can create a multidimensional, compelling training program for the company.
- A broker should treat every sales meeting with great importance, making the meeting energized, fun, and informative with a 10- to 15-minute training session on a timely and interesting subject.
- A broker should think about his or her own expertise and experience, developing six to eight one-hour training sessions covering subjects that the broker is confident about. These training sessions can serve as the backbone of an in-house monthly training program.
- Brokers and agents alike should take advantage of the designation programs available in the industry today.
- A reimbursement program is a great way for a broker to encourage agents to attend seminars and designation programs, effectively outsourcing the broker's training department.

- A broker will need to find a source for a remediation program to support underperforming agents.
- A broker's new licensee training program should include a basic skills element, a coaching element, and a mentoring element.
- Office mentors should be handpicked with character traits that demonstrate the mentor's desire to help others succeed.
- A broker should keep fresh and informed on the most current trends by attending the national conventions offered by a franchise or the annual convention/expo of the National Association of Realtors.

14

RETENTION

Retention comes from the heart, not the head.

—CLIFF PEROTTI

A t the core of a real estate company's value are the agents of the firm. Brokerage profitability and valuation is directly linked to the ability of the broker to retain agents. Nothing is more devastating to a company than losing its productive agents to the recruiting efforts of a competitor. Consequently, most brokers around the globe live in constant fear of their agents "walking out on them." The fierce competition for agents has resulted in brokers giving more and more of their gross commission dollars to their agents, in spite of the increasing operational expenses of the company. As agent commission negotiations become the primary retention focus for brokers, the result has become diminished services being provided to agents and a perception that the highest commission split will "win" agents. Brokers have lost sight of the real value proposition they offer and have become vulnerable to the fear of losing agents.

WHY AGENTS *REALLY* SELECT COMPANIES

While common sense tells us that agents look for a firm that offers training, an appealing brand, and an opportunity for leads, they often select a company that has none of these features. Managers of offices are frequently surprised when a new company wielding a new brand under the leadership of a completely unknown broker comes into the market and proceeds to recruit 50 to 150 agents in 12 to 14 months, while they were able to recruit only 5 to 10 agents in the prior year. Since agents don't always select the company that offers the most features, there must be another reason that they select a particular company.

It has been said that retention is nothing more than constantly re-recruiting existing agents. For a company to retain and attract agents, it must create and maintain a compelling value proposition, the result being that its agents *feel* and *believe* that while there may be better features available at other offices, there is simply no better place to be than at the current company. Agents are no different from anyone working for any company in the world; they want to *feel good* about where they work, they want to *believe* in their company, and they want to *respect* the company leader. The key to retention, and the real reason agents select a company, is their own positive feelings, belief in the firm, and respect for its leaders.

UNDERSTANDING THE VALUE PROPOSITION

From a recruiting or retention perspective, a company's value proposition answers the question, "Why should I select this company?" It is a clear statement about the benefits of the company. A great majority of real estate brokers are unable to succinctly explain their own company's value proposition. They unemotionally speak about their company as if it were a bland provider of what they perceive to be the generic services offered by all real estate companies. They often have trouble expressing the points of differentiation between their own company and those of any other brokerage. This "disconnect" is a symptom of brokers' lack of understanding of the true value that their own company holds and makes them vulnerable to retention problems.

A company's value proposition is not so much a laundry list of features, but rather a textured experience of how agents will feel if they work at the company. Thus, a broker's value proposition must be explained in terms of experiential words or easily absorbed metaphors that conjure up how agents would feel if they were affiliated with the company. For example, a laundry list value proposition would state (incorrectly):

> If you are an agent at our company, you get an 80 percent commission split, company-paid open house ads, a desk cubicle area, floor time twice per month, and an affiliation with a national franchise brand.

On the other hand, a textured value proposition would state (correctly):

> We are a company that is on the move. We are transitioning from being number 54 in the market to being number 7, with all the changes in office and agent energy that such a movement would imply. We are a train about to leave the station on an exciting journey. We are on fire.

The second statement does not give mundane details about the agent's commission split or ads provided by the company. It does, however, evoke specific feelings of movement. The image of the train sitting in the station is compelling. It is something different from what other brokers are talking about. It implies leadership.

Every company, regardless of what it offers agents, has a different broker/leader who is on a unique mission. If brokers are unable to espouse the specifics of where they are going and why, then they are not on any mission and are not exhibiting strong leadership skills, which are both essential retention tools. The value proposition should evoke a sense of excitement and movement. Every agent wants to be a part of a company that is special and is being talked about—a company that is on the move rather than sitting still, exciting rather than mundane. Some key textures to consider including in a value proposition are:

- How will I feel?
- What's happening around here?
- Why is this place different?
- Where are we going?
- Will it be fun and exciting?
- How can I contribute to the mission?

EXPANSION OR CONTRACTION

It has been said that a company is either in a state of expansion or contraction. This is no more evident than in a real estate brokerage. A broker should strive to be in a constant state of expansion, not only in terms of the number of agents in the company, but also in terms of fresh ideas, innovative programs, and personal growth in leadership style. There are clues that reveal the expansion or contraction of energy in a company, as shown in Figure 14.1.

A broker who is aware of the clues to expansion and contraction can take proactive steps to create an expanding energy in the office. This is critical to keeping company workers motivated and retaining agents.

FIGURE 14.1   Energy Expansion or Contraction

Clues to Expansion Energy	Clues to Contraction Energy
Upbeat office environment	Low-energy office environment
Agents coming to the company	Agents are leaving the company
Regular training programs presented	No training activities occurring
Broker is energized and fired up	Broker is tired or just getting by
Broker is busy with people, not paper	Broker is occupied with paperwork
Broker is out and about	Broker is always in his or her office
Broker is loved by the agents	Broker is liked by the agents
Agents in the company help recruit to it	Agents do not solicit other agents
Sales meetings are well attended	Poor sales meeting attendance
No whining about the company	Lots of whining and complaining
There is a "buzz" in the market about the company	No one really cares

THE BROKER—THE SOURCE

The broker is the one sustainable competitive advantage in each company and the primary retention tool of the firm. The broker's style, energy, focus, humor, and a hundred personal character traits are the source of inspiration for the company's agents and staff. It is essential that a broker keeps this in mind when walking through the office, leading a sales meeting, teaching a group of agents, or going to open houses. A broker is like a pebble being dropped into the company pond; as the pebble delivers energy into the pond, it disseminates its energy in waves throughout the agents and staff. Remember, while it is easy for an agent to leave a company, it is difficult to leave a broker who is respected and valued.

While each broker will have his or her own way of giving positive energy to the company, here are some ideas to consider:

- Walk through the office, talking with agents and asking, "What's going on?"
- Arrive first to the office and greet staff as they arrive.
- Occasionally take an agent or staff member to get coffee.
- Tour with an agent or a small group of agents.
- Post inspirational sayings on bulletin boards, flipcharts, and in the workrooms.
- Make a point to have lunch with one person from the office each week.
- Reread the vision statement daily to keep focused on the goal.
- Hand out personal development books as closing gifts to agents.
- Leave the office when in a funk.
- Laugh!

As the source of leadership energy for a company, a broker will often feel emotionally drained at the end of each day. It's important to remember that the demand being made on the broker will require him or her to be in good physical and mental health. Staying fit, eating right, and spending time having fun away from work are all important things brokers should incorporate into their weekly lives. In addition, a broker should keep mentally fresh by attending educational programs (such as the CRB designation courses) and reading personal development or inspirational books. Brokers cannot lead anyone if they cannot stay healthy and happy. (See Personal Exercise 36.)

BRINGING YOUR "A" GAME

- Write down at least three to five ways you can bring positive energy to your staff and agents on a weekly basis.
- Write down three to five actions you can take on a weekly basis to improve or maintain your personal good health and attitude.

RETENTION IDEAS

There are several basic ideas that a broker should implement to keep a high level of energy and a spirit of unity within the company. Here are some ideas for a broker to consider in building an impenetrable retention fortress. (See Personal Exercise 37 at the end of this section.)

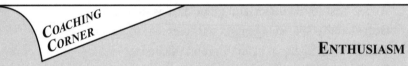

COACHING CORNER

ENTHUSIASM

Vince Lombardi once said, "If you are not fired with enthusiasm, you will be fired with enthusiasm." Agents expect you, as their leader, to be fired up with enthusiasm. You cannot ask them to work late hours, do lots of prospecting, or deliver high levels of production if you are not willing to do the same. Leadership by example is the best tool you have for commanding loyalty and respect from your agents. Your enthusiasm for the mission and vision is highly contagious and invaluable to the agents and company. Take care of yourself physically so you can handle the stress of building your company, stay focused on your vision and the mission of the company, and finally, be an enthusiastic leader when you're around the office. I don't mean be a cheerleader; cheerleading and enthusiasm are not the same thing.

Sales Meetings

Effective and informative sales meetings will be well attended and are a positive retention tool for brokers. As previously mentioned, a broker should first start by closing sales meetings to outside vendors. The broker should then develop a standing agenda that might look like this:

- Premeeting
  Play upbeat music 10 to 15 minutes prior to the meeting
  Have quality food and beverages available before the meeting
- Start the meeting on time
- Cover production since the last meeting
  Closings (gives recognition)
  Pendings and listing price changes
  Open escrows
- Recognition of team members
  Recognize professional or personal accomplishments of agents or staff since last meeting
- Report and update on company vision and make company announcements
  10- to 15-minute discussion on status of one goal or update on issues from last meeting
- Contest update
  Give update on any company contest that may be running
- Training or motivational segment
  10 to 15 minutes on a specific issue
  Have handouts for agents
- Staff contributions
  Set aside 5 minutes for transaction coordinators and/or marketing assistants to contribute
- Agent contributions
  Give agents an opportunity to mention anything "for the good of the order" (limit segment to two to three announcements)
- Adjourn meeting

Contests

A broker should hold a sales contest at least two to three times per year. These contests should run for at least one month, to allow time for everyone to get involved, and should have prizes that are announced at the outset of the contest. Contests that place the agents together in teams are effective and help to encourage teamwork in the office. If using teams, the broker should mix top producers with lower producers in order to create more balanced teams and in hopes of inspiring production from the lower producers.

"GIVE ME 90 DAYS"

A broker announced in a sales meeting that he had sold the company to another brokerage. The agents were emotionally hurt and totally shocked at this news, feeling that their broker had abandoned them. Within minutes of the announcement, the broker's agents were receiving phone calls from competitors, offering interviews and incentives if the agents were considering changing companies. The broker's staff members advised the broker of all the conversations that were occurring between the agents and the competitors. The broker knew that the sale of his company was hanging on the successful transition of the agents to the new company owner.

In an effort to do some damage control, the broker called a meeting for the next morning. All the agents were present. The broker let the agents know that he understood that the sale of the company was a surprise to them, but he had been very careful about selection of the new owner, and he believed that the new owners were going to be able to take the company to new heights. He said, "Please trust me in this selection. Give me 90 days before you consider changing companies. By then, you will have experienced the benefits of the new leadership, or I'll be the first to encourage you to find a new broker because I would have failed you."

The agents honored the 90-day period, and they were surprised by the commitment and energy they felt from the new owner. In short, only 2 agents out of 40 left the company. Asking for a 90-day trial period is a great way to buy time and an opportunity to build trust. Most agents will be willing to wait this three-month period.

Training Calendar

While this subject is covered thoroughly in the chapter on training, it is important to remember that an active training calendar is a great retention tool because it indicates a sense of caring, and it is an opportunity for all agents to grow together.

Positive Staff Attitude

A broker should encourage the development of a positive attitude in the staff members of the firm. Office administrators, receptionists, marketing assistants, and transaction coordinators should exhibit a constant helpfulness and work as a team to accomplish the company's mission.

Office Cleanliness

A broker and the office staff should encourage a clean office, taking steps to constantly police the common areas for used coffee cups, papers left in meeting rooms, and so forth. Agents will become more aware and take pride in their office if they see the broker picking up after them.

Quarterly Company Events

A company should hold quarterly company events that are both fun and value-oriented. A quarterly event may be a luncheon or a full-day event. Here are some examples of quarterly events that have been used by brokers:

- **Sales rally day.** A three-hour training session that focuses on buyers (changes in laws, attracting buyers, increasing closure rates, etc.).
- **Listing rally day.** A three-hour training session that focuses on sellers (changes in laws, effective communication, getting price reductions, managing expectations, etc.).
- **State-of-the-company luncheon.** An annual event in January, giving a report on goals from the prior year and goals for the coming year.
- **Annual awards dinner.** An annual dinner where the broker gives out annual production awards to agents and key staff members.
- **Movie in the park.** A perfect event for a warm summer evening, the broker hosts an outdoor barbeque and outdoor movie in the park for agents and their family members.
- **A day at the races.** Rent a bus and take the people at the company to a local racetrack.

Agent Advisory Roundtable

The broker selects four to five agents, of varying production levels, to meet on a quarterly basis to provide feedback, give ideas, and discuss issues that need to be addressed in the office. This is an advisory group only; the broker still makes the final decisions for the company.

Recognition Program

A company should have a production award system that provides awards to agents achieving specific production levels. There should be some awards that are noncompetitive (i.e., if agents hit the production level, they receive the recognition award) and some that are competitive (i.e., only one agent will receive the recognition). Here is a sample of one company's production awards program:

- **Noncompetitive awards:**
  Platinum agent: Achieves $250,000+ in gross commissions
  Gold agent: Achieves $150,000 to $249,999 in gross commissions
  Silver agent: Achieves $100,000 to $149,999 in gross commissions
- **Competitive awards:**
  Top producer, sales volume: Number 1 agent in the company by sales volume
  Top producer, units: Number 1 agent in the company by closed sales
  Top listing agent: Number 1 agent in the company by number of listings taken
  Rookie of the year: Honors the top new licensee

PERSONAL EXERCISE 37

RETENTION IDEAS

Write down at least five ideas that will increase the emotional bond of your agents to the company, thus increasing the likelihood of your retaining them.

KEY POINTS

- Retaining agents is critical to a company's profitability.
- Agents select and stay with companies that offer a solid value proposition.
- A company's value proposition answers the question, "Why should I select or stay with this company?"
- A value proposition should be textured and create a sense of movement for the company.
- Agents want to *feel good* about where they work, they want to *believe* in their company, and they want to *respect* the company leader.
- The most important element of a company's value proposition is the broker.
- A company is either in a state of expansion or contraction; there is no status quo.
- A broker needs to focus on creating an impenetrable fortress, meaning that no other broker is able to recruit from the office.

15

MARKETING

*If you're attacking your market from multiple positions
and your competition isn't, you have all the advantage
and it will show up in your increased success
and income.*

—JAY ABRAHAM

For the real estate company, marketing is the cumulative actions of carrying the company's brand and value proposition to potential customers in an effort to differentiate the company from other companies in the minds of prospects. Marketing is one of the greatest expense items that brokers face, so they must apply their best efforts to avoid wasting money, spending only on the most efficacious marketing programs. Brokers are constantly facing pressure by both agents and clients to increase marketing expenditures, sometimes recklessly, but seemingly always without consideration for the effectiveness or cost. Real estate brokers must be vigilant against overspending on inappropriate or ineffective marketing. They do this by establishing an annual comprehensive marketing plan that is designed to create maximum exposure for the company to a target prospect group. The broker's marketing goal is to have the company come to the mind of prospective customers when they think of real estate.

SEEK FIRST TO UNDERSTAND

In order to know where and how to spend money on marketing, brokers should determine (1) how their brand is perceived by the company's current customers, (2) how customers found the company, and (3) why customers selected the company as their real estate agency. This information can most easily be obtained through a survey of the broker's past customers. A survey can be conducted by phone, mail, or e-mail or through the Internet. Use of an online Internet survey service is inexpensive, easy to use, and quick. By using an online survey provider, such as "Survey Monkey" (found at www.surveymonkey.com), a broker can create a complete online survey within a few minutes, upload e-mail addresses, and send the survey to past customers. The results are then tracked and tabulated into easy-to-read reports. Figure 15.1 can be used as a sample to provide the company with a significant amount of information about its current clientele, such as how clients found the company, what services are most important, how the brand is perceived, client satisfaction levels, and so on.

Another way to learn about client behavior is to hold a focus group, bringing together 10 to 12 of the company's past customers and having a structured question-and-answer session. While a broker can personally run such a focus group, it is recommended that a third-party marketing firm be used to provide objectivity.

Once a broker has determined how customers are initially exposed to company services and what services are most important to those customers, the broker is ready to launch a marketing plan that will imprint the firm's brand into the minds of potential customers.

FIGURE 15.1   Sample Customer Survey

1. How did you first come in contact with ABC Realty?
   - Property sign
   - Newspaper sd
   - Internet
   - Open house
   - Home magazine ad
   - Seminar
   - Referred by a friend
   - Bus stop ad
   - Kiosk
   - Craigslist
   - Realtor.com
   - Community event
   - Other:_____
2. Would you refer ABC Realty to a friend or colleague?____Yes ____No
3. What words would you use to describe ABC Realty's service?
4. What words would you use to describe ABC Realty's brand image?
5. Before your recent transaction, were you aware of ABC Realty? ____Yes ____No
6. As you were getting ready to buy/sell, what marketing resources did you use to find a property or real estate company?
7. What is the most important thing you look for in a real estate company?

THE INTERNAL MARKETING LADDER

In *The 22 Immutable Laws of Marketing*, authors Al Ries and Jack Trout present a concept called "the law of the ladder." It essentially says that within each prospect's mind is retained a limited list of ideal products or service providers for each category of product or service that is typically used. For example, if a person is asked to provide a list of automobile brands, the person might say (1) BMW, (2) Mercedes Benz, (3) Toyota. Then the person might pause before continuing with (4) Ford and (5) Lexus. A person can typically cite one to three brands relatively quickly, indicating that these brands are embedded in the person's internal marketing ladder. A person is most likely to investigate one of these brands first, if he or she were in the market to buy the product. A pause in the listing of brands would indicate that the person has to actively think about secondary options, having already given the primary preferred brands. A broker's marketing efforts should be designed to get the company on the top three rungs of a prospect's marketing ladder for real estate.

A real estate brokerage initially gets its brand onto a prospect's marketing ladder by exposing the prospect to a consistent marketing message five to seven times in a relatively short period of time, using a variety of media. This means that the broker cannot exclusively rely on just one type of marketing medium, such as direct mail, classified ads, radio ads, or open houses, but rather needs to include a variety of these approaches to create an effective marketing program.

THE MARKETING PLAN

A company's marketing plan is a comprehensive set of objectives to be met and action steps to be taken during the year. It is composed of three segments, which are (1) creating awareness, (2) delivering services, and (3) evaluating effectiveness. (See Personal Exercise 38 at the end of this section.)

Creating Awareness

There are several traditional ways that real estate companies create awareness of their firm in the minds of prospects. In order to be effective, a brokerage should use a mix of methods and not rely on any one method alone.

Newspaper Advertising

Real estate companies spend more money on newspaper advertising than any other single category of marketing. Ironically, studies have shown that less than 14 percent of potential buyers find their homes through newspaper advertising. Brokers feel an enormous amount of pressure from agents to maintain a significant presence in the newspaper. More often than not, this is because a competitor is spending money by running newspaper ads, and agents want their broker to keep up with the competition.

Here are some recommendations to consider when advertising in newspapers:

- **Classified advertising.** Often referred to as *scatter ads*, classified ads for individual listings are the most common method of newspaper advertising for real estate companies. To increase brand awareness, a broker should include the company logo in all classified advertising.

While this will add an additional 10 to 15 percent to the cost of ads, it will create a strong sense of the company's market presence.

- **Display ads.** Often referred to as *the company ad*, a display ad is a block ad in the newspaper in which the company provides a branded shell that contains numerous listings from the firm. Typically, a display ad is a minimum size of one-eighth of a page (accommodating 1 to 6 listing ads) to a maximum of one full page (accommodating 20 to 30 listing ads). Maintaining a weekly large display ad can be a drain on the broker's advertising funds. Display ads are not encouraged for a start-up company during the first year of the company's existence because of the high cost and poor return. If a company is going to use a display ad, the broker may wish to consider limiting the size to a half page, running it only biweekly.

- **Open house ads.** The highest and best use of newspaper advertising is the open house ad. Typically, this is a three- to four-line advertisement for a Sunday open house and appears in a specific open house section of the newspaper on Saturday and Sunday only. Not all newspapers have open house sections, but if one is available, the broker should take advantage of this tool every week.

- **Local versus regional papers.** In many marketplaces, there are both regional and local newspapers. For example, in Marin County, California, residents can read the countywide regional newspaper *The Marin Independent Journal*, or they can read a local newspaper such as the *Mill Valley Herald*. The cost of advertising in regional news-papers is greater than in local newspapers. Ironically, local newspapers are often more thoroughly read than regional ones because they carry more community-oriented information, such as local high school events, Little League game results, and programs at the senior center. If a broker is attempting to create a strong local presence, advertising in local newspapers might be a good option and an even better value.

- **Controlling costs.** A broker placing consistent advertising into a specific newspaper may wish to consider taking advantage of the newspaper's bulk rate discounts by signing a contract to place a certain dollar amount of advertising or certain number of ad lines during a six-month or one-year period. Once a broker is under a bulk-rate contract, then all advertising placed by the broker's agents will be billed at the broker's lowest advertising rates, and the broker should receive credit toward the company contract obligation from ads placed by its agents.

| Tales from the Real World |

REDUCING COSTS

A local broker consistently ran a half-page display ad every Sunday in a regional newspaper at a cost of $2,500 per week. This ad featured 16 properties, one community service announcement, and an invitation for readers to visit the company's Web site. After tracking results from this ad for six months, the broker realized that this single advertising source accounted for only 10 percent of the company's inbound leads, but was 50 percent of the company's advertising budget. Naturally, this weekly ad was perceived by the broker's agents as an invaluable part of their company's marketing efforts.

In an effort to reduce the cost of this expense and to analyze the impact of a potential cutback in this single advertising item, the broker reduced the number of times the ad would be run to twice per month. The broker's agents were never aware of the change until the broker told them about it six months later. They were amazed because there had been no change in their business.

Thus, with a little courage, the broker was able to reduce the company's newspaper expenditures by $60,000 per year.

Magazine Advertising

The most common form of magazine advertising is the "homes" kind of magazine, which is generally used to advertise specific properties, featuring color pictures of homes. However, brokers can differentiate their firms from the competition by advertising in other types of magazines that are read by potential home buyers and sellers. Here are some points to consider for magazine advertising:

- **Homes magazines.** There is typically a two- to three-week lead time for putting listings into homes magazines. In a fast-paced market where listings sell within 7 to 10 days, placing ads in homes magazines may be a waste of money for a broker because most of the listings presented in the magazine ad will have been sold by the time the publication hits the stands. This can be a frustration for the consumer. As an alternative to the traditional magazine property ads, a broker might advertise buyer or seller seminars, informational pamphlets (e.g., *10 Steps to Saving Thousands on Your Next Home Purchase* or *9 Ways to Make Your Home More Marketable*), or a scheduled Webinar on a vital home-buying or home-selling topic.
- **Other magazines.** Most brokers fail to think about non-real-estate-related publications when they consider magazine advertising. The key

point to remember is that buyers and sellers of real estate also read other types of publications, such as cooking magazines, golf magazines, architectural magazines, and lifestyle magazines. While advertising in these types of publications is more costly than advertising in local homes magazines, such magazines present an opportunity for the broker's company to be seen by potential prospects before they start to look at real estate publications.

Internet Marketing

Internet advertising offers a broker the unique opportunity to be seen by thousands of potential customers at a very reasonable cost. Because of the fast-paced changing nature of Internet use by consumers and competitors, a broker should constantly be evaluating the effectiveness of the company's Internet presence. The basic types of Internet advertising to consider are (1) a Web site designed to inform consumers about the company's services and induce them to contact the company, (2) search engine advertising to drive consumers to the company's Web site, (3) fee-based lead-generation Web sites that provide a company with the names and contact information of potential home buyers and sellers, (4) online advertising of properties, and (5) e-mail newsletters.

- **Company Web site.** A real estate brokerage should maintain an active company Web site that contains information about the services offered, agents, current listings, the marketplace, community resources, job opportunities, and instructional how-tos for buyers and sellers. While a broker can spend thousands of dollars and countless hours developing a customized Web site, it is recommended that a broker take the more economical path and seek out a customizable template-based Web site. There are hundreds of providers for such Web sites, which can be found by simply inputting the term "real estate Web sites" into a search engine.

  It's extremely important for a broker to include the Web site address in every piece of promotional literature that is distributed, every sign that is installed, every ad that is placed, and every business card that is handed out. This will help drive traffic to the Web site and create a secondary opportunity to put the company's value proposition in front of a prospect.

- **Search engine advertising.** Search engines such as Google and Yahoo! offer various advertising programs to help drive Internet traffic to a broker's Web site. The primary advertising tools available from a search engine are keyword ads and banner ads.

  By purchasing a *keyword ad program*, the broker's Web site link and a one- to two-line message will appear at the top of the Web page when a search is performed by a consumer using specific keywords that a broker has selected, such as "Chicago real estate," "Milwaukee homes," and so on. In a keyword ad program, the broker can control the amount of advertising dollars spent on a daily basis as well as the potential placement of the broker's ad on the search engine page. Selected keywords can be changed, so search phrases that are not producing results can be deleted and changed in favor of more productive words or phrases. Further information on this type of advertising can be found by entering the term "Google Adwords" into any search engine.

Banner ads are the boxes that appear around a Web page when a consumer is performing a search using specific keywords. By clicking on a banner ad, the consumer is taken directly to the broker's Web site. While banner ads can be run on search engine Web sites, they may be more effective if they appear on Web sites that share the same consumers as a real estate brokerage, such as mortgage Web sites, contractor Web sites, and community Web sites.

- **Lead generation Web sites.** These are Web sites that charge a monthly fee in exchange for providing the names, e-mail addresses, and other contact information of potential buyers and sellers of real estate. Companies such as housevalues.com and homegain.com will charge the broker a set fee for each zip code for which the broker wishes to receive leads. The fee will increase if an exclusive relationship for a zip code is desired, that is, where the broker is the only real estate broker receiving leads in that zip code. The caveat for this type of service is that the broker must monitor the quality of the leads being provided; it's not uncommon that prospects provide inaccurate names, e-mail addresses, or phone numbers. Also a broker should remember that the key to successful closure on these types of leads is to follow up with the prospect within a couple of hours; the more time that passes, the less likely it is that there will be closure.

- **Online property advertising.** Because of the high level of exposure and the low level of cost, brokers should always provide online advertising for each of their listings. The advertising may appear in any one of the following venues:

Company Web site. All the broker's listings, whether active or pending, should appear on the Web site. This provides cross-selling opportunities to potential buyers and is an essential requirement for most sellers in today's marketplace.

Realtor.com. This is the most popular Web site in the United States for consumers to view property listings online. For some marketplaces, the listings are automatically uploaded onto realtor.com once they are placed in the local multiple listing service. This is an arrangement that has been created between realtor.com and the local MLS. Brokers can add highlights or improve their page placement on realtor.com by paying additional fees.

Craigslist.org.   Craigslist has become a phenomenon throughout the major markets in the United States. A broker can advertise a property listing for free on Craigslist. The listing advertisement is easily uploaded, including multiple pictures of the property. By using some minimal HTML coding, the broker can improve the appearance of the Craigslist ad, which can provide the broker's contact information as well as a link to the broker's Web site. Brokers are often amazed by the number and quality of leads generated from Craigslist ads.

Property Web site.   A growing trend is to create temporary posting of a Web site based upon the property address, for example, "123HawthorneStreet.com." This sort of property Web site is most appropriate for high-end estate properties, but it can certainly be used for lower-priced homes. The Web site address is used on all the marketing materials for the property, steering potential buyers to the Web site.

COACHING CORNER

HELP YOUR AGENTS; HELP YOURSELF

Brokers often forget that one of the most effective ways to get a bigger bang for their marketing dollars is to train their agents to market themselves. You should conduct regular training sessions on marketing to help them become more effective in the use of their time and money. If agents are more effective in their marketing efforts, the company will see more productivity, increased market share, and greater profits.

Typical trouble areas for agents' marketing efforts include:

- **Following up with Internet leads.**   Consider bringing in outside Internet marketing specialists to teach your agents to maximize their Web sites and to follow up with Internet leads.
- **Conducting effective open houses.**   After working with hundreds of agents, I can tell you that only about 30 percent of agents conduct truly effective open houses.
- **Handling floor calls.**   Historically, agents are notoriously bad at getting the name and phone number of potential prospects calling in on floor time.

- **E-mail newsletters.** While the e-mail spamming of potential prospects is not encouraged, the use of periodic e-mail newsletters is encouraged. A broker should consider developing a monthly newsletter that is e-mailed to past customers and current prospects. E-mail newsletters should contain an opt-out feature for recipients who do not wish to receive the newsletter, and it should be filled with information of value to the reader. Recipients will continue to accept newsletters that contain valuable information. Brokers can find several services online that provide templates for e-mail newsletters by inputting the term "e-mail newsletters" into a search engine.

Regardless of which online method is used to advertise listings, a broker should consider including photographs of and virtual tours for any property listing page. Such visual images will help buyers evaluate properties from the comfort of their homes.

Direct Mail

Direct mail campaigns can be used by brokerages to deliver a specific message to a targeted select group or area. Brokers should consider the following uses of direct mail in their marketing plan:

- **Just listed or just sold cards.** A broker should develop a consistent campaign of just listed or just sold postcards that can be sent out by either the company or its agents upon receiving a new listing or a successful close of escrow. This type of localized marketing is extremely effective in generating additional listing opportunities. Quality postcards can be ordered from such providers as PrintDepartment.com, QuantumMail.com, or several other online postcard providers, which can be found by using the search phrase "real estate postcards" in a search engine.

- **Printed newsletter.** A printed informative newsletter targeted to a specific neighborhood can be a useful tool in building a broker's local image and increasing potential listing opportunities for agents. Several providers of template newsletters can be found by entering the search phrase "real estate newsletters" in a search engine. Some of these template newsletters will allow customization for the broker's company. The key to using a printed newsletter campaign is to be consistent, sending the newsletter out on a monthly or quarterly basis.

Movie Theater Advertising

Anyone who has been to a movie theater in recent years has seen a local real estate company's ad on the movie screen prior to the showing of previews. While this sort of advertising will generally not make the phone ring, it does create brand recognition in the marketplace. The broker should consider advertising in movie theaters that are located only in the marketplaces served by the brokerage. If this sort of advertising is used, the broker's listing presentation manual should point out the fact that the company is using this sort of brand advertising. Potential sellers who have seen the movie theater ads will often respond with, "Oh, I've seen those ads!"

Billboard and Exterior Sign Advertising

For the average start-up company, billboard advertising is simply too expensive to consider. In addition, there are some marketplaces where there is no billboard advertising available. Billboard advertising should be considered only if the available billboard is on a major artery or freeway leading into the marketplace served by the brokerage.

There are a couple of other exterior sign opportunities that should be considered by a start-up broker. These are (1) sponsoring a local Little League for which the brokerage receives a sign at the local baseball field and (2) sponsoring a local high school athletic field scoreboard. While it is unlikely that the broker will receive a phone call from such exterior signs, they do establish that the company is supportive of local community activities and help to build brand recognition.

Mall Kiosks

The popularity and use of mall kiosks by real estate brokers fades in and out in various marketplaces. An attended kiosk that contains computer screens or televisions showing properties will attract numerous leads for the company and its agents. Typically, a shopping mall will allow only one real estate brokerage to have a kiosk within it. However, depending upon the size of the mall, kiosks can be extremely expensive to maintain, and the broker will find it a constant challenge to keep it staffed with an agent. A brokerage with fewer than 25 to 30 agents should not consider taking on the burden of a mall kiosk.

Radio and Television Advertising

The key to achieving results from local radio or television advertising is consistency and maintaining ads for several weeks. Because this can be extremely expensive, they are not recommended for a start-up brokerage.

Community Participation

The company's marketing plan should include participation by the brokerage and its agents in various community organizations and events.

- **Chamber of commerce.** Local chambers of commerce offer an opportunity for business-to-business networking and a chance to increase the company's involvement in the community. A broker should either volunteer personally or ask for an agent volunteer from within the company to get involved with the board of directors of the local chamber.
- **Special events.** Every community has its annual special events that offer a broker an opportunity for the company to get involved at a grassroots level. This could mean having a float in the Fourth of July parade, participating in a walk-a-thon benefiting some organization, or pouring beer at a fall Oktoberfest. Participation in special events also offers a unique opportunity for brokers to increase their agents' team spirit.
- **Civic organizations.** Organizations such as the Rotary or Lions Club offer additional opportunities for the broker to get involved with the local community, either personally or via one of the company's agents.
- **Local sports teams.** A broker may want to consider sponsoring a local sports team, such as Little League or soccer, as a means of increasing brand awareness in the community. Such sponsorship will also provide opportunities to host celebratory events for the players and their families, thereby strengthening the relationship between the company and the community.

Public Relations

Every broker should consider the use of press releases to local media for any newsworthy event, such as the hiring of an agent, the presentation of a real estate seminar, or the increase of market share. Initially, the broker's press releases may be ignored, but as editors or producers see the broker's name more consistently, they will begin to consider the broker as a potential source of real estate information. This will eventually lead to an interview opportunity, with a reporter asking for comments on the current marketplace or predictions about market activity.

Office Front Windows

If a broker's office is located on the ground floor of a building, the broker should consider putting some sort of plasma television screen in the front window of the office. This screen should be connected to a computer and should constantly show the company's available listings.

PERSONAL EXERCISE 38

MARKETING PLAN

Using some of the ideas presented in this chapter and ideas of your own, create a marketing plan for your company for the next 12 months. Include a minimum of five marketing objectives that you want to accomplish, plus two to three steps that will have to be taken to accomplish each marketing objective. Following is a sample of the format to use.

Objective 1: Run open house ads weekly for all open houses held by agents.

Action Steps	Time Frame
1.1 Marketing assistant to create open house sign-up sheet	January 10
1.2 Agents to be trained to use sign-up sheet in a sales meeting	January 14
1.3 Ads to be placed by marketing assistant on Thursdays	Weekly
1.4 Open house ads proofed by agents on Friday mornings	Weekly
1.5 System evaluated for effectiveness	February 15

Delivering Real Estate Services

The most essential element of any marketing plan is the delivery of the actual service by the company's agents, staff members, and broker. The best marketing plan in the world will not deliver effective results if the agents, staff, and broker are not capable individuals who truly care about their customers and deliver competent and professional service. It is for this reason that the broker's recruiting efforts are directly tied to the company marketing plan. All members of the company should be constantly searching for additional ways to improve the delivery of the service to customers.

Evaluating Effectiveness

Without obtaining feedback and evaluating the effectiveness of a broker's marketing plan, the broker is spending money without any sense of accountability or accuracy. There are two primary sources for effectiveness feedback, the agents within the company and the customers of the company. As discussed earlier, surveys are one way to obtain feedback from customers and agents. There are some additional methods that should be considered:

- **Floor time sheet.** For companies that use floor time, the floor agent should report the marketing source of any call or walk-in received from a potential buyer or seller. This reporting should be done on a floor time activity sheet, which should be placed in the manager's in-box at the end of the floor time shift. The information contained on the sheet will let the broker know which marketing activities are generating results. (Figure 15.2 is an example of this sheet.)

- **Queries from staff.** If a company does not use floor time but has all inbound phone calls and all walk-in prospects greeted by a staff member, then the staff member must be trained to ask, "How did you find out about the listing?" or "How did you find out about our company?" before referring the prospect to an agent. The answer should be noted on an activity sheet similar to the one that might be used for floor time, with the activity sheet being turned in to the manager at the end of the workday.

- **Listing/transaction submission forms.** To further understand the source of a broker's business and its potential link to the broker's marketing efforts, the company's listing or transaction submission forms should include a question such as, "Where did this client come from?" which must be answered by the agent at the time the agent turns in the listing or transaction.

- **Co-op agent feedback.** In an effort to provide a better level of customer service and to help agents stay on top of their marketing efforts for listing, a broker should consider the use of services such as those provided by HomeFeedback.com. These services are online, relatively inexpensive, and provide instant feedback to the listing agent and broker after the property has been shown or previewed by a co-op agent. The listing agent enters the co-op agent's e-mail address into the feedback system, which then sends an e-mail to the co-op agent, asking for feedback on pricing, showing condition, or other factors that the listing agent has input into the system. Once the co-op agent responds to the e-mail, both the seller and the listing agent are informed of how that feedback had been obtained on the listing. They can now, using a password, review the comments posted by the co-op agent. Sellers like this service because it is Internet-based, and they can obtain the feedback instantly from anywhere in the world that has Internet access. Listing agents like these services because the feedback comes directly from a third party, making the information more credible in the seller's mind.

FIGURE 15.2 Sample Floor Time Activity Sheet

Date	Time	Agent	Property Inquired About	Source of Prospect					
				Sign	Newspaper	Magazine	Flyer	Open House	Walk-in

KEY POINTS

- A broker should consider surveying past customers to learn how those customers first discovered the company.
- A goal of a broker's marketing plan should be to get the company on the top three rungs of a prospect's marketing ladder for real estate.
- A marketing plan includes three segments: (1) creating awareness, (2) delivering services, and (3) evaluating effectiveness.
- A broker should be constantly evaluating the effectiveness of any marketing activity and eliminating activities that are costly or not generating good results.

16

FINANCIAL PLANNING

*Good fortune is what happens when opportunity
meets with planning.*

—THOMAS EDISON

The ability to understand the finances of a real estate brokerage is a skill set that takes time to grasp. Most brokers are sales agents who have risen to the level of broker, without any accounting, bookkeeping, or financial planning training. If brokers have no prior accounting or financial management experience, then they may want to consider hiring a bookkeeper and an accountant to review the financial performance of the company on a monthly basis.

The journey of understanding the financials of a real estate company begins with the two basic reports that a broker will become familiar with, the income (profit and loss) statement and the balance sheet.

FIGURE 16.1   Sample Income Statement (Profit and Loss)

Gross revenues		
Gross commission income	$1,200,000	82.8%
Desk fees received	250,000	17.2%
Total revenues	**$1,450,000**	**100.0%**
Costs of sale		
Franchise fees paid	$ 87,000	6.0%
Agent commissions paid	960,000	66.2%
Referral fees paid	120,000	8.3%
Total costs of sale	**$1,167,000**	**80.5%**
Gross profit (company dollar)	**$283,000**	**19.5%**
Operating expenses		
Salaries and wages	$ 80,000	5.5%
Payroll expenses	21,600	1.5%
Marketing expenses	65,000	4.5%
Rent	60,000	4.1%
Telephone	6,000	0.4%
Dues and subscriptions	1,200	0.1%
Utilities	1,800	0.1%
Total operating expenses	**$235,600**	**16.2%**
Net operating income	**$47,400**	**3.3%**

Figure 16.1 is a sample income statement and shows the revenues (income), the costs of sale (commissions paid for each transaction), and the operating expenses (the company's bills). In other words, the income statement shows how much money came into the company and how much went out of the company to pay its obligations. A broker should examine the company's income statement at least weekly to keep up with the activity. By conducting a weekly review, the broker will be aware of any unnecessary expenses sooner rather than later.

The sample balance sheet in Figure 16.2 shows your assets (what you own), your liabilities (what you owe), and your equity in the company. A broker should review the company balance sheet at least once a month.

CREATING THE COMPANY BUDGET

As a start-up company, a broker is at a slight disadvantage in projecting revenues and expenses because there is no track record from which to base estimates for future revenues and expenses. However, the task is not

FIGURE 16.2   Sample Balance Sheet

Assets *(What you have)*	
Current assets	
Bank account	$33,000
Trust account	4,000
Total current assets	**$37,000**
Fixed assets	
Furniture	
Original basis	$18,000
Depreciation	(3,400)
Furniture current basis	$14,600
Computers	
Original basis	$3,500
Depreciation	(850)
Computers current basis	$2,650
Phone equipment	
Original basis	$7,500
Depreciation	(1,200)
Phones current basis	$6,300
Security deposits	$5,000
Total assets	**$65,550**
Liabilities *(What you owe)*	
Accounts payable	$25,000
Trust funds held for others	4,000
Business line of credit	15,000
Total liabilities	**$44,000**
Equity	
Broker/owner	
Initial capitalization	$50,000
Equity draws	(45,000)
Remaining equity	5,000
Retained earnings	(30,450)
Net income/(loss)	47,000
Total equity	**$21,550**
Total liabilities and equity	**$65,550**

impossible. In many ways it's easier because the broker will get to use best guesstimates for each line item in the budget. Creating a company budget will take time, so a broker should anticipate spending 20 to 30 hours in compiling the first budget. (See Personal Exercise 39 at the end of the next section.) When creating a budget, it is recommended that the broker use a simple spreadsheet program such as Excel. Once the budget has been reviewed by the broker's accountant, then it should be put into the book-keeping software, allowing an ongoing comparison between the budget and the actual operational revenues and expenses.

The budgeting process begins by projecting the company's revenue. To start with, a broker should assume that he or she will produce approximately the same level of income as the prior year, with the same timing of that income throughout the year. Figure 16.3 is a projection of a broker's income based on a prior year.

The next step is to estimate the number of agents who will be joining the firm and assume that they will be either experienced (E) or new licensees (N) because each type of agent will require a different financial projection. In the example shown below, the assumptions are:

- Experienced agents (E) will start putting properties into escrow within 30 days of joining the company.
- Experienced agents (E) will average 6.0 sales per year, or one sale every other month.
- New licensees (N) will not open an escrow until their third month after joining the company.
- New licensees (N) will only have 3.0 sales per year, or one sale every four months.
- The average sales price will be the same as for the broker, shown in Figure 16.3.
- The average commission will be the same as for the broker, shown in Figure 16.3.
- The broker will recruit a total of three experienced agents (E) and six new licensees (N) in the first year of operation.

Note that in Figure 16.4, the hire month is noted for each agent; then the projected revenues for that agent begin to show up.

So a combination of the total projected revenues is shown in Figure 16.5.

Next the costs of sale should be projected, for which the following assumptions have been made:

- No referral costs will be owed during the year.
- The broker will be at an average split of 65 percent.
- Experienced agents (E) will be at an average split of 65 percent.
- New licensees (N) will be at an average split of 50 percent.

FIGURE 16.3 Broker Projected Income

	Jan	Feb	Mar	Apr	May	Jun	Jul	Aug	Sep	Oct	Nov	Dec	Total
Broker units opened	1	1	2	3	4	2	0	0	1	2	3	0	19
Broker units closed		1	1	2	2	3	2	0	0	1	2	3	17
Sales volume (000s)	235		342	532	421	609	700	0	0	560	465	726	4590
Average sales price (000s)													270
Projected broker units closed		1	1	2	2	3	2	0	0	1	2	3	17
Average sales price (000s)		270	270	270	270	270	270	270	270	270	270	270	270
Total projected sales volume (000s)		270	270	540	540	810	540	0	0	270	540	810	4590
Average commission rate		2.25%	2.25%	2.25%	2.25%	2.25%	2.25%	2.25%	2.25%	2.25%	2.25%	2.25%	2.25%
Projected commission income (000s)		6.08	6.08	12.15	12.15	18.23	12.15	0.00	0.00	6.08	12.15	18.23	103.28

221

FIGURE 16.4 Agent Projected Income

	Jan	Feb	Mar	Apr	May	Jun	Jul	Aug	Sep	Oct	Nov	Dec	Total
New licensees hired (N)		2	1	2	1								6
Experienced agents hired (E)	1		1		1								3
Experienced units closed (E)			1		2		3		3		3		12
New licensee units closed (N)						2	1	2	1	2	1	2	11
Total units closed—all	0	0	1	0	2	2	4	2	4	2	4	2	23
Average sales price (000s)	270	270	270	270	270	270	270	270	270	270	270	270	270
Total projected sales volume (000s)	0	0	270	0	540	540	1080	540	1080	540	1080	540	6210
Average commission rate	2.25%	2.25%	2.25%	2.25%	2.25%	2.25%	2.25%	2.25%	2.25%	2.25%	2.25%	2.25%	2.25%
Projected commission income (000s)	0.00	0.00	6.08	0.00	12.15	12.15	24.30	12.15	24.30	12.15	24.30	12.15	139.73

222

FIGURE 16.5 Combined Broker and Agent Projected Revenues

	Jan	Feb	Mar	Apr	May	Jun	Jul	Aug	Sep	Oct	Nov	Dec	Total
Projected broker revenues (000s)	0.00	6.08	6.08	12.15	12.15	18.23	12.15	0.00	0.00	6.08	12.15	18.23	103.28
Projected experienced agent (E) revenues (000s)	0.00	0.00	6.08	0.00	12.15	0.00	18.23	0.00	18.23	0.00	18.23	0.00	72.90
Projected new licensee (N) revenues (000s)	0.00	0.00	0.00	0.00	0.00	12.15	6.08	12.15	6.08	12.15	6.08	12.15	66.83
Total gross commission income (000s)	0.00	6.08	12.15	12.15	24.30	30.38	36.45	12.15	24.30	18.23	36.45	30.38	243.00

When the costs of sale are subtracted from the gross revenue projections, the broker can see the projected gross profit, often referred to as *company dollar* as shown in Figure 16.6.

With a clear estimate of the company's anticipated gross profit, the broker can now estimate operating expenses and plug those expenses into the spreadsheet. By then subtracting the operating expenses from the gross profit, the net operating income is revealed, as shown in Figure 16.7.

In Figure 16.7, the broker is projecting a profit of only $570 (shown as 0.57) in the first year of operation. This is essentially a breakeven projection, which means that the company *must* achieve the projected revenues and keep expenses at the target levels (or below) or the company will lose money. A broker should *never* budget to lose money overall for the year. In the event that the company were to lose money, the broker would typically take home less in commissions, leaving the commission money in the company to cover operating expenses.

In developing an annual budget for their company, brokers will become more and more accurate each year, as they understand the subtleties of their company.

PERSONAL EXERCISE 39

CREATE YOUR BUDGET

Using the examples provided in this chapter, follow these steps to create your budget for next year:

1. Project recruiting numbers for the company
2. Determine company revenues and costs of sale
3. Estimate monthly operating expenses
4. Combine the above to project monthly and annual profit/loss

CHART OF ACCOUNTS

A *chart of accounts* is the master list of categories for all company bookkeeping items, including assets, liabilities, revenues, and expenses. When brokers are initially setting up the company budget and books, they may wish to talk with their accountant or bookkeeper to set up the initial chart of accounts to be used by the company. (Use Figure 16.8 as a sample to get started.)

FIGURE 16.6   Projected Gross Profit (Company Dollar)

	Jan	Feb	Mar	Apr	May	Jun	Jul	Aug	Sep	Oct	Nov	Dec	Total
Projected broker revenues (000s)	0.00	6.08	6.08	12.15	12.15	18.23	12.15	0.00	0.00	6.08	12.15	18.23	103.28
Projected experienced agent (E) revenues (000s)	0.00	0.00	6.08	0.00	12.15	0.00	18.23	0.00	18.23	0.00	18.23	0.00	72.90
Projected new licensee (N) revenues (000s)	0.00	0.00	0.00	0.00	0.00	12.15	6.08	12.15	6.08	12.15	6.08	12.15	66.83
Total gross commission income (000s)	**0.00**	**6.08**	**12.15**	**12.15**	**24.30**	**30.38**	**36.45**	**12.15**	**24.30**	**18.23**	**36.45**	**30.38**	**243.00**
Costs of sale (000s)													
Broker commissions	0.00	3.95	3.95	7.90	7.90	11.85	7.90	0.00	0.00	3.95	7.90	11.85	67.13
Experienced agent (E) commissions	0.00	0.00	3.95	0.00	7.90	0.00	11.85	0.00	11.85	0.00	11.85	0.00	47.39
New licensee (N) commissions	0.00	0.00	0.00	0.00	0.00	6.08	3.04	6.08	3.04	6.08	3.04	6.08	33.41
Total costs of sale	**0.00**	**3.95**	**7.90**	**7.90**	**15.80**	**17.92**	**22.78**	**6.08**	**14.88**	**10.02**	**22.78**	**17.92**	**147.93**
Gross profit (company dollar) (000s)	**0.00**	**2.13**	**4.25**	**4.25**	**8.51**	**12.45**	**13.67**	**6.08**	**9.42**	**8.20**	**13.67**	**12.45**	**95.07**

FIGURE 16.7 Net Operating Income—a Breakeven Projection

	Jan	Feb	Mar	Apr	May	Jun	Jul	Aug	Sep	Oct	Nov	Dec	Total
Gross profit (company dollar) (000s)	0.00	2.13	4.25	4.25	8.51	12.45	13.67	6.08	9.42	8.20	13.67	12.45	95.07
Operating expenses (000s)													
Salaries and wages	2.50	2.50	2.50	2.50	2.50	2.50	2.50	2.50	2.50	2.50	2.50	2.50	30.00
Payroll expenses	0.68	0.68	0.68	0.68	0.68	0.68	0.68	0.68	0.68	0.68	0.68	0.68	8.10
Marketing expenses	1.00	1.00	1.00	1.00	1.00	1.00	1.00	1.00	1.00	1.00	1.00	1.00	12.00
Rent	3.00	3.00	3.00	3.00	3.00	3.00	3.00	3.00	3.00	3.00	3.00	3.00	36.00
Telephone	0.45	0.45	0.45	0.45	0.45	0.45	0.45	0.45	0.45	0.45	0.45	0.45	5.40
Dues and subscriptions	0.10	0.10	0.10	0.10	0.10	0.10	0.10	0.10	0.10	0.10	0.10	0.10	1.20
Utilities	0.15	0.15	0.15	0.15	0.15	0.15	0.15	0.15	0.15	0.15	0.15	0.15	1.80
Total operating expenses	7.88	7.88	7.88	7.88	7.88	7.88	7.88	7.88	7.88	7.88	7.88	7.88	94.50
Projected net operating income/(loss) (000s)	(7.88)	(5.75)	(3.62)	(3.62)	0.63	4.58	5.79	(1.80)	1.54	0.33	5.79	4.58	0.57

FIGURE 16.8   Sample Chart of Accounts

Account Number	Account Name	Account Type
1000	**Current asset accounts**	
1010	Operations bank checking account	Bank
1020	Franchise fee bank account	Bank
1030	Trust account	Bank
1040	Petty cash	Bank
1100	**Accounts receivable**	Accounts receivable
1200	**Other current assets**	
1210	Loans to shareholders	Other current asset
1220	Notes receivable from agents	Other current asset
1300	**Fixed assets**	
1310	Vehicles	Fixed asset
1320	Tenant improvements	Fixed asset
1322	Walls and electrical	Fixed asset
1324	Accumulated depreciation	Fixed asset
1326	Carpet and blinds	Fixed asset
1328	Accumulated depreciation	Fixed asset
1330	Office furniture	Fixed asset
1335	Accumulated depreciation	Fixed asset
1340	Telephone equipment	Fixed asset
1345	Accumulated depreciation	Fixed asset
1350	Computers and printers	Fixed asset
1360	Accumulated depreciation	Fixed Asset
1400	**Other assets**	
1410	Security deposits	Other assets
2000	**Accounts payable**	
2100	Accounts payable	Accounts payable
2200	**Other current liabilities**	
2210	Payroll liabilities	Other current liability
2220	Trust funds held for others	Other current liability
2240	Business credit line	Other current liability
2260	Other business loans	Other current liability
2400	**Equity**	
2420	Shareholder equity	Equity
2422	Initial equity	Equity
2424	Capital contributions	Equity
2426	Equity draws	Equity
2428	Allocation of earnings	Equity
2450	Capital stock	Equity
2500	Opening balance equity	Equity
2600	Retained earnings	Equity

(Continued)

FIGURE 16.8   Sample Chart of Accounts (Continued)

Account Number	Account Name	Account Type
3000	**Income**	
3100	Real estate commissions	Income
3200	Property management income	Income
3300	Referral fees received	Income
3400	Interest income	Income
3500	Training income	Income
3600	Reimbursed expenses	Income
3700	Sublease income	Income
3800	Miscellaneous income	Income
4000	**Costs of sale**	
4100	Sales associate commissions	Costs of sale
4200	Referral fees paid	Costs of sale
4300	Franchise fees paid	Costs of sale
5000	**Expenses**	
5005	Salaries and wages	Expense
5010	Payroll expenses	Expense
5020	Nonsalary administrative compensation	Expense
5040	Advertising	Expense
5041	Magazine	Expense
5042	Newspaper/classified	Expense
5043	Direct mail	Expense
5044	Business cards and letterhead	Expense
5045	Flyers and brochures	Expense
5046	Just listed/just sold	Expense
5047	Online Internet	Expense
5048	Promotions	Expense
5049	Signs	Expense
5050	Yellow Pages	Expense
5060	Automobile expense	Expense
5061	Reimbursed mileage	Expense
5063	Service/repairs	Expense
5065	Registration/license	Expense
5067	Leases	Expense
5069	Fuel	Expense
5070	Amortization expense	Expense
5080	Convention expenses	Expense

Account Number	Account Name	Account Type
5100	Bad debts and returns	Expense
5120	Bank service charges	Expense
5140	Business entertainment	Expense
5160	Business party	Expense
5180	Credit reports	Expense
5200	Depreciation expense	Expense
5220	Donations	Expense
5240	Dues and subscriptions	Expense
5260	Equipment rental	Expense
5280	Expense reimbursement	Expense
5300	Garbage	Expense
5320	Gifts—business	Expense
5340	Inspection fees	Expense
5360	Insurance	Expense
5380	Interest expense	Expense
5400	Internet maintenance	Expense
5420	Licenses and permits	Expense
5440	Multiple listing service	Expense
5460	Parking and tolls	Expense
5480	Pest control	Expense
5500	Postage and delivery	Expense
5520	Printing and reproduction	Expense
5540	Professional fees	Expense
5560	Recruiting	Expense
5580	Rent	Expense
5600	Repairs and maintenance	Expense
5600	Supplies	Expense
5600	Taxes	Expense
5601	Sales/use tax	Expense
5602	Federal	Expense
5603	Local	Expense
5604	Property	Expense
5605	State	Expense
5620	Telephone	Expense
5640	Training/education	Expense
5660	Travel	Expense
5661	Airfare	Expense

(Continued)

FIGURE 16.8   Sample Chart of Accounts (Continued)

Account Number	Account Name	Account Type
5662	Accommodations	Expense
5663	Auto rental	Expense
5664	Meals	Expense
5665	Transportation and taxis	Expense
5680	Utilities	Expense
5700	Miscellaneous	Expense
6000	**Other income**	
6100	Gain from sale of assets	Other income

INCREASING PROFITABILITY

Because market conditions change, a broker needs to understand the key strategies for increasing profits in a real estate company. There are four such strategies: (1) increase gross revenues, (2) increase gross profit (company dollar), (3) reduce expenses, and (4) convert expenses from fixed to variable. Here are the key steps to follow in each of these strategies.

Increase Gross Revenues

In order to increase gross revenues, the broker must increase the gross commission income of the company or increase desk fee revenues. There are only four ways to increase the gross commission income of a company. (See Personal Exercise 40 at the end of this section.)

Close More Units

One indicator of a company's health is known as the company's PPP, or per person productivity. To calculate the company PPP, divide the total number of sales or units closed during the year by the number of licensed agents on the roster; for example, a company that closed 100 units with 20 agents has a PPP of 5.0. As a first step to increasing profits by closing more units, the broker should focus on increasing the PPP of the company's existing agents. This is accomplished by the broker working more personally with the agents, providing increased training and accountability.

The second step in closing more units is to hire more agents, focusing on experienced agents who have a higher PPP than the broker's current agents. For example, if the broker's current agents' PPP is 5.0, then focus on recruiting experienced agents who close at least 6.0 sales per year.

Recruiting new licensees may add additional closed units to the company in the first year, but a broker should limit the ratio of new licensees to experienced agents in the company to 20 to 30 percent of the total roster because of the amount of the broker's time they consume and the slow start-up time most rookies need.

Increase Average Sales Price

Since commissions are tied to the sales price of a property, an increase in the company's average sales price will result in an increase in the company's gross commission income.

The first step in raising the company's average sales price is to target marketing activities to neighborhoods with more expensive homes. This does not mean that a broker, who primarily sells median-priced homes, has to jump into the estate market, but rather it means that the broker should select neighborhoods with homes in a price range that is 10 to 15 percent higher than the company's current average price range. This step may also involve training the agents in the company to work this higher price range.

The second step to increasing average sales price is to recruit agents who live and/or work in higher-priced markets.

Increase Desk Fees

If a broker has a desk fee model company, then gross revenues can be increased by (1) increasing the costs to agents for desk fee plans and (2) recruiting more agents to pay more desk fees. If the company already has an agent at every desk, then alternative "home office" agent plans should be developed to increase the number of agents paying fees to the company.

Increase Gross Profit (Company Dollar)

In this second strategy, the broker is focused on increasing the company's average retained portion of all commissions generated by the agents. Most brokers live in fear of changes in this area of brokerage management because it means reducing the amount of money being received by the agents, which may translate into the risk of losing agents. If a broker is providing a fair value for the agents, this is not an issue, but the fear will most likely always be there.

Charge an Administrative Fee

By charging an administrative fee of 4 to 6 percent off the top of all commissions generated, the company is adding a dramatic boost to its revenues without increasing production. The company's agents will probably grumble at this new fee, but the broker can often explain that such a fee is a needed source to increase or maintain marketing expenses. Furthermore, it should be pointed out to the agents that their individual split levels will not change, which keeps the impact of the administrative fee to a minimum. This tactic may not be available to franchised offices because they are already taking a percentage off the top of commissions in the form of a franchise fee.

Get Company Dollar Sooner Rather Than Later

By using the scratch commission plan (see Chapter 10) for agents, the company will receive its annual company dollar earlier in the agents' production year. This reduces the risk of their not seeing it at all because they have a poor year or because they leave the company.

Reduce Agent Splits

This is a difficult challenge for brokers. If a broker is going to change commission splits on agents, the broker should consider a gradual implementation across the agent roster during the year. This is accomplished by using the agent hire date as the anniversary date (see Chapter 10). Any reduction of commissions should be done slowly in small percentages of 3 to 5 percent, thus allowing the broker to explain the reductions as a cost-of-living adjustment to cover increased expenses.

Create an In-House Referral Program

A company spends a lot of money annually to generate buyer and seller leads for its agents. Typically, such leads are simply given to a floor agent without charge. The agents receiving such leads do not perceive them as valuable, often forgetting to follow up on them. The broker should consider charging a 20 to 25 percent referral fee for such leads. This will create a perception of their value and will also increase the company dollar on all such leads closed by the agents.

Pass-Through More Expenses to Agents

Increasing the number of items that are paid for by the agents, not the company, will increase the gross profit of the brokerage. A broker may want to consider splitting the costs of programs that had been previously paid for by the company. For example, if the company previously paid for 200 just-listed cards per listing, the company could reduce this to 100 cards, or split the costs with the agents (some of whom don't use the program anyway). This tactic is not available to a company that is based on desk fees where the agents have already paid 100 percent of the expenses.

Reduce Expenses

A broker should always have some expense-reducing strategies available in the event of a market slowdown. The following are the three primary ways to reduce the expenses of a real estate company.

Cut Costs

Cutting costs involves cutting back in the two areas that cost the company the most: (1) advertising and (2) salaries and personnel. Advertising can be easily reduced by just running fewer ads, participating in fewer programs, and so on, while cutting a staff position can have more negative impact on the company's morale. A broker should remember that for every dollar of revenue increased in the company, only a small percentage (the company dollar percentage) actually benefits the company; however, for every dollar of expenses cut, the full dollar is passed on to the company's bottom line.

Eliminate Programs

Where cutting back on programs might simply reduce some perks to the agents, eliminating a program is a definite take away. As such, the broker should explain to the agents why a program is being eliminated. Often, the reasons for eliminating a program are already understood—no one was using the program, it cost too much compared to the benefits, there are better ways for the company to invest, and so forth.

Tales from the Real World

THE REAL COST OF NONPRODUCERS

A multioffice real estate company, in an effort to reduce overhead in a softening real estate market, cut the bottom 15 percent of its office rosters, based upon agent company dollar contribution. This resulted in 180 agents of a 1,200-agent company being terminated in one day. Immediately, the company's PPP was increased dramatically, the number of overpriced listings in the company was reduced, and the company profit was immediately increased. Furthermore, the company started to attract more productive agents who wanted to be with other productive agents.

Nonproductive agents cost a company in many ways, including the fact that these same agents are often responsible for claims against the company because they don't do transactions frequently enough to be competent.

Having agents in a company costs the broker money, whether they are producers or not. The difference is that producers cover their costs and bring the company profit, whereas nonproducers simply cost the broker money—and time. This is important to remember when you're looking to cut expenses.

New licensees should be given special consideration until they have been with the company at least six months.

Transfer Burden to Agents

Transferring certain expenses to the agents is similar to passing through expenses to agents (see above), but in this case, the entire cost of a program is moved onto the agents' shoulders; for example, all classified ads are paid for by agents.

Convert Expenses from Fixed to Variable

By converting expenses that would normally be considered fixed to those that are more variable in nature, the broker is reducing the company's fixed monthly overhead and financial risk. A reduction in fixed expenses translates to greater profitability.

Incentive-Based Compensation

A broker can shift compensation packages for managers, trainers, and staff members from higher base fixed salaries to lower base salaries with incentive-base bonuses. This allows higher overall compensation for individuals, but only if the company is seeing higher revenues and/or profits. The incentives should be tied to milestones that can be achieved or influenced by the specific individual.

Changing Programs

As part of a strategy to convert expenses into a more variable format, a broker might consider changing the programs offered to agents so that instead of programs benefiting everyone in the company they benefit

---

PERSONAL EXERCISE 40

INCREASING PROFITABILITY

Refer to the budget you created in Personal Exercise 39. Make at least one change to increase profitability using the techniques discussed above.

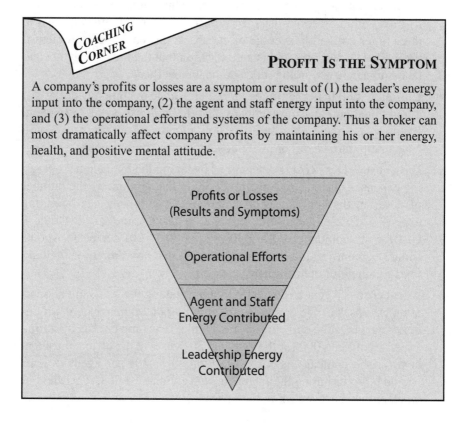

COACHING CORNER

PROFIT IS THE SYMPTOM

A company's profits or losses are a symptom or result of (1) the leader's energy input into the company, (2) the agent and staff energy input into the company, and (3) the operational efforts and systems of the company. Thus a broker can most dramatically affect company profits by maintaining his or her energy, health, and positive mental attitude.

Profits or Losses
(Results and Symptoms)

Operational Efforts

Agent and Staff
Energy Contributed

Leadership Energy
Contributed

only those agents who are productive. Such a change might include not paying for classified ads for agents until they reach a certain production level. Then the company will pay for 50 percent of such ads.

INDICATORS

There are several indicators that brokers should watch for and understand in their accounting books. The most critical ones follow:

- **Monthly burn rate.** Brokers should always know the monthly burn rate of their company, that is, the amount of money spent to keep the company going on a monthly basis. By knowing this figure, the broker will more intuitively know when there is about to be a cash flow problem.

- **Accounts payable level.** For most brokerage operations, the company's accounts payable will average around one to one and a half months of operating expenses. This means that the brokerage is paying its bills within 30 to 45 days. If the accounts payable grow to two to three times a monthly average of expenses, this could be a problem if the market slows down and is an indication that the broker may need to take immediate action to reduce company overhead.

- **Company dollar percentage.** The percentage of company dollar, for a traditional commission company, should be in excess of 23 percent. Even at 23 percent, there will be slow months where the broker will have to dip into his or her own pocket to cover some expenses.

- **Desk cost.** Desk cost is determined by taking the total annual operating expenses of the company and dividing that amount by the number of desks in the company. For example, if a company has operating expenses of $225,000 for the year and 20 desks in the office, the desk cost for the company is $11,250 ($225,000 ÷ 20) per desk. Agents should be contributing their desk cost in company dollar, or they are losing money for the company.

- **Agent cost.** Agent cost is determined by taking the total annual operating expenses of the company and dividing that number by the number of agents in the company. For example, if a company has operating expenses of $225,000 for the year and 30 agents in the office, the agent cost for the company is $7,500 ($225,000 ÷ 30) per agent. Agents should be contributing their agent cost in company dollar, regardless of whether they have a desk in the office.

BOOKKEEPING SOFTWARE

While there are several different accounting software systems available on the market, the most common software used by start-up real estate companies is QuickBooks by Intuit. This software is easily set up, and mistakes can easily be corrected.

KEY POINTS

- Every broker should establish a budget and monitor the company's progress with respect to that budget during the year.
- Budgeting starts by determining the agent roster and the anticipated units that will be generated by the roster.
- The four strategies for increasing brokerage profitability are (1) increase gross revenues, (2) increase gross profit (company dollar), (3) reduce expenses, and (4) convert expenses from fixed to variable.
- To increase commission income, a broker should focus company efforts on closing more units or increasing the average sales price.
- A broker should consider implementing an off-the-top administrative fee to increase company dollar.
- A broker should monitor several accounting indicators, such as monthly burn rate, accounts payable level, company dollar percentage, desk cost, and agent cost.

C H A P T E R

THE STRATEGIC PLAN

He who fails to plan, plans to fail.

—PROVERB

A broker's strategic business plan is divided into four key areas:

- The current situation
- Company vision
- Goals and objectives
- Financial projections

While the individual areas above have been discussed earlier in this book, they do not work as isolated areas of a company, but rather as part of an integrated whole firm. It is now time for the broker/owner to bring it all together into a cohesive, comprehensive plan, resolving potential conflicts between these areas, reducing redundancy, and uniting the individual area objectives into a first-year strategic plan. This strategic business plan provides clarity to the broker's business operations and a road map for decision making on a daily basis.

THE CURRENT SITUATION

The initial portion of a company's business plan, the current situation, is sometimes referred to as a *situation analysis* and includes a summary of several subject areas in order to provide a clear picture of the company's current situation. (See Personal Exercise 41 at the end of this section.) Areas to be covered should include:

- **Market conditions.** The broker should include some information about current market conditions and projections about the market for the coming year.
- **Office summary.** A paragraph or two summarizing the broker's current office, the management team, brand quality, market share and position, quality of agents, reputation, training programs, presentation materials, advertising presence, and the number of agents in the company. Also, a summary of any currently active issues should be included.
- **Office facilities.** A summary of current office facilities, with an evaluation of office appearance, location, parking, desk areas, and equipment should be included.
- **Leadership.** An evaluation of company leadership should be given, rating the areas of knowledge, experience, agent relations, administrative skills, employee management, transaction troubleshooting, recruiting new licensees, recruiting experienced agents, industry participation, maintaining profitability, financial management, image, planning skills, and vision.
- **Sources of business.** Looking at the broker's last 12 months, the broker should list the top four to five sources of buyers and sellers for the company and the percentage of units sold for each source.
- **Types of properties sold.** This should include a list of the top four to five types of properties sold by the company and the percentage of units sold for each type (e.g., residential/single family, residential/condo, farm, commercial/retail, etc.).

- **Agent analysis.** The broker should include a ranking of agents by company dollar (from highest to lowest).
- **Competition analysis.** The broker should create an analysis and evaluation of the current competition in the market. (See Figure 17.1.)
- **Brand ranking.** The ranking report should be created, showing the broker's company ranked by market share with its competitors. (See Figure 17.2.)
- **Threat and opportunities.** The situation analysis should include a brief list of the immediate threats and opportunities that the broker sees for the real estate business and/or the company.

PERSONAL EXERCISE 41

YOUR CURRENT SITUATION

Create an analysis of your company's current situation. Be sure to include all the areas discussed in the current situation section of this chapter.

COMPANY VISION

The importance of a company's vision is discussed in Chapter 2, and the reader was given exercises that would generate a company's vision statement, once completed. Included in the vision statement should be the company's core values and minimum performance standards. (See Personal Exercise 42.)

PERSONAL EXERCISE 42

REVISIT VISION STATEMENT

Look at the vision statement you created in Chapter 2, and make any revisions you think are necessary. Then place it in your business plan, after the current situation analysis.

GOALS AND OBJECTIVES

In putting together the company business plan, the broker is going to establish those goals and objectives deemed critical for the coming year. The broker should establish three to five objectives in each of the following areas:

FIGURE 17.1 Sample Competition Analysis (Each area is rated from 1 to 10, with 1 being the lowest and 10 being the highest.)

Competitor	Competition for Buyers	Competition for Sellers	Competition for Agents	Marketing Tools	Training Programs	Agent Compensation	Manager	Working Conditions	Overall Rating
Our company	5	6	4	7	9	9	9	8	7
ABC Realty	3	4	2	4	1	6	7	6	4
CBL	8	8	9	8	7	5	6	7	8
FHM	7	7	7	5	4	8	9	7	7
RE	10	10	9	9	9	5	10	9	9

FIGURE 17.2   Sample Market Share Ranking

Rank	Company	Units Closed	Market Share (by Units)	Sales Volume ($)	Market Share (by Volume)
1	ABC	340	34%	76,500,000	33.4%
2	CBL	280	28%	65,800,000	28.7%
3	FHM	220	22%	46,200,000	20.2%
4	RE	120	12%	30,000,000	13.1%
5	**Our company**	**40**	**4%**	**10,600,000**	**4.6%**
	Totals	1,000		229,100,000	100.0%

1. Recruiting objectives
2. Retention objectives
3. Staff and personnel objectives
4. Training objectives
5. Marketing objectives
6. Facilities objectives
7. Production objectives
8. Financial objectives

A common mistake made by brokers is that they create too many objectives to be accomplished during the year. This results in their becoming discouraged, which contributes to nothing being accomplished. If a broker creates 3 to 5 objectives for each of the above areas, there will be a total of 24 to 40 objectives, a significant challenge to meet for any broker. It's important to remember that some of these objectives are minor and require very little effort, while others may require several action steps and take several weeks or months to accomplish.

For each goal and objective established, the broker should itemize the action steps to be taken in order to achieve the objective, as well as the timing for those action steps and who is the primary person responsible for accomplishing the action step. Figure 17.3 is a sample format that a broker can use for each goal and objective. (See Personal Exercise 43 at the end of this section.)

FIGURE 17.3   Sample Recruiting Goal or Objective with Action Steps

Recruiting Objective 4

Company to send monthly e-mail newsletter to target agents. Newsletter to contain market information and company update.

Action Steps to Be Taken	By Whom	Time Frame
4.1 Provide company update, monthly.	John	Due 20th of month
4.2 Select an agent to contribute an article, monthly.	Judy	Due 5th of month
4.3 Locate monthly inspirational quote.	Terry	Due 20th of month
4.4 Create draft of newsletter for manager review.	Terry	Due 25th of month
4.5 Review and proofread newsletter.	John	Due 28th of month
4.6 Add new co-op agents to e-mail recipient list.	Terry	Due 29th of month
4.7 Mail out newsletter.	Terry	1st day of month

Figure 17.4 contains some sample goals in each of the objective areas.

FIGURE 17.4   Sample Goals

Recruiting Objectives	Retention Objectives
• Send monthly e-mail newsletter. • Create target list of experienced agents. • Create and print four-color recruiting brochure. • Contact 100 agents at open houses. • Develop recruiting incentive for agents. • Recruit 12 new licensees and 6 experienced agents.	• Broker to have lunch once a week with one to two agents. • Conduct three contests throughout the year. • Broker to walk through office daily. • Close sales meetings to vendors. • Survey in-house agents annually. • Hold "state of the company" luncheon.
Staff and Personnel Objectives	**Training Objectives**
• Conduct employee reviews every six months.	• Run 12 new licensees through training.

- Create staff incentive plan.
- Hire a marketing assistant.
- Hire a transaction coordinator.
- Create "Employee of the Quarter" award.
- Meet weekly with staff.

- Create a new licensee training program.
- Select a mentor in the office.
- Conduct monthly training for all agents.
- Create reimbursement program for Certified Residential Specialist (CRS) classes.
- Print monthly training calendar.

Marketing Objectives

- Implement Just Listed/Just Sold postcard program.
- Update Web site.
- Create lead generation referral program.
- Join chamber of commerce.
- Sponsor soccer team.
- Run half-page display ad twice per month.

Facilities Objectives

- Find and lease new office location.
- Replace fax machine and copier.
- Upgrade chairs in waiting room.
- Paint conference room.
- Hire more competent cleaning service.
- Create outdoor sitting area behind office.

Production Objectives

- Close 100 units.
- Achieve per person productivity of 7.0 or higher.
- Achieve average sales price of $286,000.
- Achieve number 4 in the marketplace by volume.
- Achieve 14 percent market share.

Financial Objectives

- Achieve closed gross commission income of $2 million.
- Maintain average 23 percent company dollar.
- Keep desk cost below $18,000.
- Keep agent cost below $13,000.
- Retain 15 percent profit for company.

PERSONAL EXERCISE 43

SETTING YOUR OBJECTIVES

Using the sample format shown in Figure 17.3, create three to five objectives and determine the action steps required for each of the following areas for your company:

1. Recruiting objectives
2. Retention objectives
3. Staff and personnel objectives
4. Training objectives
5. Marketing objectives
6. Facilities objectives
7. Production objectives
8. Financial objectives

FINANCIAL PROJECTIONS

The last segment of the broker's business plan contains the financial projections for the company. (See Personal Exercise 44.)

PERSONAL EXERCISE 44

REVISIT FINANCIAL PROJECTIONS

Look at the financial projections you created in Chapter 16 and make any revisions you think are necessary. Then place them in your business plan, immediately after the goals and objectives section of the plan.

CALENDARING THE COMPLETED PLAN

Once the broker has completed the company business plan, it's time to enter all the action steps in a calendar. The broker, or a selected staff person, should enter each action step in a company calendar on the day the step is to be completed. Some brokers use calendaring software such as Outlook or ACT!, while other brokers simply use a wall calendar. By entering the action steps onto a calendar, the broker will be reminded of approaching deadlines.

KEEPING ON TRACK

Implementation is the key when it comes to planning. When a broker's schedule becomes hectic and filled with putting out fires, time passes and it's easy for even the best business plans to be left behind and remain unfulfilled. In order to stay on track, a broker should take a few specific steps:

- Read the business plan, skimming through it in three to five minutes, at the start of the week.
- Revisit the business plan monthly with staff.
- Have each staff member report weekly on the action steps that were to be accomplished that week.

- Report weekly to staff on the action steps that were to be accomplished that week.
- Report to agents quarterly in a sales meeting on the status of the business objectives.
- Have staff members produce weekly production reports for the broker from the broker's back-end software (e.g., Lucero, Lone Wolf, etc.).
- Examine the company's financial statements monthly.

THINK ABOUT IT OFTEN

In the realm of coaching, we have long understood that you attract more of that which you think about. Using this approach, it seems only logical that if you want to achieve the objectives for your business plan, you're going to have to think about them. And the more frequently you think about them, the more likely they are to come about in a reasonable time frame.

For a start-up broker, I specifically recommend writing your recruiting goals in bulleted list form, placing them on your desk, and reading them at least once a day. By prioritizing your recruiting goals, you will move your organization along quickly and be constantly infusing the company with new agents and their energy.

BACK-END SOFTWARE SOLUTIONS

Back-end software, such as Lucero Summit or Lone Wolf, tracks the productivity statistics of the agents, makes commission adjustments and computations, and provides the broker with numerous reports for evaluating the company. Some back-end software solutions are integrated with Quickbooks, though a broker should discuss such integration with an accountant before combining the two. A broker should seriously consider early implementation of back-end software in order to provide accurate data and a high level of sophistication in analyzing company operations. This software will also help the broker monitor production objectives and certain financial objectives quickly.

┤ **Tales from the Real World** ├

18 TO 24 MONTHS

A turnaround manager for a major franchise system developed a theory that it takes 18 to 24 months to move a real estate office from nothing to being highly productive. He broke down the stages of the office's evolution as follows:

Months 1–2, Resuscitation stage. Inspire existing staff and agents with energy and hope. Get them focused on the new vision, not yesterday's failures.

Months 3–4, Leadership stage. Recruit assistant manager and office training director, creating a leadership team that share in the work and function as an attractant to potential recruits.

Months 5–12, Recruiting stage. Entire leadership team and agents focus on bringing in agents. Target a minimum of five agents per month.

Months 12–14, Training stage. Focus on training all agents to increase per person productivity, closure rates on listing presentations, lead capturing from floor calls, and so on.

Months 15–18, Production stage. Help agents focus on completing production objectives, allowing agent production to show up on the company's books.

Months 19–24, Payback stage. Enjoy the benefit of a highly productive, motivated office with exceptional energy and a healthy bottom line.

KEY POINTS

- A complete strategic business plan includes an analysis of the company's current situation, vision statement, goals and objectives, and financial objectives.

- A current situation analysis includes looking at numerous components, including the competition and market conditions.

- A broker's business plan should contain three to five goals and objectives for the areas of recruiting, retention, staff and personnel, training, marketing, facilities, production, and finances.

- Each goal and objective should include the action steps that must be taken to achieve the objective. A broker's action steps should include who is to take the action and a time frame for it to be completed.

- All action steps should be placed on a calendar.

- The broker should revisit the business plan regularly in order to stay on track.

- Consider the use of back-end software to track agent and office productivity.

18

MANAGING
YOUR RISK

*The first step in the risk management process is to acknowledge
the reality of risk. Denial is a common tactic that substitutes
deliberate ignorance for thoughtful planning.*

—CHARLES TREMPER

There are very real risks to owning and running a real estate brokerage firm. If a broker is a single-person company, then the risks are
more easily managed because the broker can control what he or she
says and does. However, a broker's liability grows with each additional
agent hired because the broker cannot control every word or action. It is
an unpleasant eventuality that a broker will have a claim filed by an
unhappy customer, an angry agent, or a disgruntled former employee.
While it is impossible for brokers to completely protect themselves from

potential claims that endanger their personal assets, there are some key strategies that can be employed by brokers to reduce such risk to more acceptable levels.

COMPANY STRUCTURE

The first strategy to consider when starting a real estate company is the ownership structure of the business, with a focus on protecting the broker's personal assets (home, savings, etc.) from a successful lawsuit.

- **Sole proprietorship.** Most start-up brokerages are sole proprietorships in which the company is owned by an individual broker, couple, or partners using a name such as "Local Town Realty." The owner or owners let the world know that they are Local Town Realty by filing a fictitious business name statement at the local county recorder's office. When working under a filed fictitious business name statement, the owners are said to be "doing business as" (dba) Local Town Realty, or "John Smith, dba: Local Town Realty." A fictitious business name statement is still required if the name of the company includes the owner's name, such as "John Smith, dba: John Smith Realty."

  A significant disadvantage to a sole proprietorship is the lack of protection afforded the broker's personal assets. If a broker is successfully sued, a broker could lose personal savings and checking accounts, personal residence, and so forth.

- **Partnership.** A partnership has two or more owners/partners, each of whom is personally liable for the risks inherent in the business. This form of business is not recommended for a real estate brokerage.

- **Limited liability company (LLC).** A limited liability company structure has grown in popularity in recent years. In an LLC, there are managing members and nonmanaging members. If the LLC is a single-person LLC, then that person is the managing member of the LLC. With an LLC, only the assets that are owned by the LLC are at risk in the event of a successful lawsuit being filed against the company. This protection is not a 100 percent guarantee and can be pierced if the owner or owners fail to follow statutory guidelines for maintaining the LLC entity.

- **Corporation.** A corporation is an ideal structure for a real estate company, but it requires more paperwork and structure than other business models. A board of directors is required (even if it is only a one-person board), and corporate officers are required, with the broker typically being the corporation president. Minutes of meetings of directors and stockholders must be consistently maintained. A corporation offers the highest level of protection possible in a business structure, but it requires that the owner(s)/stockholder(s) follow statutory guidelines to maintain the corporation protection.

A corporation may elect to file taxes under a subchapter S election, which allows the profits and losses to be passed directly through to the tax returns of the stockholders. This avoids double taxation (i.e., where the corporation pays taxes on profits, which are then passed on to stockholders as dividends that are again taxed under the stockholder's tax filing). An S corporation still files a separate tax return, but it does not pay taxes on those profits or losses that are passed on to stockholders on a K–1 form. Most start-up corporation real estate companies file under an S election.

If a corporation does not take advantage of an S election, it is said to be a C corporation, in which case it files its own tax return and pays its own taxes. Any losses accrued are retained by the corporation, not passed on to the stockholders, to be used against future profits.

Brokers should discuss which business structure would be most appropriate for their personal situation with a business attorney and tax consultant before opening the doors of the business. (Figure 18.1 gives the fundamental advantages and disadvantages in an easy-to-use table.)

FIGURE 18.1 Advantages and Disadvantages of Different Business Structures

Type of Ownership	Advantages	Disadvantages
Sole proprietorship	Easily created.	No protection for personal assets.
	No additional tax returns (uses schedule C).	Schedule C is frequently audited.
	No formal structure required.	All business is conducted under the owner's social security number.
	No double taxation of profits.	

(Continued)

FIGURE 18.1 **Advantages and Disadvantages of Different Business Structures (Continued)**

Type of Ownership	Advantages	Disadvantages
Limited liability company	Can be a one-person LLC. Provides potential barrier for risk to personal assets. Simpler structure to maintain than a corporation. Business conducted under the LLC's tax identification number, not the owner's personal social security number. No double taxation of profits.	Tax return filed for LLC and a K–1 form is given to owner. K–1 figures in a one-person LLC are still entered on schedule C. Additional minimum entity tax in some states.
Corporation (with S election)	Can be a one-stockholder corporation. Provides potential barrier for risk to personal assets. Business conducted under the corporation's tax identification number, not the owner's personal social security number. No double taxation of profits. Profits and losses are reported on K–1 as dividends to stockholders.	Cost of tax return filed for corporation. Additional minimum entity tax in some states. Requires more structure, with board of director(s), officers, etc.
Corporation (C corporation, no S election)	Can be a one-stockholder corporation. Provides potential barrier for risk to personal assets. Business conducted under the corporation's tax identification number, not the owners' personal social security number. Dividend income only.	Double taxation of profits. Cost of tax return filed for corporation. Additional minimum entity tax in some states. Requires more structure, with board of director(s), officers, etc. Profits *not* passed through to stockholders' tax returns except upon dividend distribution.

ADVISORS

The problem with being a sole business owner is that, at the end of the day, the broker must be the individual decision maker. In order to ensure the best decision possible in a couple of critical areas, a broker should consider using quality, knowledgeable advisors.

Legal Counsel

There are dozens of situations that arise in which a broker will want the advice of a good real estate attorney. For this reason, a broker should consider locating such an attorney at the outset of forming the company. Referrals to potential attorneys can usually be obtained from the broker's tax accountant, friends, or other non–real estate attorneys.

It may also be a good idea for a broker to find a general corporate counsel who is a business generalist to help the broker with such areas as policies, employment laws, harassment issues, and so forth.

Tax Consultant

Many brokers throughout the United States pay more taxes than they have to simply because they don't take advantage of available tax laws for business owners. A good tax consultant will be expensive and worth every dollar paid. A broker should interview and select a tax consultant before starting a company.

INSURANCE

As part of a broker's defense strategy to protect against catastrophic loss from an unseen event, a broker needs to develop a comprehensive strategy to manage the risks of business operations.

Errors and Omissions Insurance

Commonly referred to as *E&O insurance*, errors and omissions insurance is something a broker should maintain as part of a strategy to protect company and personal assets. The costs of E&O insurance will vary widely, based upon the broker's experience, the number of agents in the company, the average experience of the agents in the company, the volume of real estate sold, the number of units closed, the type of real estate services offered by the company (e.g., residential, commercial, property management), whether or not the company has a policies and procedures manual and training programs offered workers. Brokers with no prior claims against them can expect their first E&O policy to cost between $8,000 and $12,000 for one year. The cost of the annual policy will be affected by the deductible of the policy, ranging from $5,000 to $25,000 per claim.

Risk Management Programs

In addition to E&O insurance, a broker may also participate in a risk management program, which is sometimes offered by home protection or home warranty companies. Risk management programs are not E&O insurance. They offer access to a real estate attorney for questions and answers on potential claims.

General Liability Insurance

A broker will need a general liability insurance policy to cover the office location and employees of the company. This policy covers the brokerage for a variety of general business risks, such as an injury to a customer or thieves stealing computers from the office.

Automobile Insurance

The issue of automobile insurance occurs because the broker has agents driving customers around in their private vehicles. The broker needs to make sure that the agents have automobile insurance coverage and that the agents provide evidence of the brokerage having been added as an "additionally insured" on the policy. Some insurance companies will charge the agent a nominal fee of $25 to $75 for adding the brokerage onto the coverage. Agents who have not properly insured their vehicles for business use will potentially face a higher insurance premium. However, this is one area in which the broker must insist on compliance.

POLICIES AND PROCEDURES

Maintaining a thorough policies and procedures manual, as discussed previously in this book, can be a critical element to a broker's risk management strategy.

HEALTH AND SAFETY

A broker should maintain a keen eye for health and safety issues in the facilities used by the company. Such minimal things as tripping or slipping hazards, ingress/egress obstacles, on-site access to a complete first-aid kit, and open house safety measures should be considered.

Tales from the Real World

WHAT AGENTS DON'T SEE CAN COST MONEY

A broker received a claim from a buyer six months after the close of escrow because the broker's listing agent had failed to disclose the fact that the property had a history of settling and that the living room had dropped an inch in one corner of the house. In addition, the house turned out to be 50 square feet less than had been represented in the property flyer. At the market value of $800 per square foot, the buyer felt that she had overpaid by $40,000.

The seller had given no disclosure about any settling history to the agent, and the agent used a square footage calculation provided by the seller. The broker, along with the agent, visited the property to look at the settling damage. While walking around the exterior of the house, the broker noticed that the stucco exterior of the house, while freshly painted, showed signs of patching with cracks repaired in no fewer than 40 places. The agent indicated that he didn't think anything of the cracks because they had been repaired. The broker also noted that the walkways around the house had extensive settlement cracks. The agent said he didn't believe that the cracked walkways were a sign of anything; they were just old walkways. The broker knew that the condition of the stucco and walkway cracks were a potential indication of active settling. The broker contacted the local building department, where the broker learned that there had been many settlement problems in that particular neighborhood.

The broker settled the claim for $30,000.

TRAINING DOCUMENTATION

Most brokers do a great job of training their agents, but a poor job of documenting what training has been given to the agents. In the event of a negligence claim being made against an agent, the agent may use a defense of improper or inadequate training by the broker, which may potentially transfer a greater portion of liability onto the broker or the company. A broker should document the training given to any agent in the agent's personnel file, including an outline of the basic training program and any subsequent training programs attended by the agent. This becomes increasingly important for a broker's training of management team members. This sort of documentation may help avert potential liability.

REAL ESTATE CONTRACTS

A broker should develop a consistent procedure for reviewing contracts, addenda, contingency removals, and disclosures. Frequently, an agent creates a provision in a document that says one thing, but a different meaning was intended. A broker's review process may catch such things, thereby reducing potential liability.

AGENT VISUAL INSPECTIONS

Brokers often provide inadequate training for their agents on how to visually inspect a property for potential signs of trouble. Most states require agents to perform a minimal visual inspection on properties they sell, but without any training for potential red flags, they frequently miss visual clues to costly issues.

SQUARE FOOTAGE MEASUREMENTS

In some marketplaces, agents are required to measure the square footage of homes in order to enter the property into the multiple listing service. The problem is that most agents have never been trained on how to properly measure the square footage of a property. If a broker is in such a marketplace, he or she needs to provide training on how to take such measurements.

CLAIMS—TO FILE OR NOT TO FILE

It is inevitable that you will be faced with a claim from a disgruntled customer at some time in your brokerage ownership experience. This will immediately cause you to ask the question, "Should I file a claim with my E&O insurance carrier?"

If you file a claim, the insurance company will retain the record of a claim, even if it was settled without the insurance company having to pay out any money. In addition, the claim will be shared with future insurance companies. The more claims you have filed with insurance companies, the higher your premium costs will be at insurance renewal time.

Because most companies require a claim to be filed within a short time of receiving the first communication of a potential claim, if you delay in filing a claim, coverage under your policy may not be available at a later time, even though you paid for insurance.

With each claim received, you must balance the risk of the potential damages/cost of the claim against the potential increase in your annual premium. Here's a short list to consider when you are faced with this decision:

- Your policy deductible versus the amount of the claim being made
- The potential for the claim to expand into a larger problem
- The volatility of the customer
- The agent involved in the claim
- Potential violations of law

RISK MANAGEMENT AUDIT

Every year, a broker should conduct an in-house risk management audit to determine if there are areas of vulnerability for the broker or the company concerning the issues discussed above. This will help the broker to be constantly reducing risks that might otherwise go undetected. (See Personal Exercise 45.)

PERSONAL EXERCISE 45

RISK MANAGEMENT AUDIT

After your office has been up and running for at least six months, conduct a risk audit for the company in the areas discussed in this chapter, asking:

- Do I have any potential liability exposure in this area?
- What can I do to reduce my exposure in this area?
- Have I done all I can to protect myself and the company in this area?

KEY POINTS

- Risk management begins by the broker using an appropriate ownership model that limits the broker's personal liability.
- A broker should select an attorney and a tax consultant to work with before launching a company, giving these consultants an opportunity to help protect the broker.
- A broker should carry the appropriate types of insurance, including errors and omissions and general liability.
- All of a broker's agents should be required to have the brokerage added as an "additionally insured" on their auto insurance policies.
- Standardizing systems to be followed by agents and employees is an important element in risk management.

19

DEVELOPING COMPANY LEADERSHIP

The growth and development of people is the highest calling of leadership.

—HARVEY S. FIRESTONE

When brokers start a company, they take on a responsibility for themselves, their employees, their agents, and their families to keep the business running as a viable operation. This means that brokers must have a contingency plan to deal with the possibility that they may not always be able to, or want to, run the office. In the United States today, the real estate industry is experiencing a crisis of leadership for two specific reasons:

1. There are a significant number of broker/owners who want to retire.
2. There is a perception that it is getting more difficult to find competent managers for growing companies.

Brokers who have no pool of leadership talent at their disposal are unable to expand their companies. In order to properly address the leadership issue in their companies, they must first be willing to look at a "team" approach to leading the office.

LEADERSHIP MODELS

There are evolutionary steps in a company's growth that require the broker to share leadership duties, or the company's growth will be limited by the broker's ability to handle ever more duties, agents, stresses, and so forth. As the company grows, a broker should delegate the daily managerial activities to members of a team. There are three primary models of leadership for a real estate office.

Sole Branch or Office Manager

An office of between 1 and 16 agents can typically be managed completely by one branch manager or broker. The broker/manager in this size company derives his or her primary income from selling real estate, and the agents' production typically covers only the operational costs of the company.

Branch Manager or Assistant Manager (Two-Person Team)

As a company grows to between 17 and 35 agents, the broker/manager will need help in the managing and training of agents, as well as the administrative duties of the company. Without help, the broker/manager will often become inundated with putting out fires, thus reducing the broker's recruiting activities and causing increased personal stress.

Assistant managers (or branch managers) are typically selling managers (i.e., they still sell real estate as their primary source of income) and should be focused on the recruiting and training of new licensees, leaving the broker time to focus on recruiting experienced agents, supervising the activities of the experienced agents in the office, and making strategic business plans.

Full Leadership Team (Three-Person Team)

Once an office has 36 or more agents, a broker should consider implementing a three-person leadership team that consists of (1) the broker, (2) the assistant manager, and (3) an office training director.

Under this model, the office training director (OTD) assumes responsibilities for the recruiting and training of new licensees and acts as a mentor for these agents.

The assistant manager now assumes primary responsibility for recruiting and supervising the experienced agents in the office.

The broker's responsibilities become more focused on strategic initiatives that influence the entire company, seeking additional opportunities for the firm, whether in the acquisition of competitors or the enhancement of company services.

FINDING LEADERSHIP TALENT

When the need arises for leadership team members, they will, and do, show up. The challenge for brokers is to expand their thinking to recognize the appearance of such leaders. The perception that new leaders are difficult to find is accurate only if brokers seek someone like themselves, a path that dooms the company to "yesterday's" thinking. While new leaders in a company should share core values with the broker, they should also offer new ways of looking at, and implementing, those core values. (See Figure 19.1.)

In searching for leaders of the team, a broker should look for individuals who already demonstrate a tendency to lead. Potential candidates might already be an agent who is the unofficial "go to" person when the broker is not around—the person whom the agents seek out for answers to transactional or marketing problems when the broker is unavailable. Often, future leaders are the voices that are listened to by the agents in a company, the respected ones. They can be seen teaching new licensees how to do a better listing presentation or attending a meeting at a local association of Realtors or volunteering for nonprofit community organizations. Leaders don't have to be found. They're right in front of us.

Following are some ideas for finding leadership talent:

- **Within the company.** A broker should look for an agent who is supportive of the company, believes in the direction and vision of the firm,

FIGURE 19.1   Attributes of a Real Estate Leader

Some key attributes to seek in potential leaders are:

- **Vision-oriented.** A vision-oriented leader will be able to maintain focus.
- **A mindset of change.** A real estate company leader should be able to adapt to change and be comfortable serving as an instrument of change in a company.
- **A desire to win through others.** An ideal candidate should enjoy helping other agents succeed.
- **Effective communication.** A leader must be able to communicate both good and bad news, obtaining buy-in from agents.
- **Public speaking.** A leader should be comfortable speaking in front of groups of agents.
- **Teaching.** A leader with solid teaching skills is a strong asset to a company.
- **Toughness.** A real estate leader is under a constant barrage of demands from agents, vendors, and clients. A strong leader is tough, but fair.
- **Sense of humor.** Sometimes you just have to be able to laugh.

and respects the broker. Leadership candidates should be solicited by the broker in an office sales meeting, allowing a few days for interested candidates to contact the broker.

- **Within a competitor's firm.** A broker should also solicit from agents the names of potential candidates that currently work for other firms. The broker should then make a personal call to any candidates to invite them to a meeting to discuss the leadership opportunity. A broker should also look for potential leaders who are currently teachers at a local college or real estate school or leading committees at their local association of Realtors.

JOB DESCRIPTIONS

Assuming that a broker develops an entire leadership team, the job descriptions of each member of the team might look something like the following.

Broker or Branch Manager

In a three-person leadership team (see Figure 19.2), the broker or branch manager's duties include:

FIGURE 19.2   Three-Person Leadership Team

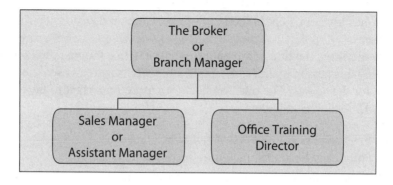

- Guiding the company vision, planning, and overall operations
- Handling budgetary responsibilities for the office
- Supervising office administration and staff
- Sharing recruiting activities with other leadership team members
- Supervising and training other leadership team members

Sales Manager or Assistant Manager

The key function of the sales manager or assistant manager is to provide primary support for the agents in the company, allowing the broker or branch manager the opportunity to continue developing the firm. Key duties include:

- Supervising experienced agents in the office
- Handling overall transaction management for all agents
- Recruiting experienced agents
- Backing up the broker or branch manager when he or she is not available
- Participating in the broker's leadership development program

Office Training Director (OTD)

Brokers sometimes use a mentor position to provide field training for new licensees. Sometimes a potential problem arises with this position because this mentor, by assisting new licensees with their transactions, is in a sense creating company policy but is not a member of the company leadership team. This could result in erroneous actions because the mentor has not been kept in the loop of management decisions or changes in policies.

By elevating the title of a mentor to that of office training director and including this person in the leadership team, there is a greater sense of continuity for the agents. The position becomes more important to the office, as the OTD's duties include:

- Primary responsibility for recruiting new licensees
- Training new licensees, including acting as their mentor
- Backing up the sales manager or assistant manager when that person is not available
- Participating in the broker's leadership development program

LEADERSHIP COMPENSATION

While the broker/branch manager, as the owner of the company, receives all company profits, a compensation plan should be set in place for the other leadership team members.

Sales Manager Compensation

The sales manager is compensated in three basic areas, based upon the desired objectives of the company:

- **Sales commission split.** A broker may want to establish a generous fixed-commission split for the sales manager, acknowledging that the sales manager will have less time available to do his or her own personal sales. A commission split of 80 to 85 percent is not unusual, depending upon the market area and the size of the office.
- **Base compensation.** Typically, this is a monthly stipend of $1,000 to $2,000, varying with marketplaces. Base compensation is further acknowledgment that the sales manager will spend time doing administrative duties that negatively affect his or her personal sales income but that is essential for company operations.
- **Recruiting bonuses.** A common way to encourage a sales manager to spend time on recruiting activities is to provide an incentive program

for the job. Any incentive program should be based upon the recruited agent's production level prior to coming to the firm, with higher bonuses paid for higher-producing agents (based upon company dollar contributed to the firm, not gross commissions generated by the agent). Bonuses might range from $500 to $5,000.

Office Training Director Compensation

The position of office training director is compensated in three basic areas, based upon the desired objectives of the company:

- **Sales commission split.** A management-tier commission split is appropriate, (e.g., an 80 to 85 percent split for the individual) depending upon the market area and the size of the office.
- **Trainee referral compensation.** As the office training director assists new licensees in closing transactions, a portion of the commission on the transaction is assigned as a referral fee to the office training director, in the 20 to 25 percent range (which is subject to the OTD's commission split). This referral fee arrangement often lasts for the first three closed transactions of the new licensee. Some brokers establish a lower referral fee of 5 to 10 percent, but then they have it apply to the new licensee's entire first year of production.
- **Recruiting bonuses.** An office training director might receive a recruiting bonus of between $200 and $500 per new licensee recruited, since that is one of the primary functions of the position. A broker may also desire to offer a recruiting bonus program similar to that of the sales manager's, to encourage additional recruiting of additional agents to the company.

THE LEADERSHIP DEVELOPMENT PROGRAM

Once the company has a clear idea of the attributes desired in its leadership candidates, job descriptions for leadership positions, and compensation plans for each position, the company's leadership development program should be created.

A leadership development program should include three essential elements: (1) classroom instruction, (2) field-training or on-the-job training, and (3) performance-based accountability.

EMPOWERING YOUR LEADERS

As you hire and train future leaders for your company, you are going to have to get comfortable with the idea of "letting go" and giving control of tasks to your managers and trainers. If you are a bit of a control freak, this can be challenging. You will always believe that you can do it better than they can, which may or may not be true. The truth is that they will do tasks a little differently from the way you would have done them. Ultimately, this will add a greater dimension to the company's style and make for a stronger brokerage.

If you want to have strong leaders in your company, you must gradually empower them to do everything you do, making you completely "replaceable" for the day-to-day tasks. Remember, you'll never be truly replaceable; it's your company, and you'll always be respected and looked at as the head of the company.

Give your leaders the responsibility and the power to get the job done. Then hold them accountable if they fall short of expectations and acknowledge them if they handle the job properly. By micromanaging leaders, you may kill their spirit.

Classroom Instruction

A company should provide formal classroom instruction for leadership trainees. The primary ways of providing this instruction are:

- **CRB courses.** These are courses offered by the Council of Real Estate Brokerage Managers, a nonprofit organization whose mission is to provide high-quality training and resources for brokers, managers, and potential managers. There are four to five core courses that every broker/manager should take, covering such subjects as strategic planning, financial planning, managing sales associates, marketing a company, and recruiting. While some of these courses can be taken via CD-ROM, brokers are encouraged to attend programs in person, allowing networking and information-sharing opportunities among brokers from across the globe.

    Brokers can provide these courses for their company leaders by subsidizing the tuition costs of the programs, which typically run in the $500 to $1,000 range.

- **Broker training sessions.** The broker should require leadership trainees to attend a weekly training session, taught by the broker, and lasting 1 to 2 hours. These sessions should cover the hands-on, how-to's of running an office. A training schedule should be created that would be retained by the broker as documentation of what subjects were covered in these sessions. A broker could use a binder or manual to document such training or acquire a template product, such as the Manager's Development Record (TheBrokerCoach.com) that offers 20-plus pages of subjects to cover during such broker training sessions. Upon completion of all broker training sessions, the training record should be placed in the leadership trainee's personnel file.

Field Training

The purpose of a field training element in a leadership development program is to provide an opportunity for the trainee to learn firsthand from the broker by working closely with the broker during real-life aspects of office operations for a period of time. In a field training environment, the broker typically works two to three times with the trainee on each type of scenario that arises. The first time through a scenario, the broker models the desired behavior, and the trainee simply observes; the second time through a scenario, both the broker and the trainee participate in the solution process; and the third time through, the trainee is in charge of the situation, with the broker observing and being present to step in should the trainee make a mistake. Again, the broker should document such training and the trainee's performance. After each training experience, the broker should debrief the trainee, asking, "What did you observe or learn?"

Performance-Based Accountability

In this phase of a broker's leadership development program, the trainee is given the opportunity to be fully in charge of a certain aspect of company operations. As the trainee masters each challenge, the broker assigns increased responsibility, culminating in the trainee running all aspects of the office operations. Each week, during the broker training sessions, the trainee is questioned about what has transpired in these areas of responsibility and what he or she has learned. (See Personal Exercise 46.)

PERSONAL EXERCISE 46

YOUR COMPANY LEADERSHIP

Given the information you have learned in this chapter, do the following:

1. Define the attributes you would look for in a sales manager and an office training director.
2. Write down your office leadership model and the duties of each leadership team member.
3. Write a job description for each leadership team member and include a compensation plan.
4. Write down the top 10 things you would want a manager-trainee to learn during a leadership development program.
5. Outline your leadership development program.

Tales from the Real World

IMPACT OF THE RIGHT SALES MANAGER

A manager took over a dying office and immediately proceeded to find a sales manager to help in the recruiting effort that would be required to rebuild the office. The manager first solicited names of potential candidates from his current agents, and one candidate's name, Mary S., was submitted by several agents.

Mary S. was a mentor at the number 1 office in the marketplace. As a mentor for the last two years, she had trained over 20 agents. The broker met with Mary S. and offered her the position of sales manager, with the promise of a strong training program and the eventual leadership of the office.

Mary S. joined the firm as a sales manager and within 120 days had recruited over 20 agents from her former firm. Most of these agents had worked with Mary S. as their trainer, so they were just starting to really launch their careers. She further recruited an office training director, marketing assistant, and transaction coordinator from her prior firm.

Within another six months, she recruited the top producer in the marketplace, who also happened to work at her former firm. And within 18 months, the broker's office was the number 1 office in the marketplace, with 62 agents on the roster.

Never underestimate the power of hiring the right sales manager.

KEY POINTS

- Brokers should start thinking about a leadership team from the outset of their business.
- Leadership team members should be sought whose personalities complement the broker but are not the same as the broker.
- Brokers should solicit their own agents as leadership candidates.
- Eventually, a broker should hire a sales manager and/or an office training director, or the broker will slow down the growth of the business.
- Leadership compensation plans may include a generous commission split, base compensation, recruiting bonuses, and trainee mentor referral fees.
- A leadership development program should include classroom instruction, field training, and performance-based accountability.

CHAPTER

KEEPING FRESH AND AVOIDING BURNOUT

If you feel burnout setting in, if you feel demoralized and
exhausted, it is best, for the sake of everyone, to withdraw and
restore yourself. The point is to have a long-term perspective.

—DALAI LAMA

R eal estate has its cycles like any other business. In slow times, brokers are challenged to manage their expenses, retain agents, recruit more productive agents, and increase production. In a fast-paced market, brokers are challenged by volumes of transactions, increased numbers of agents, demanding clients, marketing differentiation, and maintaining a perceivable value proposition. And whether the market is slow or fast, the demands of a broker's private life are piled on top of the business demands. It all adds up to the same thing—stress. If left unaddressed, stress consumes a broker's energy and leaves the broker feeling tired or overwhelmed. This can lead to depression, overeating, high blood pressure, and risk of heart disease or stroke.

Brokers often treat their personal energy level as a symptom of the activities going on in their lives meaning that if things are going well, they are happy, and if things are going poorly, they are upset. This is exactly the opposite of the truth: the activities in their lives are a result of their thinking and feeling. Thus, if brokers want companies that are energized, focused, productive, and profitable, they must bring a more empowered self to the game.

Dr. David Hawkins, in *Power vs. Force*, wrote, "One individual who lives and vibrates to the energy of optimism . . . will counterbalance the negativity of 90,000 individuals who calibrate at the lower weakening levels." While a broker may not need to balance the negative thinking of quite this many people, the broker does need to be aware of the influence and impact of his or her own personal energy level on the attitudes and results of the staff, agents, and company. If a broker exhibits being upset, depressed, or angry, the broker's staff will be tenuous and then pass this same energy to the agents around them. And, like a virus, the lower energy of the broker will be spread throughout the company. On the other hand, if the broker arrives at work exhibiting happiness, lightheartedness, focus, and high energy, then the staff and agents will react accordingly; the company will be a productive, energized place. The importance of a broker's energy level and its impact on the company should not be underestimated.

ELEMENTS OF POSITIVE LEADERSHIP ENERGY

In order to create a positive energy level, brokers should encourage the following elements in their lives (see Personal Exercise 47 at the end of this section).

Potential-Oriented Thinking

The broker should develop clarity of vision and constantly try to focus on the outcome before it occurs, as if it were already in place. This approach helps to achieve the result by the broker exhibiting an ongoing commitment to success by thinking successful thoughts. The broker should avoid whining about an outcome or situation that doesn't work out quite the way he or she thought it would. The broker should accept responsibility for the outcomes and always remember that the potential that existed on the first day the company opened its doors still exists—and always will.

Training Mentality

A mindset of always learning is critical to the broker's constant growth, an essential element to maintaining a positive attitude. The ongoing gathering and sharing of new information is invigorating. Brokers should maintain a training schedule in the office, offering regular, methodical learning opportunities for their agents. Furthermore, brokers should attend classes regularly themselves—always being open to new ideas and always growing.

Congruence in Actions

Brokers who guide a company must demonstrate congruence between their actions and what they are saying to their agents and staff. If brokers are telling their agents that they should be increasing productivity and helping to recruit agents and should avoid whining, then the brokers must personally demonstrate these attributes on a regular basis. Brokers must be the physical manifestation of their vision, refocusing if they get sidetracked and adapting and overcoming obstacles.

The Right Support System

Successful brokers surround themselves with the right support system, including supportive friends and family. Brokers should endeavor to select carefully those people whom they integrate into their company and personal lives, surrounding themselves with achievers, not low-energy people. Brokers' support systems could include a coach or business mentor with whom they can discuss objective solutions to business challenges.

Conduit of Positive Energy

Brokers should think of themselves as conduits of positive energy that recharges the office staff and agents merely by their presence. This means maintaining a high level of personal energy. Brokers can accomplish this by watching what they eat and drink (i.e., what is put "in" the system), keeping their metabolism high by exercising regularly, and associating with high-energy people. These steps will enable the broker to emanate an upbeat and motivating energy that is shared with everyone.

Inspiration

Brokers should genuinely like and care about the people in their offices. Furthermore, a broker needs to demonstrate resilience during challenging times, staying focused on the vision for the company. A broker should work to see opportunities where others don't and work to stay inspired, when everyone else is not. This "eye of the tiger" will pass on to the agents and staff, translating into a positive, driven, and highly productive organization.

PERSONAL EXERCISE 47

YOUR LEADERSHIP ENERGY

Refer to the topics discussed above and write down 10 ways that you will demonstrate positive leadership energy in your company.

REENERGIZING

In the midst of managing a company, putting out fires, recruiting agents, training new licensees, doing their own personal production, and keeping up with the responsibilities of their families, brokers spend little time reenergizing themselves. There are many subtle ways that brokers can use to reinvigorate and refresh themselves that don't consume a lot of extra time (see Personal Exercise 48 at the end of this section). Some of these follow:

- **Develop healthy eating habits.** Brokers should try to make healthy choices in their diet and activities. Simply making better choices at restaurants will help a broker maintain a healthier lifestyle. A broker should make an effort to avoid excess consumption of anything, be it bread or wine. Also brokers should avoid the quick lunch at their desk; it wreaks havoc on the digestive tract. As we have all heard, it takes at least 30 days to begin to create a new habit. Start today!
- **Do something physical every day.** This can be as simple as a 10-minute walk around the block or as involved as a gym workout.

- **Get enough sleep.** One of the major contributors to stress-related illness is lack of sleep. Brokers who are actively building a company should strive to get a minimum of seven to eight hours of sleep each night.

- **Learn something new.** Education and expanding the mind are two simple ideas for brokers to help them reconnect with renewed potential.

- **Read personal development books.** Personal development books, sometimes referred to as "good food books" can offer brokers new insights and provide them with fresh ideas to motivate themselves and their agents.

- **Listen to uplifting music.** Every person has music that makes him or her feel good. Whether it is a song by Meatloaf or Vivaldi, there is an uplifting tune for everyone. Brokers can have music readily accessible on their computers with the click of a mouse. A quick three to five-minute music session can often restore some balance to an over-stressed broker.

- **Give.** If one believes in the Law of Attraction, which says that you get more of what you think and do, then by looking for a daily opportunity to give, brokers are attracting giving into their lives. This sort of giving doesn't have to be some large financial donation but may mean more if it is a simple act, such as helping someone store a suitcase in an overhead bin on an airplane, picking up something that someone dropped, or simply listening attentively to someone.

- **Empower someone.** Allowing a staff member, agent, or management team member to make an important decision demonstrates a high level of trust, and this person will feel empowered. Teaching staff members and agents skills to a level where the broker can trust them is the most direct way to empower people.

- **Get out into nature.** There is a restorative quality to the experience of being out in nature. Too often brokers experience a constant, ongoing "noise" from the people, activities, and demands around them. By lunching in a park, hiking a path, or standing under the stars and looking up, a broker can reconnect with what's really important in life.

- **Be around happy, successful people.** A broker cannot afford to have agents in the office who are negative in their outlook on life. These people are a drain on the broker's energy level and toxic to the company.

QUALITY OF THOUGHT

If you want to move your company quickly toward your vision, you should be careful to control your thinking, for as you think, so shall it be. You can also maintain a positive outlook by avoiding constant exposure to negative thinkers. Here are some clues to look for in determining whether an individual is motivated by positive or negative thinking:

Negative Thinking	Positive Thinking
Negative self-talk	Positive self-talk
Arguing for limitations	Feels potential
Displacement	Accepts responsibility
Sabotaging	Empowering

- **Avoid watching the news.** Brokers who watch the daily television news are exposed to 30 minutes of strongly negative communication. A typical newscast features multiple stories about violent deaths, criminal activities, and scandals. By taking this information into their personal thinking systems, they will think about it for hours and attract more of this energy into their lives. If brokers want to keep up with financial news and information, they can subscribe to an online newspaper, with those particular articles being delivered daily to their e-mail boxes.

- **Take vacations.** Brokers should intentionally schedule and take vacations, whether a weekend at a spa or two weeks on some exotic island. This personal time will help reward family members who have tolerated the broker's demanding lifestyle, while rejuvenating the broker.

PERSONAL EXERCISE 48

HOW DO YOU REENERGIZE

Write down 10 ways that you personally reenergize yourself and exactly how you are going to integrate these into your lifestyle as a broker/owner.

MAINTAIN BALANCE

The real estate brokerage industry is demanding, and it's easy for a broker to become a slave to the business. Brokers should strive to keep

---

Tales from the Real World

A SECOND CHANCE

A broker was known for her high energy and motivating leadership style. Over a few years, she built a successful 50-agent company by spending 12- to 16-hour days at the office and frequently working on weekends. Real estate was her life. She had a loving husband and a family of three children, who frequently complained about her long hours and her absence from the family. She responded with, "There's plenty of time for family once I've created some financial security for us." She was driven, successful, and committed.

One day, while she was eating lunch at her desk, she suddenly felt nauseous and dizzy. The next thing she knew, she was in the back of an ambulance on the way to the hospital. During the ride, all she could think about was her husband and kids. She thought, "Will I ever see them again?" After examining her, doctors determined that she had experienced an "irregularity" in the activity of her heart. They told her that the constant stress that she was maintaining at work was catching up with her and that she was lucky to have avoided a serious heart attack—this time.

When she left the hospital, she vowed to reprioritize her family in her life. She would work to live, not live to work. Over the next few years, she took full advantage of her second chance by spending more time with her family. And because she was a happier, more balanced person, her business thrived.

---

clear on what's really important in their lives: health, family, and enjoying the ride. It is especially important to prioritize personal time with loved ones, making sure not to constantly sacrifice time with these special people for some real estate agent or transaction. A well-balanced broker is a more productive broker. All brokers should develop some policy with their agents, limiting calls after hours to emergencies only. After all, we are real estate brokers, not doctors; nobody dies because we take a night off.

KEY POINTS

- The most important steps that brokers can take toward achieving success of their companies are to (1) maintain a level of high energy and (2) keep their thoughts positive.
- Brokers can help maintain positive attitudes by attending classes and learning something new.

- A key element for a broker to embrace in becoming an inspiring leader is to maintain and encourage congruence between what is said and what is done in the company.
- As far as a broker's energy level is concerned, garbage in equals garbage out.
- A broker should remember that personal health, family, and enjoyment of life are more important than the company. Set and keep personal boundaries.

21

GO FOR IT!

And thus the native hue of resolution
Is sickled o'er with the pale cast of thought,
And enterprises of great pitch and moment
With this regard their currents turn awry,
And lose the name of action.

—WILLIAM SHAKESPEARE IN *HAMLET*

The excerpt in the epigraph is from Hamlet's famous "To be or not to be" soliloquy. It emphasizes that doubt and fear can deter even the greatest of enterprises from being realized. While there is a time for deliberation and planning, there is also a time for action. And that time is now.

After having read this book thoroughly and completed the exercises, a broker is ready to step forward and begin implementing his or her vision for a new real estate company. As the broker launches the new firm, there are three strategies that should be employed to help ease the transition from salesperson into broker/owner.

STRATEGY 1: THINK LIKE A BROKER

Brokers enjoy personal success through the achievements of their agents above their own personal production. If brokers find greater enjoyment in personally selling homes, instead of helping other agents to close transactions, they will grow to resent the time consumed by their agents and find it a real challenge to give their full commitment to their agents and their companies.

Brokers should also maintain a company-first mindset in their dealings with agents, vendors, and prospects. If an agent wants special consideration on a commission split, the broker needs to remember that the company has an obligation to treat all agents fairly, or such special arrangements will soon be discussed in the company's lunchroom, and the agents' respect for the firm and broker will be diminished. Company-first thinking also means that the broker, who has accepted the responsibility of leadership for the agents, must protect the company from toxic personalities, inadequate file work, potential liabilities, and anything that could endanger the company's viability and the broker's vision of success.

STRATEGY 2: CLARITY OF DESTINATION (KNOW WHERE YOU ARE GOING)

Many brokers fail to achieve the full potential of their company because they were unclear about where they were really going in the first place. There is no substitute for the attracting power of a clear vision and a thorough strategic business plan. It has been said that one hour of planning saves four hours of wasted time. It's probably more accurate to say that having a written plan saves time, money, heartache, hassles, and stress.

If a company's road map is its strategic business plan, then the goals and objectives stated in the business plan are the directions to be followed, without which the odds of making it to the destination are negligible. For each goal and objective, a plan should have three to four action steps that can be put directly into the broker's calendar, creating movement toward the goal on a daily or weekly basis.

COACHING CORNER

LEADERSHIP VERSUS MANAGEMENT

There is a significant difference between a manager and a leader when it comes to running a real estate company. Brokers often become complacent, forgetting that their agents look to them as their leaders. Agents want to be inspired and motivated by their broker, not managed. A brief comparison to remember:

Clues to Being a Manager	Clues to Being a Leader
Defers or procrastinates about recruiting	Includes recruitment into planned activities
Talks about the "features" of the company	Talks about vision and movement
Uses agents	*Empowers* agents
Goes it alone	Uses coach and leadership team model
Has a "secret agenda"	Shares vision with entire company
Shoots from the hip	Has a strategic business plan
Focuses on escrows	Focuses on the business
Hires anyone who says yes	Hires only agents who improve the company
Argues for limitations	Finds ways to make things happen

STRATEGY 3: SEEK HELP TO SAVE TIME AND MONEY

Brokers who want to achieve their vision of success sooner rather than later may want to seek the advice and counsel of other professionals in the industry. A broker may consider joining a networking group of fellow brokers from noncompeting marketplaces. Such a group can be found or created by going to classes offered by the Council of Real Estate Brokerage Managers (CRB), attending conventions, and participating in online discussion groups or blogs. Franchise affiliations may also have such groups.

A broker can also use a real estate brokerage coach as a resource for ideas, making sure that any hired coach has significant experience in brokerage ownership (not just management). By working with a coach, a broker can tap the coach's experience to save time and money in the development of in-house programs, policy manuals, commission programs, and a variety of other useful services.

Traditional business consultants can also be sought. Specialists such as a certified public accountant (CPA), tax advisor, real estate attorney, business insurance specialist, and so on can provide a broker with specific information and reduce the broker's learning and research time.

And finally, brokers should not forget to tap the talent of people working at their own companies. Once an assistant manager or office training director has been hired, a broker can include his or her input into many decisions, often discovering new perspectives and ideas. Key employees or staff members should not be overlooked as a valuable resource of information.

KEY POINTS

- **Recruit, recruit, and recruit.**   As a new company owner, the number one priority of brokers, occupying no less than 30 percent of their working hours, should be the recruiting of agents to the firm. While at first recruiting may seem like a foreign process to a new broker, it is nothing more than selling, but instead of selling real estate services to homeowners, the broker is selling real estate services to agents. Brokers often make the mistake of letting recruiting become the "back burner" chore that they deal with when they have extra time; this is a formula for disaster. Remember, a company is either in a state of expansion or contraction; there is no middle ground.

- **Keep looking up!**   The development of a successful real estate company is a worthy goal and a journey that is filled with exhilarating highs and stressful lows. During the tough times, it's very easy to get overwhelmed. The key to surviving these challenging times is to keep focused on the original, passionate vision that existed at the outset. In other words, keep looking up! By focusing on the vision, a broker will avoid looking down at current troubles and will be more resilient, seeing setbacks as a minor part of the overall journey to success.

- **Have fun!**   Some of our greatest business leaders have told us about the importance of following our joy to find success. Owning and running a real estate company is a great way to enjoy life! It's a lifestyle with unlimited financial potential that can bring countless moments of laughter with some great agents and customers. As brokers go through their day, they shouldn't forget to look around and smell the roses.

A CHALLENGE
FROM THE AUTHOR

During my 22-plus years in this business, I have worked with hundreds of brokers and spoken to thousands of agents. I have seen amazing successes and astounding failures. I have helped brokers start their companies and guided others into closing their failing firms. The most fascinating aspect of having seen all of this is that I have come to believe that it is impossible to predict a particular broker's success or failure. Each broker begins the journey with the same potential as the next; each broker comes to the table with knowledge and experience; each broker has a dream. Yet somehow, less than 50 percent create profitable businesses. Why are some brokers fabulously successful and others failing, or even worse, stuck in mediocrity?

The key is in their way of thinking and their actions (or lack thereof) that correspond to that thinking. Brokers must think and act like people who deserve success in order for success to find them. We attract in our lives that which we think about most. In other words, if brokers are whiners and constantly filled with doubt about their own ability to create a successful business, then they are attracting more doubt and insecurity from the world, resulting in lackluster recruiting results, retention problems, and a lack of profit. This doubting Thomas will attract agents who don't believe in their own abilities, can't make it as full-time agents, and sell only an occasional house.

Conversely, action-oriented brokers who daily reinforce their thinking about their impending success and visionary goals will attract that success to them. Their offices will be filled with energized full-time agents who are productive and who participate in both the company and their own lives. Profit will follow, then growth, then more profit, then more growth, and so on. The broker will be a cocreator in the outcome by attracting the right kind of energy and people from the world.

Worse than absolute failure is the mediocrity of "getting by" that exists in our business today. When most brokers open their company doors for the first time, they say to themselves something like, "I'm going to have the best company in the world!" or "I'll show them how to do it!" When looking at that same broker's office a couple of years later, it is more common than not to simply see yet another typical brokerage, filled with mediocre agents and struggling to be a profitable business.

Somewhere along the line, the broker began to compromise on the vision of excellence in favor of just another mediocre real estate company. Maybe he or she found it harder than expected; maybe the broker just got busy doing his or her own transactions. Either way, the one thing that is sure is that the internal fire in the belly or passion for an exceptional outcome was lost. So the broker's thinking and actions dwindled to the level of normal, and another boring real estate company was created.

So my challenge to you as a future leader in this real estate industry is simple:

Be exceptional. Be inspirational.

There are thousands of average business leaders in the world. Don't be one of them. Choose to be exceptional in everything you do. Average is easy and boring; exceptional is challenging and exciting. Average is an absence of legacy; exceptional is its own legacy. Live a life of inspiration, and your business will be inspirational. Your business will be a reflection of your thinking and passion.

Take the challenge!

Go for it!

APPENDIX

This Addendum A to the Broker-Salesperson Independent Contractor Agreement between ABC Real Estate as Broker and _____ as Salesperson dated _____, _____.

TERM AND ANNIVERSARY DATE. This Addendum, and the commission schedules contained herein, shall apply to all commission revenues closed by the Sales Associate on behalf of ABC Real Estate through the Sales Associate's Anniversary Date, which date is _____.

ADMINISTRATIVE FEE. Prior to the sharing of commissions hereunder, Broker shall retain 5% "off-the-top" of all commissions earned as an Administrative Fee. The remaining portion of earned commissions shall be divided between Broker and Sales Associate as set forth below.

TRANSACTION FEE. An additional Transaction Fee of $100.00 will be charged to the Sales Associate for each closed transaction (excluding residential leases and rentals). The Sales Associate is encouraged to pass this Transaction Fee on to the buyer or seller but is not required to do so. If the buyer or seller pays the Transaction Fee, then the Transaction Fee will not be deducted from the Sales Associate's portion of the commission; if the buyer or seller does *not* pay the Transaction Fee, then the fee will be deducted from the Sales Associate's portion of the commissions due hereunder.

COMMISSION SCHEDULES. ABC Real Estate and the Sales Associate have mutually agreed to the selected commission schedule option as indicated by the Sales Associate's and Broker's initials placed adjacent to the selected option.

_____/_____ Option 1: Standard Commission Schedule

Under Option 1, the Sales Associate begins at a commission percentage based on his or her net earnings for the preceding Anniversary Year, as applied to the Standard Commission Schedule below. No Sales Associate will start an Anniversary Year at a commission level greater than 80%. At the start of the Sales Associate's subsequent Anniversary Year, he or she will be placed at a commission percentage level based on the highest threshold crossed under the Maintenance Schedule column below. (Circle and initial Sales Associate's commission level.)

Standard Commission Schedule		
Gross Commission Income (from Prior Anniversary Year)	Sales Associate, Commission Percentage	Maintenance Schedule Thresholds
$0–$20,000.00	50%	$0
$20,000.01–$40,500.00	60%	$30,000
$40,500.01–$84,000.00	65%	$60,000
$84,000.01–$100,000.00	70%	$92,000
$100,000.01–$145,000.00	75%	$125,000
$145,000.01–$200,000.00	80%	$170,000
$200,000.01+	85%	N/A

_____/_____ Option 2: 100% Commission Schedule

Under Option 2, the Sales Associate's commission split is reset to 60% each Anniversary Year. There is no bonus for a Home Office Associate under this schedule.

100% Commission Schedule	
Gross Commission Income	Sales Associate, Commission Percentage
$0–$50,000.00	60%
$50,000.01+	100%

_____/_____ Option 3: Mentor Referral Program

Option 3 is available only to new licensees (under six months' experience) who join ABC Real Estate. For the new Sales Associate's first three closed transactions, he or she shall work with an experienced Sales Associate as a partner/mentor, who shall receive a 25% referral fee for such mentoring services. Thereafter, the Sales Associate shall be under the Commission Schedule otherwise selected (both this option and the nonmentor schedule should be initialed).

_____/_____ Option 4: Home Office Associate Schedule (No Assigned Desk)

Under Option #4, the Sales Associate has no assigned desk at the branch office and begins at a commission percentage based on his or her net earnings for the preceding Anniversary Year, as applied to the Standard Commission Schedule below. No Sales Associate will start an Anniversary Year at a commission level greater than 85%. At the start of the Sales Associate's subsequent Anniversary Year, he or she will be placed at a commission percentage level based on the highest threshold crossed under the Maintenance Schedule column below. (Circle and initial Sales Associate's commission level.)

Home Office Commission Schedule		
Gross Commission Income (from Prior Anniversary Year)	Sales Associate, Commission Percentage	Maintenance Schedule Thresholds
$0–$20,000.00	55%	$0
$20,000.01–$40,500.00	65%	$30,000
$40,500.01–$84,000.00	70%	$60,000
$84,000.01–$100,000.00	75%	$92,000
$100,000.01–$145,000.00	80%	$125,000
$145,000.01–$200,000.00	85%	$170,000
$200,000.01+	90%	N/A

OTHER TERMS AND CONDITIONS. The following additional terms shall also apply, unless otherwise noted, to all commission schedule options:

1. The Sales Associate's commission level will be reviewed during the month immediately preceding the Sales Associate's Anniversary Date and, if appropriate, adjusted on the first day of the Sales Associate's Anniversary Month.
   a. If a Sales Associate's commission level is adjusted, the new commission level will apply to all future closed transactions, regardless of the commission level at which such transactions were opened or otherwise pended.
2. Any outstanding unpaid amount(s) that a Sales Associate owes ABC Real Estate will automatically be deducted from commission income earned.
3. ABC Real Estate has established the following minimum commission rates for listings:
   a. 6% listing commission for resale homes or floating homes up to $400,000.00
   b. 10% listing commission for raw land up to $400,000.00, or business opportunities of any price
   c. 5% listing commission for all other properties

   Any listing commission below 5% needs prior management approval, or the commission earned will first be allocated to the company in an amount that it would have otherwise been entitled to under the commission rates set forth above.

   The Sales Associate shall *not*, without prior management approval, allow any commission earned or offered to ABC Real Estate to be reduced from the original earned or offered amount or rate. Such reductions made without prior management approval shall be deducted from the Sales Associate's portion of the commission only.
4. Any commission schedule herein may be adjusted up or down in order to keep pace with changing conditions in the marketplace. ABC Real Estate reserves the right to change, modify, adjust for inflation, or amend this agreement, in part or in total, at any time. No change will take place without prior 30-day written advance notice to the Sales Associate.

_____/_____ In-House Lead Generation Program

Subject to the approval of the Broker, by initialing this provision, the Sales Associate is indicating an interest in participating in the company's In-House Lead Generation Program. Under this program, buyer and seller leads that are generated solely by the company's lead generation marketing activities (national networking, Internet Web site leads that are not inquiring about a specific listing, etc.) are referred to the approved Sales Associates, with a 25% referral fee being due to the company. If this paragraph is *not* initialed, the Sales Associate is waiving the right to participate in the program.

ACCEPTED AND AGREED TO THIS DATE: _____

Sales Associate: _____

ABC Real Estate

By _____
    Broker

Index

About the Author

Cliff Perotti is the president of TheBrokerCoach.com, an international real estate consulting, coaching, and training company; and he is the CEO of The Perotti Group, a national real estate investment firm. Cliff is also the founder of Cliff Perotti Seminars and the Perotti Real Estate Network, which works to empower the general public through real estate investment education. Cliff's headquarters are located in Corte Madera, California.

Cliff has been referred to as a "serial entrepreneur" by those who know him. Having started his first publishing company at age 16, his business experience has crossed into many industries, including real estate brokerage, game companies, bars and restaurants, hotels, construction, and real estate investments.

Cliff has over 22 years of experience in real estate brokerage and training. Working in both independent offices and corporate franchises has given him a wide range of experience and the clear ability to "walk the talk." His brokerage leadership roles have included broker/owner, branch manager, sales manager, recruiter, estates director, and trainer for such organizations as Anthony Schools of Northern California, Jon Douglas Company—Realtors, Prudential California Realty, and the California Association of Realtors. He has earned accolades as a top recruiter, trainer, and manager, specializing in start-up companies and turning around nonproductive offices.

As an author, coach, trainer, and catalyst, he enjoys helping people unleash their potential. Cliff is a master instructor for the Council of Real Estate Brokerage Managers (CRB). He has been involved in the CRB since 1984, serving on numerous committees and the board of directors. Cliff's insights on negotiating, management, training, and recruiting have appeared in many real estate publications. He has created several educational programs and tools, including "The Recruiter Paradigm," "Launching Your Real Estate Company," "Manager's Development Record," and "Personal Coach."

Cliff Perotti has been a featured speaker on the subjects of business development and recruiting for the National Association of Realtors, the Florida Association of Realtors, and several large national real estate franchises.

He has been an active volunteer in his local community, receiving the Spirit of Marin Award for his work with the local chamber of commerce. Cliff is a lifelong resident of California and counts among his greatest personal accomplishments his roles as husband, father, and friend.